Virginia

K. M. Kostyal
Photography by Medford Taylor

COMPASS AMERICAN GUIDES
An Imprint of Fodor's Travel Publications, Inc.

Virginia

Copyright © 1994 Fodor's Travel Publications, Inc.
Maps Copyright © 1994 Fodor's Travel Publications, Inc.

Library of Congress Cataloging-In-Publication Data
Kostyal, K. M. 1951-
Virginia/K. M. Kostyal: photography by Medford Taylor.
   p. cm.—(Compass American Guides)
   Includes bibliographical references and index
   ISBN 1-878867-41-5 (paper) $16.95 ISBN 1-878867-42-3 (hard) $24.95
   1. Virginia—Guidebooks.   2. Virginia—Pictorial works
   I. Title.   II. Series: Compass American Guides
   F224.K67   1994   93-43501
917.5504'43—dc20   CIP

Although the Publisher and the Author of this book have made every effort to ensure the information was correct at the time of going to press, the Publisher and the Author do not assume and hereby disclaim any liability to any party for any loss or damage caused by errors, omissions, misleading information, or any potential travel disruption due to labor or financial difficulty, whether such errors or omissions result from negligence, accident, or any other cause.

Editors: Kit Duane, Ruth Schecter, Jessica Fisher   Designers: David Hurst,
Managing Editor: Kit Duane   Christopher Burt
Photo Editor: Christopher Burt   Map Design: Eureka Cartography
Compass American Guides, 6051 Margarido Drive, Oakland, CA 94618
Production House: Twin Age Ltd., Hong Kong
Printed in China
10 9 8 7 6 5 4 3 2 1

Cover: Pastoral scene typical of the Piedmont

The Publisher gratefully acknowledges the following institutions and individuals for the use of their photographs and/or illustrations on the following pages:
The Chrysler Museum, pp. 54, 148, 154, 205, 216, 231; Hampton University Archives, pp. 69, 239; The Library of Congress, pp. 15, 23, 39, 121, 124, 156, 173, 176, 185, 202; The Maggie L. Walker National Historic Site, p. 119; The New York Historical Society, p. 209; Underwood Archives, pp. 50, 80; The Virginia State Library and Archives, pp. 21, 25, 56, 85, 93, 94, 97, 105, 126, 141, 144, 174-175, 178-181, 225, 227.
    We also wish to thank the following individuals for their contributions to this book: Carolyn Parsons at the Virginia State Library and Archives for her help locating photographs and for information about Elizabeth Van Lew; Werner L. Janney for his expert reading; Candace Compton-Pappas, our typesetter and illustrator; and Ellen Klages, our proofreader.

To my parents, Dick and Helen Kostyal,
who bred me with Bay water in my veins
and Virginia on my mind.

C O N T E N T S

Literary Extracts

Topical Essays & Timelines

Maps

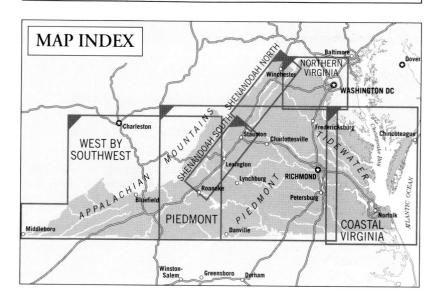

FACTS ABOUT VIRGINIA

Old Dominion

CAPITAL: Richmond
STATE FLOWER: Dogwood flower
STATE BIRD: Cardinal

Cardinal

Dogwood flower

STATE TREE: Dogwood
ENTERED UNION: June 25, 1788

POPULATION (1991): 1,234,602

White		77.4%
Black		18.8%
Hispanic*		2.6%
Asian/Pacific		2.6%

Population of Hispanic origin is an ethnic grouping and not additive to the population racial groupings.

FIVE LARGEST CITIES:

Virginia Beach	393,069
Richmond	203,056
Norfolk	202,798
Arlington	170,936
Newport News	170,045

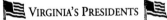 **VIRGINIA'S PRESIDENTS**

1ST.	George Washington
3RD.	Thomas Jefferson
4TH.	James Madison
5TH.	James Monroe
9TH.	William Henry Harrison
10TH.	John Tyler
12TH.	Zachary Taylor
28TH.	Woodrow Wilson

Dogwood

ECONOMY:

Principal industries:
services, trade, government, manufacturing, tourism, agriculture

Principal manufactured goods:
textiles, transportation equipment, electric and electronic equipment, food processing, chemicals, printing

Principal crops:
tobacco, soybeans, peanuts, winterwheat, corn, far grain, tomatoes, apples, summer and sweet potatoes

Per capita income (1991): $19,976

GEOGRAPHY:

Size: 40,767 sq. miles (117,000 sq. km)

Highest point: 5,729 feet (1,736 meters) Mount Rogers, Grayson-Smyth County

Lowest Point: Altantic Ocean sea level

CLIMATE:

Highest temperature recorded: 110°F (43°C) at Balcony Falls on July 15, 1954

Lowest temperature recorded: -30°F (-35°C) at Mtn. Lake Bio Station on January 22, 1985

Wettest place:
54.39" annual rainfall at Wallaceton in Norfolk County

Driest place:
33.89" annual rainfall at Woodstock in Shenadoah County

FAMOUS VIRGINIANS:

Richard E. Byrd ♦ Patsy Cline ♦ Robert E. Lee ♦ Booker T. Washington
Willa Cather ♦ Thomas J. "Stonewall" Jackson ♦ Meriwether Lewis and
William Clark ♦ Edgar Allan Poe ♦ Maggie Walker ♦ Patrick Henry

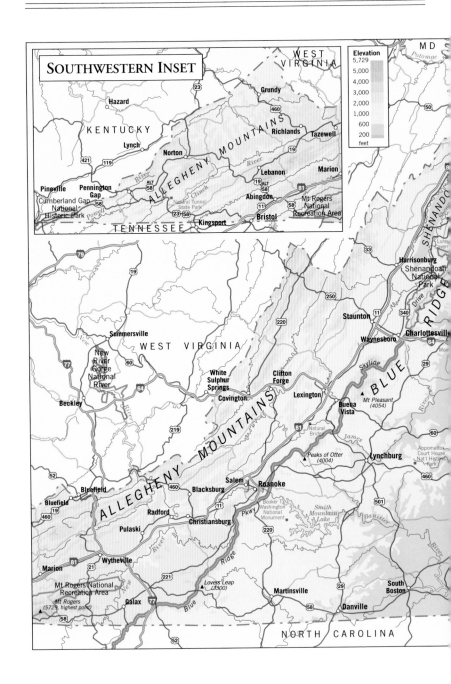

VIRGINIA

0 5 10   20   30   40

miles

P R E F A C E

LIKE MOST PEOPLE I KNOW, I have gone through stages in my relations with my home state. When I was young—until I was 19, in fact—it was all I had ever known. Not so much home as the universe. Then I had a full, rich wandering taste of the wider world, and Virginia became a little passé to me, a little too provincial. In fact, just too *Virginia*.

Now, at 40-something, I simply wallow in this state, because it *is* so very Virginia. As a travel writer, I have to leave it a lot, and at every new destination I visit, I wonder, as all travelers do, whether I could live in this new place. No, not really. Because, in the end, it's just not Virginia.

What makes Virginia is something too subtle for words to contain, but I have tried to embed it somehow between the lines of this guide. The past clearly gives Virginia its essence. You simply can't escape it here. Every town has its historic homes, its old monuments, its gravestones, its local history museum. Every town's history is unique, full of tales and heroics, absolutely worth the telling. But there is simply too much to tell about Virginia in one guide, so I have had to be selective. I've tried to keep the Virginia essence always alive, at the same time portraying the state's remarkable diversity. Every corner of Virginia, from the coast to the mountains, has its own geography and its own personality. It was a sheer joy to wander through all that diversity, to meet so many different variations on Virginia and Virginians.

I hope that all travelers wandering Virginia will share some of that joy with me.

■ ACKNOWLEDGMENTS

Heartfelt appreciation goes first to the many public affairs people at visitors centers, museums, and historic homes across the state. They were as a group unstinting in providing insight, research materials, and general encouragement. The Virginia Department of Tourism also offered endless information and guidance, as did the Virginia State Library, the Arlington libraries, and the Lloyd House historical library in Alexandria. My thanks also to my editor, Kit Duane, who so appreciates the subtleties of the Virginia psyche that I consider her an honorary Daughter of the Old Dominion. Thanks also to Tobias Steed for his consummate professionalism and understanding of the writer's world. For leading me down the esoteric paths of grammatical finesse, and for his fine literary sensibilities, my thanks to Werner Janney.

Finally, I want to thank my husband, Buzz, for his never-ending support for and patience with an often absent spouse. And to my son, Will, a thanks for simply being himself.

THE PORTRAICTUER OF CAPTAYNE IOHN SMITH ADMIRALL OF NEW ENGLAND.

Æta 37
A° 1616

These are the Lines that shew thy Face: but those
That shew thy Grace and Glory brighter bee:
Thy Faire-Discoueries and Fowle - Overthrowes
Of Salvages, much Civillizd by thee
Best shew thy Spirit: and to it Glory Wyn;
So, thou art Brasse without, but Golde within.
If so, in Brasse,(too soft smiths Acts to beare)
I fix thy Fame, to make Brasse steele out weare.

Thine as thou art Virtues.
John Daunes. Heref:

H I S T O R Y

HISTORY HAUNTS VIRGINIA LIKE A LOST LOVER. Images, mementos, whispers of the past float along her rivers, get tangled in the thick press of her forests, stand beside the too-gallant statues that posture in her courthouse squares.

So much history, and so many of them. Native American and European, male and female, black and white. Every little borough has its own story, as does every long-standing Virginia family. It's fair to say that the first 250 years of this state's recorded history read like a saga filled with its own theatrics: heroes, devils, tragedies, comedies, victories, and defeats. After all, Virginians trace themselves back to the first colonists, to major players in the Revolution, to "founding fathers" of the new nation. And then the state was capital of the Confederacy and the primary battleground for the Civil War. For octogenarian Virginians—and younger ones who cleave to the Commonwealth's past—that war, regardless of its cost, was a moment of glory.

Glory clearly tinges Virginia's past, sometimes to the Old Dominion's detriment. Virginians have had a deserved reputation for courting old traditions, for looking backward more often than forward. But that old-line conservatism seems itself to be receding into the past. While Virginia can't be counted as one of America's most progressive states, she has learned in recent decades to move forward, with the past as a sort of patina about her. She may not be an angel, but her charms are considerable.

■ FRUITFULLEST VIRGINIA

The Virginia saga actually began somewhere in the vaguest past, when bands of nomads drifted out of Asia and into the area. When they reached the Atlantic they could drift no farther. And so they spread out along its tributaries, settled into the endless coastal forests, lived off the abundance of the land, slowly resolving themselves into tribes and kingdoms. We know little of their culture except that they were a prosperous people and members of the Algonquian language group. Some tribes built temples and lived in protected, palisaded towns; others lived in homesteads dispersed along rivers. To the west, in the Shenandoah

Robert E. Lee's statue graces Monument Avenue in Richmond.

▪ HISTORY TIMELINE ▪

1607 Group of 105 English colonists reach Cape Henry, after a journey of 18 weeks. They establish the Jamestown settlement.

1609 The colony's leader, Capt. John Smith, returns to England. Relations with the Powhatan Indians become hostile.

1610 Jamestown reduced to 60 survivors after winter famine; saved by the arrival of Gov. Thomas West (Baron De La Warr) with new colonists, needed supplies, and strong leadership.

1614 Pocahontas marries John Rolfe, tobacco enthusiast.

1619 First democratically elected legislative body in New World, the House of Burgesses is formed. Unmarried women are sent from England to marry colonists; and first recorded black colonists arrive on a Dutch man-o'-war.

1644 Peace treaty with the Powhatan after attack by Chief Opechancanough fails.

1675 Nathaniel Bacon leads unauthorized attacks against Indians. He and his adherents end in open rebellion, the next year driving British governor William Berkeley out of Jamestown and burning the town.

1699 Capital moved to Williamsburg.

1774 House of Burgesses dissolved by British Gov. John Murray. Patriots reconvene at Raleigh Tavern.

1775 Patrick Henry gives his "Give me liberty or give me death" speech, predicting the start of violence. April 19, Revolutionary War begins at Lexington and Concord in Massachusetts.

1776 Virginian and North Carolinian soldiers burn Norfolk on New Year's Day. Last Revolutionary convention in Williamsburg by unanimous vote carries a resolution calling for independence. Motion passes July 2nd. Declaration of Independence signed in Philadelphia, setting forth the founding philosophy of an experiment in democracy.

1781 On October 19th, Lord Cornwallis surrenders British army to Gen. George Washington at Yorktown.

1789 Virginian George Washington becomes the first President of the United States.

1801	Thomas Jefferson of Monticello is elected the nation's third President, defeating incumbent John Adams.
1861	Virginia secedes from the Union and joins the Confederacy, causing the western counties to separate from the state. Col. Robert E. Lee becomes commander of Virginia's forces.
1865	On April 9th, Lee surrenders the Confederate army to General Grant at Appomattox.
1941	More than 215,000 Virginians serve in World War II over the next four years. 185 warships are built at Newport News shipyard.
1954	Supreme Court finds racial segregation in public schools unconstitutional.
1964	Passage of the U.S. Civil Rights Act, followed the next year by the Voting Rights Act, affects life in Virginia.
1970	State elects its first Republican governor since 1886, and its third constitution is approved.
1990	The first African American governor of Virginia and the nation, L. Douglas Wilder, begins to serve his term.

Valley, another great tribe, the Sioux Indians lived—hunting, among other animals, buffalo.

Then, in the sixteenth century another band of restless wanderers unceremoniously entered their world. These were, of course, the European explorers, intent on a kind of migration of their own, only in reverse of what the Asian nomads had done: They were pushing west toward the riches of the Indies—until North America got in their way.

In the 1560s, Spanish adventurers captured a native chief from the coast of what is now Virginia, named him Don Luis de Valasco, and brought him back to Madrid for an education. When Spanish Jesuits returned Don Luis to the Virginia coast in 1570, he reasserted his rights as a chief, and the Jesuits built a mission hoping to convert the Indians to Christ. Instead, Don Luis dispatched the Jesuits to the Great Spirit. Little was heard from Europeans until aspiring English colonists bumped up upon the shore 37 years later. The Powhatan chief who watched them land was probably Don Luis's son, and by now leader of the combined Algonquian groups along the coast.

The English, meanwhile, had moored their ships and named the area on which they'd landed after their beloved Elizabeth, the virgin queen. They called it Virginia.

Elizabeth had been dead for a scant three years, and Shakespeare had just written *Anthony and Cleopatra*. It was James I who sat the throne of England when three impossibly small ships set sail down the Thames in December 1606. Backed by the newly formed Virginia Company, the expedition was essentially a business venture. Its members were instructed to do four things in the strange, wild land that the poet Edmund Spenser called "fruitfullest Virginia": They were to locate a sea passage through it to the Orient; to search out its wealth, whatever that might be; to convert its "heathen" to the Anglican faith; and, along the way, to bring glory to themselves and their sovereign. They accomplished exactly none of their objectives. But they did manage, in spite of themselves, to plant the seeds of a New World in the immense, uncharted wilderness of North America.

■ JAMESTOWN ESTABLISHED

The ships—the 100-ton *Susan Constant,* the 40-ton *Godspeed,* and the 20-ton *Discovery*—set sail carrying aspiring adventurers, plus the ships' crews. About half of the 105 colonists who survived the trip were the younger sons of gentry who had nothing to gain by staying in seventeenth-century England, where they would inherit neither land nor wealth. This exotic Virginia held the promise of untold riches and opportunity. That they would have to work for any of this seemed to have escaped them as they set sail with high hopes, few skills, and even less of the grit they would need to survive.

The other half of the expedition was composed mostly of artisans weary of England's entrenched class structure and lack of opportunity. Unfortunately, their particular crafts and experiences weren't exactly what was needed to tame a wilderness—but who knew then what *was* needed? Only one man among the hundred on board seems to have been well-suited, both by temperament and experience, to deal with and establish a new world. A seasoned mercenary and adventurer, his name was John Smith, and he would prove to be a godsend to the expedition. But none of them knew that at the time, and, in fact, his chronic braggadocio managed to get him arrested before the ships had crossed the Atlantic.

This early illustration of the Powhatan village of Pomiooc was drawn circa 1590 by an illustrator at the time of a visit by Spanish Jesuits. (Virginia State Library and Archives)

Their crossing was plagued from the start. Before setting down the Thames, they were cursed with the ill omen of Halley's Comet streaking across the night sky. Then they spent six weeks foundering in contrary winds and wicked weather off the British coast. Those six lost weeks proved more critical than they could have known: It cost them precious provisions that would later cost many of them their lives.

Finally, after four and a half months en route, with stops in the Canaries and West Indies, they sighted the low, wooded coastline of Virginia. Coming alongside the capes at the mouth of the broad and benevolent Chesapeake Bay, the English stopped to erect a cross in gratitude. They then proceeded up a wide river that they called James, for their king.

It was late April and Virginia's new-green forests were petalled in white dogwoods. The newcomers reconnoitered the shoreline, gorging on wild strawberries and on the clams and mussels that paved the shoals. After exploring the lower James for a couple of weeks, they chose a small island 60 miles (97 km) upstream on which to build a fort. Connected by a narrow isthmus to the mainland, the island, they reasoned, would be easy to defend against French or Spanish warships, and against attacks from the hostile half-clothed natives that had already assaulted them when they landed at Cape Henry. Also, the island had good deep anchorage for their ships just offshore.

In high spirits, the small band set about transforming the island they had named Jamestown into a facsimile of Britain. They built a stockaded, triangular fort and planted crops, working communally as the Virginia Company had prescribed they do. They also searched voraciously for gold, believing optimistically that the very river sands were spangled with its glint. And very soon, they began to die. Throughout the summer, the combination of malnutrition, bad water, and typhoid, a disease they had unwittingly brought with them from England, carried away half the members of the Jamestown band. Recounting the grisly scene, one of them described "men night and day groaning in every corner of the fort . . . some departing three or four in a night . . . their bodies trailed out of their cabins like dogges to be buried."

Only John Smith, who had not been released from his bondage until a month after the expedition's arrival in Jamestown, seemed to understand the potential— and the requirements—of this new wilderness. By September he had been made president of the governing council, and he was quick to push every man, even the cosseted gentry, into action. Smith's first commandment to the surviving colonists was simple: "He that will not worke shall not eat." For a year Smith's determination and guts, his ability to deal effectively with the local natives, who were sometimes helpful and sometimes hostile, and his sheer zeal for adventure kept the struggling and diminished band afloat, against all odds.

In the fall of 1609, Smith was badly wounded when a musket accidentally discharged into his leg. Afraid the injury might be the end of him, Smith sailed for England. He never returned. Ironically, the man who, more than any other, had grafted England onto the Virginia soil, spent less than a year and a half in the New World.

Smith's departure spelled doom. Winter was coming on and new colonists had arrived, so that the band now numbered 500. Though they had laid in new stores and livestock, they couldn't reach their own livestock corralled outside the fortress because of the Powhatans' unrelenting aggression. Laying siege to Jamestown, they kept the colonists prisoners inside their own fortress. That grim winter of 1609–10 is remembered as the "Starving Time." When spring came again, only

THE FIRST DAY AT JAMESTOWN.

"He that will not worke shall not eat," proclaimed Virginia's founder Capt. John Smith in order to cajole the landed gentry to do their share of the work at Jamestown. (Library of Congress)

CAPT. JOHN SMITH AND POCAHONTAS

When John Smith was born in Lincolnshire, England, in 1580, the Elizabethan "age of wonder and delight" was in full cry, with Asia, Africa, and the Indies only recently "discovered." A soldier of fortune, Smith proved a formidable fighter. In the Balkans he became something of a legend, particularly after he took the heads of two Turkish noblemen in successive hand-to-hand duels. Soon after that, though, young John found himself a captive of the Turks, then sold as a slave to a Turkish pasha. The wily Smith managed an almost impossible escape and made his way slowly back across Europe to England.

He returned home just as the fever for the New World was sweeping London. At 27, Smith set sail with the first band of colonists—and managed to get himself arrested before ever setting foot in Virginia. There was even talk on board of hanging the outspoken braggart.

Once in Virginia, the expedition opened sealed orders from the King's Council, which named seven men to head up the colony. John Smith was one of them. Still, at first he had little say in how things were run. Instead, he watched disdainfully as the colonists grappled ineffectively with the frontier and occupied himself by making river forays into the interior. From these expeditions, he created remarkably accurate maps and charts of the Virginia coastline.

It was on one such trip that he and an Indian princess first met. Taken prisoner by a Powhatan hunting party, Smith staved off his own execution by captivating his captors with the "magic" of his compass. Eventually, the Indians presented him to their powerful chief, also called Powhatan. According to Smith, the Indians were "ready with their clubs, to beat out his braines," when Pocahontas "got his head in her armes, and laid her owne upon his to save him from death: whereat the Emperour was contented he should live . . . ." After that encounter, Pocahontas apparently developed a devotion to Smith and visited Jamestown a number of times. In fact, the girl even saved him—and the colonists—a second time when she warned them of a Powhatan plot to attack the fort.

Smith may have had a strong ally in the Indian princess, but he was not so highly esteemed by his own colleagues. One detractor described him as "an ambityous, unworthy, and vayneglorious fellowe." Ambitious, yes; vainglorious, oh, yes; But unworthy? No. It was John Smith's "worthiness" that kept Virginia alive through its first struggling year.

If Smith saved Jamestown through stamina and vision, the Indian princess Matoaka saved it through charm. The favored daughter of the powerful Powhatan chief, she has come through history under her nickname, Pocahontas—"playful one."

From the first, she seems to have been captivated by English ways. Though the English actually kidnapped her after Smith left for England, she still chose to wed a colonist, John Rolfe (the same man who gave Virginia a smokable tobacco), and their union resulted in the "Pocahontas Peace"—almost eight years of good relations between the Powhatans and the English.

The couple and their infant son, Thomas, sailed for England in 1616, where the exotic and dignified "Lady Rebecca," as she had been christened, soon became a London celebrity. When she was presented at court, her regal bearing induced English gentlewomen to curtsy before her and to back out of a room in her presence. She also had a brief reunion with her old friend John Smith, who by then was devoting all his time and energy to promoting Virginia.

After 10 months in England, Lady Rebecca reluctantly left behind the delights of Britain and set sail with her husband for Virginia. But a short distance down the Thames, she took ill. Very soon, Pocahontas the "playful one," favored lady of court—both the Powhatan one and the English one—was dead at 21. Her son, Thomas, however, returned to prospering Virginia as a young man and married a well-placed colonial damsel. Their descendants have kept alive the legacy of Pocahontas.

America's first legend: Indian princess Pocahontas rescues adventurer John Smith in 1608. (Virginia State Library and Archives)

60 souls, half-dead themselves, remained to greet it. They also greeted a ghastly new problem: A fresh contingent of colonists suddenly arrived from England. Expecting to find a thriving settlement, they had brought only scant provisions with them. Their leader, the newly appointed Governor Gates, took a long look at the forlorn survivors and the devastated fortress, whose wood had been pulled down for fires over the course of the winter. He decided that Jamestown couldn't be saved. On June 7, the English abandoned their only foothold in America and sailed away.

But not far. On their way down the James, they met an advance party of yet another group of incoming English. This group, they were assured, was a well-provisioned relief expedition of some 300 men and women. Gates brought his ships about and headed back to Jamestown.

John Smith had considered the 1,500-acre island of Jamestown "a verie fit place for the erecting of a great cittie." No cittie, of course, ever went up here in what was little more than a low-lying, malarial miasma. Hardly a propitious place on which to build a New World, the island unquestionably took more lives than was its due. In the first dozen years of the settlement, aspiring colonists faced a one in seven chance of survival. Inexplicably, they poured out of England anyway, many apparently ignorant of the hardships ahead and others willing to stake their lives on the chance to make a new beginning at the edge of the known world. Also inexplicable was their inability to adapt to, or make use of, the resources of this rich land. In the face of woods teeming with wild game and rivers full of fish and shellfish, they still starved, though some of that can be explained by the almost constant threat of Indian attack.

Finally, in 1611, the colonists founded a new settlement upriver on higher, healthier ground. Jamestown remained the main hub of colonization, but this second settlement, Henrico, brought new hope to the settlers. At about the same time, the Virginia Company ordered a halt to its misbegotten experiment in communalism. Settlers were now issued their own plots of land and could reap the profits from their own sweat. Sooner than they could have predicted, that sweat begin to produce gold for them—not the cloying yellow metal but Virginia gold: tobacco.

Like many eighteenth-century Europeans, the Powhatan natives were devotees of the "esteemed weed," but the variety that grew in Virginia was too harsh for European tastes. An enterprising colonist named John Rolfe, however, experimented and found that he could cultivate a milder type of West Indian tobacco popular in Europe. Soon the fortunes of the colonists were secured. Even the streets of Jamestown were patched with sprouting tobacco plants, as Europe clamored for what King James, an early and ardent nonsmoker, called "the horrible Stigian smoke of the pit that is bottomless."

Though attacks from the natives, disease, and the hardships of the wilderness still plagued the early Virginians, they could now smell in that "Stigian smoke" their own success. They pushed out farther into the frontier, establishing small tobacco farms along the James and York rivers. In 1622, many of the families in those scattered farms were slaughtered in a violent massacre plotted by Powhatan chieftain Opechancanough. Still the settlers persisted, and two years later, King James officially declared Virginia a colony, taking it out of the hands of the private company. A renewed spirit of hope and opportunity fueled the colonists.

Even in those early years, the idea of self-determination was becoming the backbone of the colonial esprit. Virginia already had its own elected assembly of representatives—and a growing sense of "inalienable rights." In some vague way, these people already seemed to sense that they were in the process of creating both a New World and a new world order. The old entrenched oligarchy of England wasn't the way of Virginia. A man could arrive here as an indentured servant, pay off his seven years' indenture, then go on to become a prospering and prominent colonist. In those halcyon years, when slavery was not yet a sickness on the soul of the Commonwealth, even the first Africans who arrived in Jamestown in 1619 apparently came not as slaves but as indentured servants.

■ VIRGINIA LEAVES THE CROWN

The colonists' growing sense of independence from English authority came to an unexpected head in 1676, when Virginians staged a short-lived but portentous rebellion against the king's arrogant governor, William Berkeley. A virtual war had been raging between the Native Americans and the colonists, but Berkeley had refused to organize a force to go against the Indians. A charismatic newcomer named Nathaniel Bacon took matters into his own hands, and with a band of followers, he attacked a Powhatan village. Berkeley was enraged by this upstart behavior and labeled Bacon a traitor. Bacon's Rebellion was on. Throughout the summer and early fall of 1676, Bacon's growing army of rebels fought surprisingly

(following pages) A map drawn in 1630 based on Capt. John Smith's original map of Virginia.

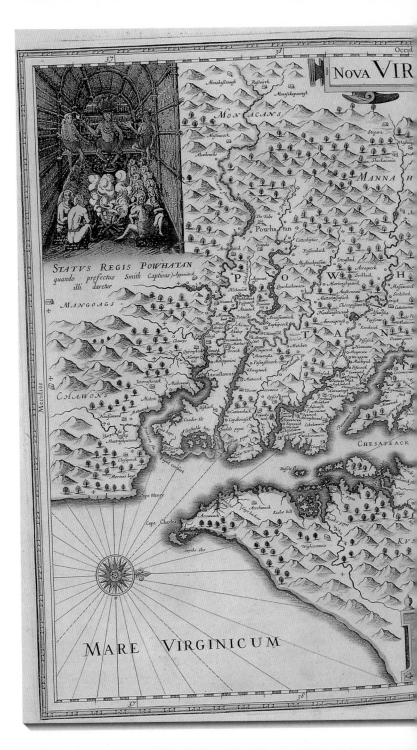

Monahassanugh   Rassawck
Monasukapanough

MONACANS

Massinacak
Mowhemencho   Stegora

Shackaconia

MANNAH

The Fales
Powhatan

Arroheteck   Orapaks
Catachtplco

Passaunkack   Meghughquassunk   Uttensstauk   Accopeeck

POW   Appecant

Nichtanse   Quackohowaon   Mortoughquand
Nichtanse   Mattanquond
Matastecoani   Ascranock

Pamunck   Matanquisack
Chicopissto   Nantaughtacund

Aurenaposogh   Papiscono
Kerehook   Matau

Massawomeck
Socbbeck
Cattowtone

Chawops   T A N

MANGOAGS   Matchut   Ozenick   Piffasecke   Nconesuck

Menapucunt   Menaskunt   Newntown   Mangoraca

Jamestowne   Matchut   Nawnautough   Wcaycomoco
Pataromerke   Weapanock

COHAWONS   Warraskoyack   Machawait   Mokete   Kiskack   Uttamuffak

Nandtaughtacund   Kechoughtan   Ceader Ile   Gosnolds hope   Centanieck   Paanke

Sharpes Ile   Mattanock   Capahowsick   Tindals poynt   Nepawaock

Chesapeack   Forcon de Poynt comfort   Deep Water   Wosapake   Echahowa
Mortons baye   Kithowanack   Chischiacomoco

CHESAPEACK

Cape Henry   Russels Ile

Vigrohoconck   Arrohoteck   Keales hill   Keales poynt   KUS

Cape Charles   Arrowmeck   Wighcocomoco

Smyths Iles

MARE VIRGINICUM

STATVS REGIS POWHATAN
quando prefectus Smith (Captivus) Appomattck
illi darctur

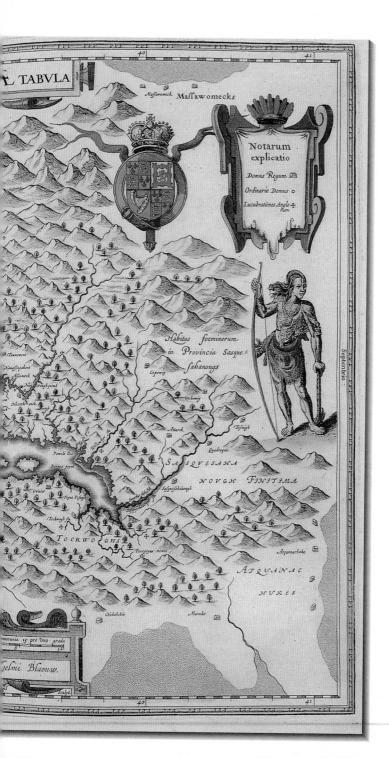

L TABVLA

Massawomeck Massawomecks

Notarum
explicatio

Domus Regum
Ordinarie Domus
Lucubrationes Anglo-
rum

Habitus foeminarum
in Provincia Sasque-
sahanougs

Cepewie

Onehowie

Atuesk

Tesinigh

Quadroque

SASQVESAHA
NOVGH FINITIMA

Sasquesahanough

Powels Iles

Osinies

Point Pisinge

Tockwogh fl.

T O C K W O
G H S

Peregryns mount

Atquanachuke

A T Q V A N A C
H V K E S

Chickahokin

Matocks

communis. 15 pro Uno gradu

elnii Blaeuw.

Sculpt.

Septentrio

well against the governor's forces. At times, a victory even seemed possible. But Virginia was not yet ripe to overcome her British overlords. By October Bacon was dead and Berkeley had reclaimed his authority. The governor spent the rest of his rule bludgeoning the colonists and avenging himself on the "rebels." He had 23 of them killed for their part in the rebellion, leading King Charles II to comment that, "That old fool has hanged more men in that naked country than I did for the murder of my father." In Bacon's Rebellion, English authority had won one round. But the fight had just begun.

As Virginia's first century came to a close, the untrammeled wilderness—and its opportunities—were already passing. Tobacco, a greedy weed, had an insatiable appetite for both land, which it quickly exhausted, and labor. Tragically, that high labor demand had begun to mire the colony in the horrors of slavery—an institution that ultimately enslaved blacks and compromised the whole of Virginia society. By the early eighteenth century, a nouveau gentry had seeded itself across Virginia. In the east, yeoman farmers became an increasingly rare breed, as wealthy tobacco planters, backed by legions of African slaves, claimed the countryside. The wealthy also became serious land speculators, buying up northern and western lands, then reselling smaller plots to those willing to settle into the hardships of a new frontier. For better or worse, Virginia's landed aristocracy had been born.

Jamestown, malarial and star-crossed, was finally abandoned as the capital in 1699, and a new town—Williamsburg—took its role as the hub of colonial culture and politics; it even had its own college, named after the beneficent monarchs, William and Mary. But while Tidewater society had became entrenched and gentrified, the western reaches of the known frontier were home to small, industrious farmers. In the 1730s a flood of Scotch-Irish and Germans, Quakers and Mennonites, streamed out of Pennsylvania and down into the grassy, open sea of the Shenandoah Valley. The coastal Virginians, recognizing these immigrants' grit, were happy to have them there as a buffer against the Indians—and against the French, who were inching ever south and east into British-claimed territory.

In 1752 war broke out, and the Crown called up the Virginia militia to fight against the French and Indians along the western front. When the fighting ended with a British colonial victory, the courageous young commander-in-chief of the colony's militia emerged from the fray a hero. His name was George Washington.

Having just supplied the British with men and equipment for the French and Indian War, the colonists were less than pleased when, in 1765, Parliament imposed a new tax on them. The infamous Stamp Act raised the hackles of liberal Virginians who were tired of the Mother Country's demands. A firebrand orator named Patrick Henry stood in the Virginia House of Burgesses and admonished the Crown in shocking terms. " . . . Caesar had his Brutus, Charles the Third his Cromwell, and George the Third may profit by their example. If this be treason, make the most of it."

In less than a decade, Virginia and her sister colonies were definitely making the most of it. The 1773 Boston Tea Party, another outburst against British taxation, was followed in 1774 with the convening of the First Continental Congress in Philadelphia. By the time the Second Continental Congress met a year later, British and colonial forces had exchanged fire at Lexington and Concord. The Revolution was on. To lead its forces, the congress unanimously elected one of the colony's few proven military heroes—George Washington.

While Washington struggled to turn ill-equipped and untrained colonial farmers, merchants, and artisans into a fighting force, another Virginian was distinguishing himself in the Philadelphia corridors. Thirty-three-year-old delegate Thomas Jefferson had been charged by his colleagues to draft a paper that would explain the colonists' position to King George. On July 4, 1776, the congress adopted the "Declaration of Independence." Written and adopted over the course of only a couple of weeks, the document reflects Jeffersonian clarity and humanism:

> We hold these truths to be self-evident, that all men are created equal, that they are endowed by their Creator with certain unalienable Rights, that among these are Life, Liberty and the pursuit of Happiness . . . .

For its first half-dozen years, the Revolution raged largely in the colonies to the north and south of Virginia, though the British did harass the colony's easily accessible coastline. In the midst of the war, Virginia's capital was moved for a second time, out of Williamsburg to the more centrally located village of Richmond. By 1781, though, the war was driving deep into Virginia, as turncoat Benedict Arnold led his troops against Richmond. Jefferson, the governor at the time, ordered the General Assembly out of the defenseless town and west into Charlottesville. Looking to corral the impudent author of the Declaration of Independence, the brilliant British commander Lord Cornwallis sent troops in pursuit. But a farmer named John Jouett spotted the redcoats moving along the moonlit roads of the Piedmont. Suspecting their intent, Jouett mounted his horse and dashed through the night

A British Gentleman Reflects on General Washington

*H*e undoubtedly pants for military fame, and, considering the little military knowledge and experience he had before he was made a general, he has performed wonders. He was generally unfortunate (indeed I may with propriety say always) in every action where he was immediately concerned until the affair at Trenton in the Jerseys. Since that unlucky period (for us) he has only been too successful.

His education is not very great nor his parts shining, his disposition is rather heavy than volatile, much given to silence. In short, he is but a poor speaker and but shines in the epistolary way. His person is tall and genteel, age between forty and fifty, his behavior and deportment is easy, genteel, and obliging, with a certain something about him which pleases everyone who has anything to do with him. There cannot be a greater proof of his particular address and good conduct than his keeping such a number of refractory, headstrong people together in any tolerable degree of decorum.

His house is at a place called Mount Vernon, about twelve miles below Alexandria on the banks of the Potomac River in Virginia, where he has a very fine plantation and farm, but, by the best accounts I could get, his estate, altogether, before these troubles did not amount to more than £300 a year in Virginia currency. But estates in this country are seldom valued by the year; it is some difficulty to know exactly what they are worth where they keep great numbers of Negroes and make large crops of tobacco. His friends and acquaintances reckon him a just man, exceedingly honest, but not very generous. Perhaps they may give him this character because he manages his estate with industry and economy, and very seldom enters into those foolish, giddy, and expensive frolics natural to a Virginian.

He keeps an excellent table, and a stranger, let him be of what country or nation, he will always meet with a most hospitable reception at it. His entertainments were always conducted with the most regularity and in the genteelest manner of any I ever was at on the continent (and I have been at several of them, that is, before he was made a general). Temperance he always observed, was always cool-headed and exceedingly cautious himself, but took great pleasure in seeing his friends entertained in the way most agreeable to themselves. His lady is of a hospitable disposition, always good-humored and cheerful, and seems to be actuated by the same motives with himself, but she is rather of a more lively disposition. They are to all appearances a happy pair.

He has no children by his wife, but she had two by her first husband, a son and daughter. The daughter died unmarried; the son, Mr. John Custis, a very worthy young gentleman, is lately married and lives with his mother at Mount Vernon. He lives entirely as a country gentleman; has no post, civil or military.

—Nicholas Cresswell, *Journal,* 1777

on backroads to warn Jefferson and the others in Charlottesville that the British were coming.

Defeated in this little foray, Cornwallis settled his forces into the Virginia port of Yorktown, near the mouth of the Chesapeake Bay. Washington, still fighting in New York, saw a chance to do the British irreparable harm, particularly with the aid of his new French allies. Sneaking his troops out of New York, he pushed them on a relentless march south into Virginia. By early September his army of 16,000—some ragtag, war-weary Colonials and others French reinforcements— had Cornwallis cornered at Yorktown. French warships hovered at the mouth of the Bay, cutting off a British escape by sea. Washington's army laid siege to York- town, as Cornwallis, vastly outnumbered, pulled back and waited for British rein- forcements to arrive by sea. They never came. After several weeks, the English lord admitted defeat. But with characteristic disdain, he refused to appear in person for the surrender ceremonies. The opposing forces gathered on an open field for the ceremony, and as the redcoat fifes and drums played "The World Turned Upside Down," British Brig. Charles O'Hara surrendered what turned out to be almost a quarter of a continent to Washington. Though the war would drag on for another year and a half in New York, Yorktown marked America's decisive moment.

■ FROM COLONIALISM TO MODERNISM

With peace came all the freedoms and foibles of independence. Under the loosely knit Articles of Confederation, each of the new states operated virtually on its own. After a decade of foundering along in 13 different, often contentious directions, the barely united states recognized the need for some central authority, particularly to manage commerce, banking, and foreign affairs. A Constitutional Convention was held, again in Philadelphia, and after much wrangling among delegates, the outcome was the United States Constitution—still the Bible of American law and government. The newly formed union also voted unanimously for the unimpeachable hero of the Revolution, George Washington, to become the country's first President. After more wrangling, the Congress empowered Washington to establish a new "federal city" somewhere in the southern precinct. He chose a spot on the Potomac River about 15 miles (24 km) upstream from his beloved Mount Vernon. A slice of Virginia, including the thriving port town of Alexandria, was included in the diamond-shaped federal tract.

During the country's first decades under the Constitution, Virginia continued to hold a place of prominence, contributing seven of the nation's first 12 Presidents. But, while its soil seemed to grow good statesmen, it did not grow much else, especially in the populous east, where tobacco had exhausted the lands. Throughout the early nineteenth century, there was a mass exodus of younger Virginians to the unspoiled lands in the west. With its depleted population and soil, the state still remained rural and agrarian. The few pockets of early industrialization were located in Tidewater and in cities near the fall line—Fredericksburg, Petersburg, and Alexandria. The capital, Richmond, located right at the fall line of the James River, had also put its power to good use, becoming a major tobacco-processing and flour-milling center, as well as the home of the redoubtable Tredegar Ironworks. In the West, coal, iron, and salt-mining were burgeoning, as was a growing disaffection with the Eastern "Tuckahoes"—the gentry that still relied on slave labor and had a disproportionate hold on the reins of Virginia's political power. The Western "Cohees" (from "Quoth he") of the Shenandoah Valley and surrounding mountains lived virtually in another world from that of the old Tidewater. And the state did nothing constructive to knit its two halves. When the age of railroads arrived in the mid-1800s, Virginia could have regained its prosperity by building rails that linked the goods of the West with its ports and markets in the East. But rivalry between cities like Richmond, Petersburg, and Norfolk resulted in small "short lines" that went only from here to there, with no real intrastate network.

Then there was the question of slavery. It hung ominously over the state—and over the century—just as Jefferson had predicted it would. He had called it "a fire-

George Washington as a young man. A third-generation Virginian, his great-grandfather had emigrated from England in the mid-1600s.

bell in the night" that "awakened and filled me with terror. I consider it at once a knell of the Union." By the mid-nineteenth century, many other Virginians had come to share Jefferson's terror. In 1859, John Brown launched his famous raid on Harper's Ferry, now in West Virginia, but then part of Virginia. The moment that Jefferson had dreaded was fast approaching.

With Lincoln's election in 1860, the moment was at hand. In quick succession the seven "cotton states" seceded from the Union. But not Virginia. Only a quarter of Virginia's white population owned slaves. Ironically, the state that suffered most from the war waited three more months to secede. Not until Lincoln ordered up local militia to fight on the side of the North did Virginia leave the Union, refusing to do battle against its Southern brethren. Richmond soon became capital of the Confederacy, and the state chose a brilliant young lieutenant, Robert E. Lee, to lead its forces. It would be a year into the war before the Confederacy's president, Jefferson Davis, made Lee commander of the Army of Northern Virginia.

Almost from the beginning of the war, the fighting was on top of Virginia. Yankee forces quickly moved on Norfolk, burning buildings and scuttling several of the South's precious few ships. In July, members of Congress packed their picnic baskets and drove south to Manassas to watch their Northern troops whomp the Southern upstarts. Soon, they jested, they'd all be dancing in Richmond. They might have been, too, had they not come up against a stonewall. The battle looked like it was going to be a Northern rout, when suddenly an eccentric professor from the Virginia Military Institute turned it around. Thomas Jonathan Jackson and his men managed to hold onto an impossible position on the high ground of Henry House Hill. Seeing him there, South Carolina's General Bee rallied his own retreating troops by calling, "There stands Jackson like a stone wall! Rally behind the Virginians!" The Rebels, letting loose for the first time with their blood-curdling yell, took Manassas against all odds. And the war dug deeper into the soul of Virginia.

After Manassas, the redoubtable Jackson went on to wage his legendary Valley Campaign. For three weeks his band of 6,000 to 19,000 men outmaneuvered, outfought, and outwitted 65,000 Union forces, frankly making fools of the Northerners up and down the Shenandoah Valley—and keeping them away from already beleaguered Richmond. By now Lee was in command of his "Army of Northern Virginia," and he was intent on shoving the Yankees that were crawling all over the Old Dominion back across the Potomac and into Washington. By August he had managed to do just that, but it was to little avail. The North could simply regroup, resupply, and come at the South again. But every battle cost Lee men and supplies he couldn't replace. In late August of 1862, when the North and South squared off again at Antietam, the Confederacy suffered a serious blow.

In the year that followed, the South's fortunes turned up again with stunning victories at Fredericksburg and Chancellorsville, sites within 10 miles (16 km) of one another in northern Virginia. But Chancellorsville was bought at an immense cost, because it was here that the seemingly invincible Stonewall fell. Riding out at dusk after a victorious day, Jackson was mistakenly shot by Southern sentries. His wounded arm was partially amputated, and he seemed to be recovering when pneumonia set in. Within the week he was dead.

Perhaps if Jackson had lived the Southern devastation at Gettysburg could have been avoided, or at least lessened. In any case, the human cataclysm that occurred in that small Pennsylvania crossroads claimed 28,000 Southern casualties and 23,000 Northern ones. After Gettysburg, Lee and his generals knew the war was lost, but they fought on. By late spring, Richmond was virtually surrounded and nearby Petersburg under siege. On a fine April morning, the old Confederate capital was abandoned and much of it put to the torch by its own people. There was nothing left to fight with, or for. On April 9, Lee met with Grant in a small house in the central Virginia town of Appomattox, and the two generals worked out the terms of surrender.

The war was over, the Union restored, and the Old Dominion a vast, unremitting wasteland. Her farmlands were ruined, a seventh of her white men were either dead or disabled, her currency was utterly worthless, and she had no capital with which to rebuild. What Virginia did seem to have in abundance was a tough and inordinately proud bunch of people. The survivors of the "War Between the States," as old Virginians still call it, adapted to a new age. Ex-slaveholders in the southeast slowly turned their farms over to share-croppers, parceling out small plots in return for a portion of the harvested crop. While the system helped get the state back on its feet, it was only a step above the slavery that blacks had suffered.

In the western part of the state, however, farmers wisely diversified, turning to wheat, vegetables, and livestock. Mining also slowly recovered, and by the turn of the century the Hampton Roads ports were world leaders in coal exporting, thanks in part to the railroads. Finally, the state had a viable network of rails that connected its eastern ports to its western products.

GRANT MEETS LEE AT APPOMATTOX

On April 9, 1865, Gen. Ulysses S. Grant met with Gen. Robert E. Lee at Appomattox to accept the surrender of the Confederate army. Brig. Gen. Horace Porter, Grant's aide-de-camp, wrote an account of the meeting.

*T*he contrast between the two commanders was striking and could not fail to attract marked attention as they sat ten feet apart facing each other. General Grant, then nearly forty-three years of age, was five feet eight inches in height, with shoulders slightly stooped. His hair and full beard were a nutbrown, without a trace of gray in them. He had on a single-breasted blouse, made of dark-blue flannel, unbuttoned in front, and showing a waistcoat underneath. He wore an ordinary pair of top boots, with his trousers inside, and was without spurs. The boots and portions of his clothes were spattered with mud. He had had on a pair of thread gloves, of a dark-yellow color, which he had taken off on entering the room. His felt, "sugarloaf," stiff-brimmed hat was thrown on the table beside him. He had no sword, and a pair of shoulder straps was all there was about him to designate his rank. In fact, aside from these, his uniform was that of a private soldier.

Lee, on the other hand, was fully six feet in height and quite erect for one of his age, for he was Grant's senior by sixteen years. His hair and full beard were a silver-gray, and quite thick, except that the hair had become a little thin in front. He wore a new uniform of Confederate gray, buttoned up to the throat, and at his side he carried a long sword of exceedingly fine workmanship, the hilt studded with jewels. It was said to be the sword that had been presented to him by the state of Virginia. His top boots were comparatively new and seemed to have on them some ornamental stitching of red silk. Like his uniform, they were singularly clean and but little travel stained. On the boots were handsome spurs, with large rowels. A felt hat, which in color matched pretty closely that of his uniform, and a pair of long buckskin gauntlets lay beside him on the table. We asked Colonel Marshall afterward how it was that both he and his chief wore such fine toggery and looked so much as if they had turned out to go to church, while with us our outward garb scarcely rose to the dignity even of the "shabby genteel." He enlightened us regarding the contrast by explaining that when their headquarters wagons had been pressed so closely by our cavalry a few days before and it was found they would have to destroy all their baggage except the clothes they carried on their backs, each one, naturally, selected the newest suit he had, and sought to propitiate the god of destruction by a sacrifice of his second-best.

General Grant began the conversation by saying: "I met you once before, General Lee, while we were serving in Mexico, when you came over from General Scott's headquarters to visit Garland's brigade, to which I then belonged. I have always remembered your appearance, and I think I should have recognized you anywhere." "Yes," replied General Lee, "I know I met you on that occasion, and I have often thought of it and tried to recollect how you looked, but I have never been able to recall a single feature."

—Brig. Gen. Horace Porter, 1865

Robert E. Lee surrenders to Ulysses S. Grant at Appomattox on April 9, 1865. (Library of Congress)

Still, a vast majority of the state remained rural—and deeply attached to old traditions. Through the first decades of the twentieth century, Virginia adhered to the discriminatory "Jim Crow" laws that haunted much of the South. The result was a dual culture—separate schools, separate stores, separate neighborhoods, and separate colleges and universities (the state had several nationally known black institutions). In spite of, or maybe because of, the state's segregationist policies, in some parts of Virginia—notably Richmond and the Tidewater—black businesses and black culture flourished. The state produced such remarkable figures as educator Booker T. Washington and musicians like Ella Fitzgerald, Pearl Bailey, and opera star Camilla Williams. At socials and barbecues across eastern Virginia, fine local bluesmen improvised on the distinctive, soulful sounds of the Piedmont blues. "Ever been down, you know 'bout how I feel. Ever been down, you know 'bout how I feel. Like a soldier lying here on some battlefield."

Like their white counterparts, African American Virginians suffered with the Depression and prospered with the World Wars. World War II created a major boom in Northern Virginia, where the hydra-like tentacles of nearby Washington have forever fueled the local economy. The Hampton Roads area, with its strong military and shipbuilding tradition, became a national focus of incoming and outgoing men and matériel. At war's end, those areas continued to thrive, and Virginia as a whole moved slowly but inexorably away from its antebellum affectations.

When the issue of segregation came to a head with the Supreme Court's 1954 *Brown vs. Board of Education* decision, Virginia reacted much as it had during Civil War secession. Always more "Virginian" than strictly "Southern," neither the state nor its schools ever became armed battlegrounds over the issue. Still, the governor postured like a diehard segregationist and the General Assembly enacted a law that withheld state funds from any school honoring integration. The battle over integration raged in Virginia for half a decade, and during that period, some public schools closed. Then in 1959, a handful of black children were admitted to white schools in Norfolk and Arlington, heralding the gradual end to a racial system whose roots went back 300 years, to the early days of slavery.

Today, Virginia is an amalgam of its own history. Proud of its past, it carefully tends its colonial homes and its Civil War heroes, of which, in both cases, there are many. The state no longer "makes the painful impression," as British historian Arnold Toynbee wrote in 1940, "of a country living under a spell, in which time has stood still." Time and change are moving rapidly here now. In 1990, Virginia elected the first African American governor in the nation, L. Douglas Wilder. And the state's influential "Golden Crescent," the urban corridor that stretches from northern Virginia south to Richmond, then east to Hampton Roads, has become a major chunk of the eastern megalopolis.

In most of the Old Dominion, enlightened thinking plays as much a part in local goings-on as does conservatism. Certainly, there are still pockets of never-say-die traditionalism, but they only add to the state's divinely eccentric personality. Pinch most any of Virginia's natives, whether liberal or conservative, and they'd probably agree with former governor J. Lindsay Almond: "The only sane and constructive course to follow is to remain in the house of our fathers—even though the roof leaks, and there be bats in the belfry, rats in the pantry, a cockroach waltz in the kitchen and skunks in the parlor."

COASTAL VIRGINIA

COASTAL VIRGINIA IS DOMINATED by the huge pulsing heart of the Chesapeake Bay. Its veins and arteries web the land in a network of creeks and marshlands and wide tidal estuaries that flow back and forth to its tidal beat. This vast shallow inland sea, named for a Native American tribe, encompasses several thousand miles of coastline and averages a depth of only 20 feet (6 m). It connects, of course, to the Atlantic, and the Atlantic in turn defines the eastern extreme of Virginia, blessing it with some fine ocean beaches. But the ocean is enormous, somewhat overwhelming, and the property of so many. The bay—or at least its broad southern expanse—belongs solely to the Old Dominion. (Maryland, to be fair, claims ownership of its upper half.)

It was a Marylander, actually, H. L. Mencken, who defined the bay best. He called it "that great protein factory." It certainly was that in Mencken's day, but in recent decades it has suffered tragically from pollutants. Fish and shellfish harvests have fallen off dramatically since the 1950s, leading private citizens, conservation groups and government entities to band together to save the bay. In recent decades, the bay has begun a slow resuscitation. Flounder, croaker, spot, and rockfish are making a gradual comeback. New oyster beds are being planted, sea grass is returning, and more white-sailed ketches and sloops billow across its chop than ever before.

For centuries the bay has meant three things to Virginians: a rich mine for seafood, a limitless watery playground, and a strategic military arena. If you wander its three peninsulas—known locally as the Northern Neck, the Middle Neck, and the Peninsula—you'll soon discover the simplicity, and complexity, of life along the Virginia coast.

■ EASTERN SHORE

Bounded by the Chesapeake on the west and the Atlantic on the east, this alluring tongue of land probably best preserves the old coastal style of Virginia. Its prairie-flat fields of corn and vegetables never lie fallow; in winter they seem to grow flocks of Canada geese and other wintering-over birds. As elsewhere in rural Virginia,

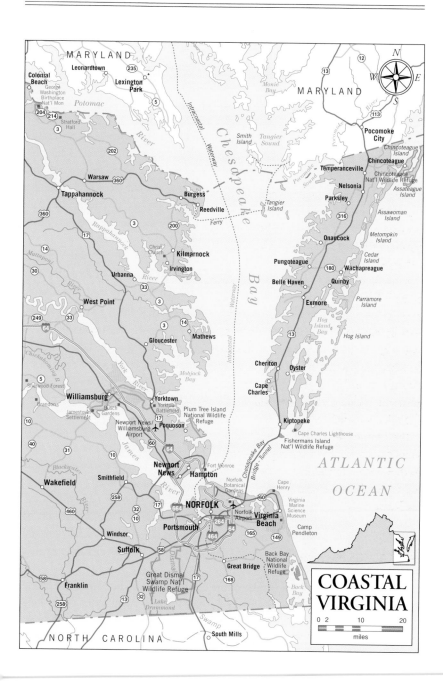

COASTAL VIRGINIA

0 2   10   20
miles

small towns with long histories suddenly appear out of nowhere, and a few water-men still work the creeks and inlets of the bay. Part of what is called the Delmarva (Delaware, Maryland, and Virginia) Peninsula, the Eastern Shore is simply its own place—blessedly provincial and still remarkably pure.

Chincoteague Island—just south of the Maryland border on U.S. 13 then east on Route 175—is this area's best known attraction, made famous by its oysters, its cowboys, and a pony called Misty. For almost 70 years now, the island's firemen have been minding a herd of wild ponies that spend most of the year grazing on adjacent Assateague Island. But once a year, during the last week of July as the firemen herd the young ponies across the inlet that separates the two islands, half the East Coast gathers on Chincoteague to watch. There, the foals are auctioned off in a lively sale.

Local legend holds that ponies first arrived on the island in the sixteenth century, when a group of horses swam ashore from a Spanish galleon shipwrecked offshore. In the 1940s, writer Marguerite Henry spent some time here and made the island's ponies famous with her classic *Misty of Chincoteague.* The book was later turned into a popular movie, and the pony penning has been a standing-room-only affair ever since.

The area is well worth a visit at any time of year. Chincoteague itself charms with its well-weathered but tidy island homes and its abundant seafood restaurants. For those interested in collector-quality decoys, the island also boasts a number of well-respected carvers.

The Chincoteague National Wildlife Refuge, with parts on both islands, is off Route 175 on the east side of town. Over on Assateague Island, the refuge supports a wealth of migratory birds, as well as such graceful year-round shorebirds as egrets and herons. Beyond it, the **Assateague National Seashore** offers a magnificent 37-mile (60-km) stretch of unsullied, undeveloped beach, a rare find on the Atlantic. The old candy-striped Assateague Lighthouse still warns mariners of the Chincoteague shoals, as it has since 1857. Because these islands sided with the Union during the Civil War, this was one of the few Virginia lighthouses that operated throughout the war.

Floating in the gray-green flatness of the Chesapeake Bay, **Tangier Island** barely raises its head above the level of the sea. Yet this two-and-a-half-mile (4-km)-long strip of land manages persistently to survive against time, weather, and the bay.

Life moves slowly here, the watermen in their white dead-rises still plying the islands' reed-lined channels. Neat houses stand crammed into narrow lanes, and soft-crab "plantations"—little sheds raised on stilts above the water—present a picturesque image along the main Tangier boat channel. Most visitors arrive by cruise boat, and spend a few hours poking around the local gift shops and eating very satisfying seafood, particularly at Hilda Crockett's Chesapeake House. This island landmark sets guests down at long family-style tables and starts passing platters of crab cakes, ham, potato salad, clam fritters, cole slaw, home-baked bread, and more.

Besides its seafood and watermen, the island is known for a famous prisoner. In 1814, Francis Scott Key was a captive of British forces, who were using Tangier as a base. From the island, he was transported up the bay to Baltimore, and, while witnessing the Battle of Baltimore, was inspired to write what we now know as the "Star-Spangled Banner." Cruises depart daily May to mid-October from Reedville, Virginia, off Route 360. For reservations call (804) 453-BOAT.

OLDE ENGLISH ON TANGIER ISLAND

Listening to the Tangier Island watermen chatting together in Ray's café or on the boats, many English listeners could imagine they were in Devon or Cornwall. Their pattern of speech has many characteristic West Country intonations. As one fisherman remarked, "Our voice, our language, hasn't changed since people first moved to Tangier Island, or so some people have told us . . ."

The Tangierines—approximately 800 residents—say that their island was first settled in 1686 by a certain John Crockett, a Cornishman. There are no records of this, but the evidence of the Tangier Island speech is overwhelming. To English ears, they sound West Country. Most striking of all "sink" is pronounced *zink*. *Mary* and *merry* have a similar pronunciation, though this is common to much of the tidewater district. "Paul" and "ball" sound like *pull* and *bull*. For "creek" they will say *crik*. And they have a special local vocabulary: *spider* for "frying-pan," *bateau* for "skiff" and *curtains* for "blinds."

—Robert McCrum, *The Story of English*, 1986

Wild ponies of Chincoteague (top). Shucking a Chincoteague oyster (bottom).

An aerial view of Tangier Island.

■ CHESAPEAKE BAY BRIDGE-TUNNEL

More than just a transportation corridor, this 17.6-mile (28.3-km) man-made phenomenon allows you to drive out onto—and into—the sea, with gulls wheeling overhead and enormous oceangoing ships passing in front of your car.

Cutting across the Chesapeake Bay from the Virginia Beach area to the Eastern Shore, the bridge signifies that can-do spirit so characteristic of the early 1960s when it was built. The original design called for an above-water bridge all the way across the bay, with higher spans to allow shipping in and out of Hampton Roads. But navy strategists wouldn't go for that. They claimed that if an enemy chose to destroy one of the high spans, the resulting debris would block navigable channels, and effectively put the Norfolk Naval Base out of business. And so today, what we have is an elaborate complex of four man-made islands connected by 12 miles (19 km) of trestled roadway, two mile-long tunnels, two bridges, and two miles (3.2 km) of causeway. The resulting engineering feat cuts out the 95 miles (153 km) it used to take to go *around* the bay, instead of across it. And it has given local anglers a new option. A 625-foot-long (1,006-km) fishing pier juts out from Sea Gull Island, the complex's southernmost island and the only spot where you can get out of your car and experience being "on the bay."

In 1987 the name of the local Eastern Shore businessman who masterminded the bridge-tunnel was affixed to it. It is now officially known as the Lucius J. Kellam, Jr., Bridge-Tunnel.

■ VIRGINIA BEACH

Virginia Beach is just that—miles of Atlantic beach, boardwalk, and highrise resort hotels. The city also happens to be the state's most populous metropolis, and it's still growing. The *Wall Street Journal* declared it a "Boom Town of the '90s." To visitors, it is first and foremost a beach, a place to come to watch dolphins disport just offshore, to loll in white sand, to beachcomb, rollerblade, bar hop, or . . . take in yet more of Virginia's history.

The resort area, centered along Atlantic Avenue between Fifth and 31st streets, is now in the process of reconstruction. Connecting park areas, wider sidewalks, and a generally more gracious appearance will result. Away from the built-up beach bustle and usual tacky shops are a few unexpected finds to check out when the sun and sand get to be too much.

LOW, SORROWFUL BEAUTY

*R*iding down to Port Warwick from Richmond, the train begins to pick up speed on the outskirts of the city, past the tobacco factories with their ever-present haze of acrid, sweetish dust and past the rows of uniformly brown clapboard houses which stretch down the hilly streets for miles, the hundreds of rooftops all reflecting the pale light of dawn; past the suburban roads still sluggish and sleepy with early morning traffic, and rattling swiftly now over the bridge which separates the last two hills where in the valley below you can see the James River winding beneath its acid-green crust of scum out beside the chemical plants and more rows of clapboard houses and into the woods beyond.

Suddenly the train is burrowing through the pinewoods, and the conductor, who looks middle-aged and respectable like someone's favorite uncle, lurches through the car asking for tickets . . . and when you ask him how far it is to Port Warwick and he says, "Ab*oot* eighty miles," you know for sure that you're in the Tidewater . . . .

You look out once more at the late summer landscape and the low, sorrowful beauty of tideland streams winding through marshes full of small, darting, frightened noises and glistening and dead silent at noon, except for a whistle, far off, and a distant rumble on the rails.

—William Styron, *Lie Down in Darkness,* 1951

Virginia Marine Science Museum, located at 717 General Booth Boulevard just south of the Rudee Inlet Bridge, is now in the process of renovation and expansion. It offers a wealth of exhibits, from a 50,000-gallon aquarium to examples of local wildlife, explanations of weather movements, and a chance to tong oysters like a real waterman. An outdoor boardwalk crosses a pristine salt marsh, with explanations of what life is like in a Virginia wetland.

The Association for Research and Enlightenment (67th and Atlantic Avenue) is well known to new age cognoscenti as the house that Edgar Cayce built. Sometimes called the "father of holistic medicine," Cayce was an early twentieth-century psychic who, while in a self-induced sleep, could diagnose and treat the ailments of people who sought his help. This Virginia Beach center, founded in 1931 on Cayce's spiritual principles, seeks to help visitors explore such topics as dreams, ESP, reincarnation, and holistic health.

Christian Broadcasting Network, meanwhile, pushes "that old-time religion." Broadcast evangelist Pat Robertson founded the network, and uses it as a base for his Family Channel, his "700 Club," and his Founders Inn.

Cape Henry defines the northern end of Virginia Beach, its windswept tip now safely surrounded by well-guarded Fort Story. It is well worth showing your driver's

A fashionable Virginia Beach seaside resort, circa 1920s. (Underwood Archives)

license to the gatehouse guard so that you can drive through the base and down to the historic hub of Virginia's Atlantic Coast. Here, the buff-brick **Old Cape Henry Lighthouse,** built under orders from George Washington, points its head toward the ocean. The oldest government-built lighthouse in the country, it was replaced in 1881 by the "new" black-and-white Cape Henry Lighthouse, which stands just across the road. That fortuity means that today visitors may actually explore the defunct colonial light, climbing its dizzying 84-step circular staircase, then up a ladder into the tower. From here, the Atlantic reaches endlessly off toward Europe. To get to Cape Henry, take Route 60 to northern Virginia Beach and look for signs to Fort Story.

Across from the lighthouse stands the **First Landing Cross,** commemorating the place where that 1607 band of Englishmen first landed on Virginia soil. Here, too, stands a **Battle of the Capes Monument** and a statue to the French Comte de Grasse. Both honor the critical Revolutionary sea battle between British Rear Adm. Thomas Graves and the French commander Joseph Paul de Grasse. De Grasse and his fleet of 24 ships managed to repulse the 19 British ships that were intended to reinforce Cornwallis at Yorktown. Because the British fleet never made it, Washington and his allies were able to defeat Cornwallis at Yorktown, a battle that turned the British Empire upside-down.

The southern end of Virginia Beach is blessed with the **Back Bay National Wildlife Refuge,** a 4,600-acre playground for winter waterfowl, summer-nesting osprey and songbirds, and fall and spring migratory flocks following the Atlantic flyway.

Virginia Beach also boasts several historic houses that offer public tours. These include the **Francis Land House,** an eighteenth-century brick plantation house located at 3131 Virginia Beach Boulevard; **Upper Wolfsnare,** a simpler farm home at 2040 Potters Road; and the **Adam Thoroughgood** and **Lynnhaven houses,** at 1636 Parish Road and 4401 Wishart Road, respectively. These last two well-preserved architectural gems break with the manor house norm. Both resemble English cottages and reflect a lifestyle common in the colonies before the tobacco barons began building their palaces. Gardens and interpreters enhance the historic experience at each.

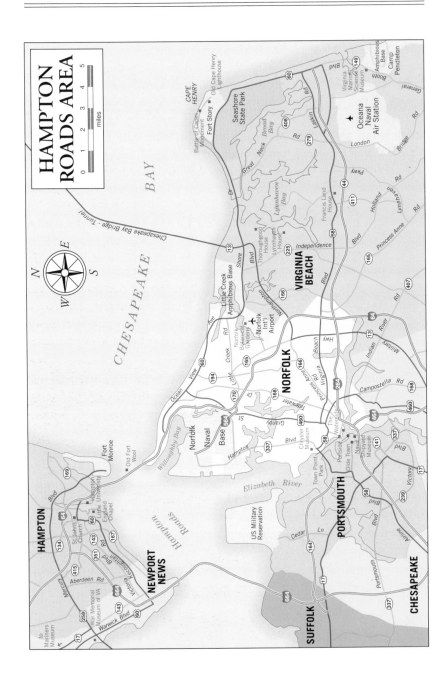

HAMPTON ROADS AREA

■ HAMPTON ROADS

Virginians use the term Hampton Roads in ways that may seem inordinately confusing to non-Virginians. In brief, Hampton Roads is the large natural harbor into which the James, Elizabeth, Hampton, Nansemond, and Lafayette rivers flow. But Hampton Roads can also mean the lands surrounding this body of water. That's where lines begin to blur. Some people call only the area on the south side of the harbor Hampton Roads, referring to the north side as the "Peninsula." Other people call the south side simply that—"south side," technically meaning everything south of the James. Whatever the coasts of Hampton Roads are called, they have in common a mutual regard for the military-industrial complex, a long history, and a similar conservative sentiment.

As to the history, the Powhatan Indians were here long before that first band of Englishmen arrived in the spring of 1607. Though the English did not linger long at the time before continuing upriver to Jamestown, they returned and established a fort at Old Point Comfort within three years. Shortly after that, they attacked a Kecoughtan village, drove out the natives, and "opened up" the general terrain for settlement. Soon a smattering of colonists had settled in what is now Hampton.

Lightning crackles between the old and new lighthouses at Cape Henry.

The shipyards at Norfolk in 1936. (The Chrysler Museum)

Situated as it was near the entrance to the bay, the region quickly developed as a shipping and maritime hub.

But war, more than anything else, has sealed the fate of this area. When the Revolution broke out, Hampton Roads' strategic position was not lost on the British. Norfolk, Portsmouth, and Hampton were attacked and badly ravaged. Even the dastardly quisling Benedict Arnold stopped in the area on his way up the James to attack Richmond. Not long after him, the British Lord Cornwallis arrived in Portsmouth with his entire force, planning to set sail from here to New York. But his superiors ordered him to establish a post somewhere on the Virginia coast, and after some thought, he chose Yorktown. History has recorded what happened there.

The Civil War struck Hampton Roads hard as well, tearing the area in two. From the beginning, the Union held onto Hampton's Fort Monroe, using it as a stronghold in the midst of Confederate territory. Soon, much of the rest of the region was in Federal hands. Even the history-making "battle of the ironclads" was waged in the waters of Hampton Roads.

Ironically, recent wars have brought only prosperity to this area, as men, matériel, and money have flooded in. Even in these post-Cold War days, the navy, air force, and army are all well-represented here, and Hampton Roads remains one of the greatest shows of military might on earth.

■ NORFOLK

Most urbane of the Hampton Roads cities, Norfolk owes its cosmopolitan air to two things—a huge and profitable naval omnipresence and the Chrysler Museum. A sophisticated institution by any standards, the Chrysler sets a certain "tone," as well as extending its refined arms out to administer other historic sites in the city.

Norfolk Naval Base, the largest naval base in the world, is the place to go to "see some navy." More than 150 ships call this home port, and at any given time, the base's 15 piers resemble a bristling battlescape of subs, tenders, destroyers,

BATTLE OF THE IRONCLADS

In 1861 Portsmouth sat safely in the middle of the Confederacy, and the Union troops stationed in its federal shipyard were essentially surrounded. Given their situation, they judiciously decided to "jump ship," as it were, but before they did, they torched everything of worth, including several ships in for repairs. One of these, the unremarkable steam frigate *Merrimac,* rose phoenix-like from the ashes.

The secretary of the Confederacy's non-existent navy had ordered that an "unsinkable" ship be built, reasoning that "inequality of numbers may be compensated by invulnerability." So, the half-burned *Merrimac* was raised and resurrected as something her re-creators liked to call an ironclad. Though she made less than six knots and drew 22 feet (7 m) of water, she did seem unsinkable, with her iron-plated hull. She was duly christened the CSS *Virginia.*

Word of this indomitable threat reached Northern ears, and soon the Union, too, was at work on its own unsinkable warship, the *Monitor.* The *Virginia* struck first. On March 8, 1862, the ironclad ran out of the Elizabeth River and into Hampton Roads, making for the five federal warships that had blockaded Virginia's most important ports. At battle's end she had effectively destroyed or run off all five of them.

Two days earlier the *Monitor* had left New York under tow. As she rounded Cape

continues

Henry, her men could hear the cannon booming in Hampton Roads, but they arrived too late to join the fray. The *Monitor* got her chance, though, the following day. Spectators lined the shores as the two ironclads took to the ring. For four hours the ships stalked and sparred with each other, but apparently they were fairly evenly matched because their duel ended in a draw. The *Monitor* crept back to Union-held Fort Monroe, while the *Virginia* returned to Portsmouth. Though both ships stayed in Hampton Roads for two more months, they never engaged again, mostly because President Lincoln had ordered that the *Monitor* "be not too much exposed."

When Norfolk fell to the Union in May 1862, the *Virginia's* commander wanted to take her up-river to safety in Richmond, but he was warned that her draft was too deep to get past the Jamestown flats. On May 11, the legendary ironclad was blown up by her own forces. The *Monitor* survived until the following December, when she went down in a storm off North Carolina's Cape Hatteras.

The recently opened Merrimac and Monitor Bridge across Hampton Roads commemorates the battle of the two ships. It also angers all diehard Southerners, who believe it should be called the "Virginia and Monitor Bridge."

The Virginia (Merrimac) *and the* Monitor, *the nation's first ironclad ships, in battle. (Virginia State Library and Archives)*

(opposite) Chincoteague resident, Walt Clark, poses with Old Glory (the flag, not the pickup).

cruisers, oilers, landing ships, and even an aircraft carrier (five are homeported here.) Stretching for 15 miles (24 km) along the Elizabeth River and Willoughby Bay—off of Hampton Boulevard or I-64, this huge complex of naval facilities requires more than 100,000 military and civilian personnel to keep it going.

Besides its run-of-the-mill brass, the base also claims two four-star admirals: the Commander-in-Chief, Atlantic, who is also in command of NATO'S Atlantic operations; and the Commander-in-Chief, Atlantic fleet. Together, these two are responsible for the defense of the eastern half of the country as well as a considerable chunk of the Western Hemisphere. Both they and other high-ranking elite live in a line of gracious old homes that are left over from the 1907 Jamestown Exhibition held on this site. The exhibition drew attention to the naval potential of the area and planted the seed for the base. But no real construction began until 1917, the final year of World War I. By Armistice Day the following year, 34,000 enlisted men were stationed here.

The navy presence in Norfolk has grown steadily ever since, and even recent base closings have left this huge facility virtually unscathed. Currently, it stands to lose only one small facility and will probably gain in stature as other bases close. The base is accessible by guided tours that begin at The Waterside or at the base's tour office off Hampton Boulevard.

Downtown Norfolk is something of a mishmash today. Parking lots sprawl at the edge of historic homes, some new highrises loom above dilapidated storefronts, but the waterfront—the waterfront thrives. An inviting brick promenade follows the shoreline of the Elizabeth River (from downtown take Tidewater Dr.), where work boats and smaller naval vessels slide by. **Town Point Park,** a seven-acre greensward and outdoor concert site, sits between the **Waterside Festival Marketplace** (333 Waterside Drive) with its 120 shops and eateries, and the city's new gun-metal gray **Nauticus.** This high-tech/Disneyesque/virtual reality "museum" allows visitors to explore the rich life of the ocean realm; human uses of the seas through shipping, naval technology, and energy exploration; and the role the port of Hampton Roads has played in world maritime affairs. Long in the making, Nauticus is a joint venture between government agencies, universities, and private donors.

Inland from this "new Norfolk," but within walking distance of it, are several sites from the city's long past. One, of course, is a church. The brick wall enclosing it bespeaks **St. Paul's** colonial past. Inside are graves dating to the seventeenth and eighteenth centuries. The large brick church itself (corner of St. Paul's Boulevard and City Hall Avenue), built in 1739, is the only structure that survived British Lord Dunmore's destruction of the city on New Year's Day 1776. But St. Paul's did take a hit. A rusting British cannonball remains lodged high up in the southern wall of the church exterior.

Moses Myers House holds a unique place among Virginia's endless historic homes. This dignified old Georgian/Federal-style brick home, located at 323 E. Freemason Street, portrays the life of a Jewish family in colonial Norfolk.

A boot-straps entrepreneur, Moses Myers came to Norfolk from his hometown of New York in 1787 when he was in his mid-30s. The recent Revolution had already forced him into bankruptcy once, but no quitter, Myers believed Norfolk would provide good business opportunities. Migrating south with his bride, Eliza, they established themselves as the first Jewish family in Norfolk. Within five years Myers's merchandising business was doing so well that he was able to erect the first stage of this impressive home. However, the gods of fortune, then as now, proved fickle, and the War of 1812 again destroyed Myers financially. He lost everything but his house and its furnishings.

For five generations, until 1931, the home stayed in the Myers family. Now owned by the city and administered by the Chrysler Museum, it is furnished mostly with Myers family pieces, from the exceptional mahogany case clock that Moses and Eliza brought with them from New York to portraits by such masters as Gilbert Stuart and Thomas Sully. Apparently, the Myerses' fortunes have again been reversed—positively—and their home has become a shrine to fortitude and good taste.

The **MacArthur Memorial**, on Bank Street and City Hall Avenue, represents a shrine of a wholly different cast. Begun through a grassroots effort of local admirers of Gen. Douglas MacArthur, the memorial opened in 1964, in Norfolk's old, domed, neo-classical city hall (1850). (Thomas U. Walters, designer of the U.S. Capitol dome, acted as a consulting architect on the building.) Now enshrined in the rotunda are the remains of the general, with surrounding rotunda walls bearing his quotes. The rest of the building traces MacArthur's meteoric rise to five-star general and his critical role in the Pacific theater.

The Chrysler Museum sits amid the decorous eclectic-style mansions of the city's Hague neighborhood at 245 W. Olney Road—for hours call (804) 622-1211. Housing one of this country's finest art collections, the serene Italianate marble structure holds exceptional exhibits of antique and art glass; Greco-Roman, Egyptian, and pre-Columbian antiquities; and art nouveau and art deco works. Its wide-ranging collection of paintings includes works by Americans Charles Willson Peale, Asher Durand, Winslow Homer, Edward Hopper, Jackson Pollock, and Richard Diebenkorn. Works by European masters from the fourteenth to the twentieth century are also displayed, including pieces by Filippino Lippi, Gauguin, Renoir, and Matisse.

The museum traces its origins to two schoolteachers—Irene Leache and Anna Cogswell Wood—who arrived in Norfolk after the Civil War and started a female seminary. Their love of art eventually inspired local citizens to found the Norfolk Arts Society, which in turn led to the construction of this building. Completed in 1939, it was called the Norfolk Museum of Arts and Sciences and it thrived as such until 1971. That was the year Walter Chrysler bestowed his bounty on the city of Norfolk, giving it a major portion of his redoubtable art collection.

Son of the founder of the Chrysler Corporation, Walter seems to have been a born collector. At the tender age of 14, he bought his first serious piece—a Renoir nude. That early attempt at collecting ended tragically, when the dorm master at his boarding school destroyed the "prurient" piece. Walter did not give up. After college, he took a grand tour of Europe, collecting the avant-garde works of

The Chrysler Museum in Norfolk.

Sunset over the Jordan Bridge in South Norfolk.

Matisse, Picasso, and others. When he returned to this country and a corporate life, he continued to pursue his interest in art, helping to develop New York's Museum of Modern Art. He also found time to produce a couple of Broadway plays, including a hit called "New Faces," which catapulted actress Eartha Kitt into stardom.

In 1958 the retired Chrysler established a museum for his collections in an old church in Provincetown, Massachusetts. But soon he outgrew this space. Norfolk, hearing of his plight, offered him a home at the Norfolk Museum of Arts and Sciences. He accepted. He and his wife, who had longtime affiliations with Norfolk society, established themselves in an old brownstone mansion in the Hague within sight of the museum. Visitors to the house recall the soft glow of the Tiffany lamps, now on display in the museum, that illuminated the rooms in the Tidewater twilight. In 1988, at the age of 71, Chrysler died in Norfolk, close to his beloved collection.

Norfolk Botanical Garden blankets 150 acres in the lush vegetation of coastal Virginia. Forests of lacy conifers; rose, holly, and camellia gardens; rhododendron thickets; and banks of azaleas edge lakes and lily ponds. Some 12 miles (19 km) of walking paths thread this sylvan quietude, and visitors can tour the grounds on foot, aboard the gardens' open-air "trackless trains" or on canal boats that ply the lake.

The garden began as a WPA project in 1938, when a group of local women was hired to plant 4,000 azaleas. Gradually, more azaleas were added, as well as camellias and rhododendrons. In the 1950s, the garden gained renown as the site of the International Azalea Festival, which still is held every April. Hosted by a young "queen" and her court, the festival honors the North Atlantic Treaty Organization. Even in the forest, this city's military heritage is not forgotten. The garden is located on Azalea Garden Road, near Norfolk International Airport and east of the intersection of Military Highway and Norview Avenue.

It's worth visiting **Doumar's,** a '50s-style drive-in at 1919 Monticello Avenue, for its barbecue, ice cream, and history . The Doumars' illustrious uncle, Abe, was none other than the inventor of the ice cream cone. The inspiration came when Abe, a Lebanese immigrant, was selling trinkets at the 1904 St. Louis World's Fair. Standing near a waffle vendor, Doumar suggested that the guy roll his waffles into cones, fill them with ice cream, and call them a cornucopia. Hence, the ice cream cone megabusiness America enjoys today.

After the fair Abe invented his own four-iron waffle machine, and three years later he was in Norfolk, hawking his cornucopias at the Jamestown Exposition. Teddy Roosevelt himself, in attendance at the exposition, enjoyed a Doumar's confection. Eventually, Abe and other Doumar kinsmen settled permanently in Norfolk, selling ice cream from stands along the city's Ocean View beach. By the 1930s, the Doumars had opened the drive-in that still operates today. Now, as then, the Doumars promise you any ice cream flavor you want—as long as its vanilla, chocolate, strawberry, or butter pecan.

■ PORTSMOUTH

From its colonial days, Portsmouth has been known as a shipbuilding town. Its Gosport Navy Yard, established in 1767, went on to become the Norfolk Naval Shipyard in 1945, now the oldest and largest in the country. Though it faces potential extinction in the next round of base closings, the naval yard has enjoyed a long, illustrious history over its two centuries. It was responsible for the ironclad CSS *Virginia* (also known as the *Merrimac*), as well as for the first battleship, the USS *Texas* (1892), and the first aircraft carrier, the USS *Langley* (1922).

Cultivating an image beyond its shipbuilding one, Portsmouth these days is tempting travelers to its fair shores with its small-scale but appealing festival market, **Portside,** which overlooks the Elizabeth River and the Norfolk skyline. And its nearby Olde Towne claims "the largest concentration of restored eighteenth-century homes between Alexandria and Charleston."

The apple-red **Lightship Museum,** docked along the waterfront near Water Street, is a fine piece of the maritime past. The ship's spit-and-polish interior gives a good sense of what life was like for crews living aboard these floating beacons. This one saw service from 1915 to 1964, and among its other compelling features, it displays the old Fresnel lens from the Smith Point Lighthouse.

The first lightship ever built in this country was constructed in nearby Hampton in 1819. Within a year of that commission, four more lightships had been built and placed off dangerous shoals in the bay. The age of lightships peaked in the early twentieth century, then rapidly declined as they were replaced by buoys and lighthouses or simply deemed unnecessary. They became functionally extinct when the last one, the *Nantucket I,* was decommissioned in 1985. Its poignant final message read: "We must now look somewhere else to find the stuff that sea stories are made of."

A few sea stories can be found close by at the **Naval Shipyard Museum,** on the corner of High and Water streets, where model ships ride the immobile seas of display cases and wartime and maritime memorabilia are exhibited. A large diorama of Portsmouth in 1776 brings the colonial town to life and offers a narration on the history of the city from 1776 to the present.

You can get a full-scale taste of that period by strolling through **Olde Towne Portsmouth,** just west of the waterfront. This is the original 65-acre tract laid out as a colonial town in 1752. Its well-tended Colonial, Federal, and Victorian homes provide a wealth of architectural and historic detail. A free brochure, "Olde Towne Walking Tour," available around town, details the importance of the different homes, almost all of which are still private residences. Only the **Hill House** at 221 North Street functions as a museum and headquarters of the Portsmouth Historical Association. A dignified old brick Federal built in the early 1800s, the home holds furnishings collected by the longtime owners, the Thompson/Hill family, who lived here until 1961.

Homecoming for a U.S. carrier at Pier 12 at the Norfolk Naval Base.

Ball-Nivison House at 417 Middle Street is a good example of an architectural trompe l'oeil known as a "tax dodger's" house. Its gambrel roof and dormer windows were designed to partially disguise its second floor and thereby persuade rapacious mid-seventeenth-century British tax collectors to assess it as a one-story structure. During its long history, the house entertained some illustrious guests. The Marquis de Lafayette was feted here during his 1824 hero's tour of America. Andrew Jackson, too, came in 1833, on one of his inspections of the town's naval facilities.

Downtown Portsmouth melds into the edges of Olde Towne. These days, some of the 1950s and '60s-style buildings along High Street have been put to innovative uses. The **Commodore Theatre** (421 High Street), built in 1945 as a movie house, has been returned to its original art deco splendor—but with a twist. Its lower level now serves as a theater/restaurant where audiences can enjoy a light meal and watch first-run movies at the same time. Nearby, a defunct department store has been renovated to house the city's **Children's Museum.** Originally housed down the street in the old courthouse building, the museum is now located at the corner of Court and High streets, and much expanded. Its whimsical, hands-on approach is a great hit with elementary-age kids.

Meanwhile, the Classical Revival brick courthouse, located at 1846 Court Street between Queen and High, is now the exclusive domain of the city's **Arts Center,** which features changing multi-media exhibits of the works of both regional and international artists. Next door is the small **Virginia Sports Hall of Fame,** where mementos and sports equipment highlight great moments in the lives of Virginia teams and athletes.

■ GREAT DISMAL SWAMP

The Great Dismal Swamp hardly deserves its gloomy name. Dismal it is not, though great it is, and for that reason it's now preserved as a national wildlife refuge. Straddling the Virginia-North Carolina border, this wondrous 106,000-acre wetland supports a variety of migratory birds, as well as deer, fox, raccoons, otters, bobcats, bears, and many, many mosquitoes. Its peaty soil also supports a vast array of flora—dense evergreen shrub bogs and forests, eerie cypress swamps, with the young "knees" of new trees poking out of the tea-brown waters. Tannin in tree bark and the peat bog underlying the marsh give the swamp waters their remarkable stain.

At the heart of the marsh lies **Lake Drummond,** a 3,100-acre natural lake that is something of a hydrogeologic oddity. Most swamps form in basins that catch the water feeding into them. Lake Drummond, in contrast, actually occupies a slightly sloping hillside, and water drains out of it into manmade canals that allow canoeists and other boaters to explore the lake and its tributaries. Commercial boat tours also offer day trips through the swamp, and hikers and bicyclists can travel along a dirt road and an elaborate boardwalk raised above the wetlands.

Exactly how the swamp and Lake Drummond got their start more than 4,000 years ago remains a mystery, though the local Native Americans had a theory. They believed it had been created by a "fire bird." Scientific evidence suggests that a peat fire did cause the lake's depression, and there is even speculation that a meteor may have landed in the vicinity.

Apparently the first whites to see the lake came on a hunting expedition in 1665. One of the party was North Carolina's governor, William Drummond, after whom the lake was named. Few followed after them and those who did had little nice to say about the great marshland. Virginia's Col. William Byrd called it a "horrible desart" and advised that "Never was Rum, that cordial of Life, found more necessary than in this Dirty Place."

But George Washington, consummate explorer, surveyor, and developer, found it "a glorious paradise" and visited it repeatedly in the mid-1700s. His forays were not without entrepreneurial motive. Washington, an obsessive canal builder, wanted to build a five-mile (8-km)-long waterway through the marsh to connect commerce between North Carolina's Albermarle Sound and Virginia's Chesapeake. His plan was deferred by the Revolution, but in 1805, after Washington's death, the Dismal Swamp Canal opened. Now more accessible, the swamp began to capture the imagination of the public and of that most imaginative lot—writers. Longfellow included it in his poetry, and in 1839 Harriet Beecher Stowe wrote *Dred: A Tale of the Great Dismal Swamp,* describing the exploits of runaway slave Nat Turner. (More than a century later, William Styron brought Nat Turner to widespread public attention with his *Confessions of Nat Turner.*)

Commerce, too, came to the swamp, and throughout the nineteenth and twentieth centuries, its rich forests were heavily logged. By the 1970s, with the growing regard for conservation, the Great Dismal Swamp began to be seen as more than simply timberland. In 1973, Union Camp, the swamp's major owner for more than

Virginia's Great Dismal Swamp, which George Washington considered a "paradise" and another settler a "horrible desart" [sic].

half a century, deeded its holdings to the Nature Conservancy, which immediately conveyed the land to the U.S. Department of the Interior for a national wildlife refuge. At that time, the 49,000-acre gift was the "largest single land donation ever made to the government for wildlife conservation." Boat access is available from Feeder Ditch off Dismal Swamp Canal, on Route 17 south of Portsmouth; hiking/biking access from Suffolk, south on Route 13, then Route 32 to Washington Ditch.

■ HISTORIC HAMPTON

For all its slow, Southern style, Hampton has been the scene of some truly pioneering ventures. Site of one of the first colonial villages, it rightfully claims to be the "oldest, continuous, English-speaking settlement in America" (though it has been burned twice—by the British in the War of 1812 and the Union in the Civil War). It's also home to Hampton University, one of the country's first African American institutions of higher learning. And it was at Hampton's NASA facilities that those early Mercury astronauts trained for their Earth-shattering orbits of the planet.

In the last decade, this city has followed the trend toward festivalizing its old downtown waterfront. It's done an exemplary job, in part because it hasn't gutted and anaesthetized its seafaring soul. The wharves where seafood trawlers dock and the processing plants where they off-load still cluster along the Hampton River, yet just beyond them stretches a new brick-paved plaza. Adding its own nostalgic tone to the plaza, the 1920 carousel from the city's defunct Buckroe Beach amusement park revolves in a flash of prancing, painted horses.

The **Virginia Air and Space Center**, built in 1992, looms above the entire scene. An award-winning architectural tour de force, the glass, brick, and aluminum building is overarched by a winged roof, symbolic of the city's long association with flight—or, some say, recalling the seafaring aspect of the seagull. In either case, the building makes a strong impact. Inside, it houses two museums that essentially flow into each other: the Air and Space Center and the Hampton Roads History Center. In the latter, Hampton's history is traced through dioramas and storyboards, from its days as a colonial port right into its involvement with space flight at the city's Langley Air Force Base and NASA facilities.

The air and space exhibits clearly dominate the building. Ten historic aircraft are suspended from the building's high glass vaults. The center's piece de resistance is the Apollo 12 command capsule that allowed those lunar pioneers to make "one giant leap for mankind." An interactive space gallery gives visitors a hands-on experience of aeronautics and space travel. The center's IMAX theater, with its five-story screen, is the only one of its kind in Virginia. The center is located off I-64 and Exit 267 at 600 Settlers Landing Road.

In stark contrast to the high-tech center, small **St. John's Church** stands just a few blocks away at 100 West Queens Way. Built in 1728, it represents the only part of the old colonial town that survives, though it, too, has been burned and repaired twice. Shaped like a cross, the graceful Georgian brick chapel is surrounded by a walled graveyard, with many original eighteenth-century stones. Though the interior has been Victorianized, it still features a stained-glass window depicting Indian princess Pocahontas. The church's most prized possession is its communion silver. Crafted in England in 1618 and in continuous use ever since, it is the oldest such service in America.

■ HAMPTON UNIVERSITY

August Hampton University lies on the far bank of the river, off I-64, Exit 267, facing downtown. Its sloping, shaded grounds overlook the sailboats and workboats that thread their way up and down Hampton River. Standing on its campus, you can appreciate the feel of a civilized idea brought to elegant fruition, and imagine the dreams that went into the founding of this African American university, whose roots go back to the Civil War.

As the Union-held Fort Monroe attracted escaped slaves to the area during the

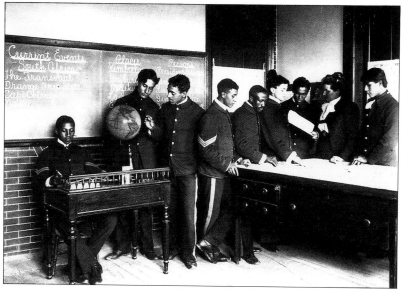

Hampton University is one of America's oldest African American universities. In 1878 it began admitting Indian students as well, a few of which are pictured in this photo from the late nineteenth century. (Courtesy of Hampton University Archives)

war, the New York-based American Missionary Association dispatched personnel to Hampton to help the growing black population. One of their first projects was to open a series of schools in the area. With the war's end the AMA pursued its efforts in education, establishing normal schools to train black teachers throughout the South. Hampton became the site of the Hampton Normal and Agricultural School.

For years the school was guided by the visionary hand of Gen. Samuel Chapman Armstrong. Born in Hawaii of missionary parents, Armstrong had become a staunch abolitionist and had fought in the war before becoming head of Hampton's Freedman's Bureau at the war's end. Armstrong believed that, beyond just training teachers, the new black institutions should teach such skills as agriculture and mechanics, and he incorporated these into a highly successful curriculum. He also apparently had a talent for raising money and managed to attract significant Northern benefactors. Perhaps his most innovative stroke was in founding the Hampton Singers, a traveling student troupe whose stellar performances garnered the school both fame and funds.

In 1878, the school extended its scope, offering to educate Indian students taken captive during the Indian Wars of the 1870s. The institution today boasts a **museum** with a fine collection of African and Native American artifacts, some the work of those early students. The museum also houses paintings by African American artists.

The university's impressive **Memorial Chapel** (1886) was designed by respected New York architect J. Cleveland Cady. The clock tower of this redbrick Italianate structure has long been a waterfront landmark for the city. Inside, the chapel's pine pews were hewn by university students themselves as part of their hands-on education. Nearby rambling **Virginia Hall** was designed by Richard Morris Hunt, the renowned early twentieth-century architect. Less showy but perhaps more moving is the university's venerable **Emancipation Oak**. More than a century ago, under this now-sprawling live oak, Lincoln's Emancipation Proclamation was read aloud.

Another city landmark associated with Hampton University is the **Little England Chapel**. The simple white clapboard church, built in 1879, represents the only existing example of the black missionary churches that proliferated in Virginia after the Civil War. This one began quite informally, when a Connecticut printer, recently employed by the Hampton Normal and Agricultural School, invited a few neighborhood kids into his home one Sunday to sing hymns. The following week, 17 children appeared on his doorstep, and in less than a year, 75 people were gathering on Sundays. At that point, the school got involved, sending teachers rowing across the river to help provide Sunday instruction. Very soon, the simple Little England Chapel that stands today was constructed and continued to hold services until 1989. Recently renovated to its 1930s appearance, the chapel is on the National Register of Historic Places.

From downtown Hampton, take Settlers Landing Road west, then left on Kecoughtan less than one mile. It's located at the corner of Kecoughtan and Ivy Home roads.

Not far from the Little England Chapel lies an arcane bit of Hampton history, this one infinitely more piratical and dating to the mid-seventeenth century. At that time, word was quickly spreading that the newly established sea lanes of the Chesapeake were rich in booty. The news lured pirates up from the Caribbean, who holed up in the endless creeks and marshes of the Eastern Shore and attacked ships passing through the Virginia capes.

Merchant and tobacco ships were forced to travel in biannual convoys to protect themselves from the brigands, the most notorious of whom was Edward Teach—or, as the world remembers him now—Blackbeard. Cultivating his reputation for ferocity, he went into battle, one eyewitness attested, with "lighted matches stuck under his hat, which appearing on each side of his face, his eyes naturally looking fierce and wild, made him altogether such a figure that imagination cannot form an idea of a Fury from Hell to look more frightful."

When British ships finally forced Blackbeard out of the bay, he sailed south to harass North Carolina shipping. At the behest of the population there, Virginia's Governor Spotswood dispatched two sloops to run the pirate down. During a pitched battle, the buccaneer, with 25 wounds in him, finally succumbed. His infamous head was then summarily detached from his body and hung from the bowsprit of one of the royal ships. When the victorious entourage returned to Hampton, the bloody "trophy" was placed on a point on Hampton River. Now known as Blackbeard Point, the site today is the placid setting for neighborhood homes—a far cry from "a Fury from Hell."

■ F O R T   M O N R O E

Fort Monroe probably has more history and more luminaries haunting its moated environs than any other place still standing in the Hampton Roads area. Embedded in the tip of Old Point Comfort, at the end of Mercury Boulevard (Route 258), the

■ BLACK LIFE TIMELINE ■

1624 Birth of William, first native-born black of Virginia.

1650 Black population of Virginia numbers 300.

1651 Anthony Johnson, bound servant, secures freedom. Imports five servants and acquires 250 acres on the Eastern Shore, making him the first black landowner in Virginia.

1653 Johnson petitions court for lifetime rights to his runaway servant, a black man who had committed no crime. First known judicial sanction in the English colonies of lifetime servitude where crime was not involved.

1698 Slave trade opens; slavery established.

1730 Black population in Virginia numbers 30,000.

1776 Slave population is 270,260. Thomas Jefferson includes in his draft of the Declaration of Independence an indictment of slavery. Clause later struck out to appease Georgia and South Carolina.

1778 Importation of slaves barred by Virginia legislation.

1782 Manumission of slaves legalized. Provision that master must continue to support freed slaves deters emancipation.

1795 Dred Scott born a slave in Southhampton County. Later moves with owners to Missouri, where in 1848 he sues to obtain his freedom on grounds he lives in free territory. Loses suit in 1857, but is emancipated and afterwards works in St. Louis as a hotel porter.

1830 Black population numbers 517,100, of which 90 percent are slaves.

1831 Nat Turner Rebellion. Turner and small band of followers massacre his master's family and about 50 other whites in the vicinity; Turner is caught and hanged.

1830s American Colonization Society transports free blacks to Liberia. 3,000 of the state's 50,000 free blacks go.

1850 As more and more slaves escape to the North, Southerners demand a Fugitive Slave Act to guarantee the return of their slaves; first invoked in the case of a fugitive from Norfolk named Shadrach, arrested in Boston. A sympathetic crowd of black Bostonians helps him escape his pursuers as lawyers prepare a defense.

1860 Union troops invade Alexandria and release slave-jail inmates, turning the building into a prison for Confederate soldiers.

1861   General Butler's Union forces move into Fort Monroe near Hampton; thousands of black refugees flock to the fort to gain freedom.

1863   President Lincoln issues Emancipation Proclamation, freeing Confederate slaves and allowing for recruitment of black soldiers; nearly 180,000 respond to the invitation.

1864   Battle of the Crater; black division charges on Confederate line. Over 1,000 blacks killed, wounded, or captured; charge fails.

1865   Confederates evacuate and set fire to Richmond. Black soldiers march in and halt without command at Lumpkin's slave jail to pay tribute to the inmates cheering through the bars. Thirteenth Amendment ratified in December, prohibiting slavery.

1868   Fourteenth Amendment ratified, declaring all persons born or naturalized in the United States citizens. Classes begin at Hampton Normal and Agricultural Institute in Hampton, a school for freedmen, later to become the scene of Booker T. Washington's early studies. He would gain fame as the director of the Tuskegee Institute.
        Fifteenth Amendment ratified, banning voting discrimination based on race, color, or previous condition of servitude.

1901   Delegates to the state constitutional convention adopt a poll tax and "understanding" requirement for prospective voters that has the effect of severely limiting the black vote.

1954   U.S. Supreme Court orders desegregation of schools.
        Virginia's Byrd Organization begins the Massive Resistance that is followed by many school closings (Prince Edward County School District closed 1959–1964).

1964   Enactment of 1964 Civil Rights Act aimed at repealing the South's Jim Crow laws, and barring racial discrimination in voting and use of public facilities.

1965   Voting Rights Act. Like the Civil Rights Act, it attempts to repeal Jim Crow laws and uphold the Fifteenth Amendment. Leads to drastic increases in the numbers of black registered voters in the South and a comparable increase in the number of blacks holding elective offices there.

1989   L. Douglas Wilder elected Virginia's and the nation's first black governor.

hexagonal stone casemate fort—still part of a functioning military base—goes back to the early nineteenth century, just after America's scare in the War of 1812. Hoping to better protect the undefended American coastline, President Madison appointed Gen. Simon Bernard, a French military engineer and one of Napoleon's former aides-de-camp, to design a system of coastal fortifications. The result was a series of forts stretching from Maine to Louisiana. Fort Monroe, one of these, was personally designed by Bernard himself. Encircled by a moat 1.25 miles (2 km) in circumference and enclosing 63 acres, it remains the largest stone fort ever built in the United States. So impregnable was it that it was called the Gibraltar of the Chesapeake.

There are countless ironies associated with Fort Monroe. One is that a young lieutenant of engineers, Robert E. Lee, was posted here early in his career and found it a post "by no means to be despised." He oversaw the completion of the fort's outworks and approaches during the early 1830s. Thirty-some years later, he may have regretted his own handiwork, because Fort Monroe became one of the Union's most critical strongholds in the South. Though it was ensconced in Virginia territory, the fort was immediately secured by the North at the outbreak of the Civil War. Thus, the North held the entrance to Hampton Roads, cutting off Virginia's major ports, all of which lay upriver.

Old Point Comfort Lighthouse—the oldest standing structure at Fort Monroe, built between 1819 and 1834.
(opposite) Ospreys nest on a channel marker nearby.

In 1861, three Hampton slaves escaped their owner and sought protection in this Union stronghold. The fort's commander, Gen. Benjamin Butler, a lawyer by training, gave them shelter. When his Southern counterpart, Maj. John Cary, demanded their return, citing the Fugitive Slave Act, the clever Butler replied that the act did not apply to "a foreign country, which Virginia claimed to be." Butler's argument was soon adopted by Union commanders throughout the country and eventually by the War Department. It also caused something of a crisis at Fort Monroe, as runaway slaves inundated "freedom fort." Nevertheless, the Union managed to shelter and clothe many and give them work. The refugees who couldn't be accommodated spread into the surrounding areas, building shantytowns.

At the end of the war, the old freedom fort got its own Moses. Harriet Tubman, heroine of the Underground Railroad, came to the Colored Hospital at Fort Monroe to serve as a nurse/matron. Another child of the South also found himself here after the war—Confederate Pres. Jefferson Davis. He came as a captive, having been apprehended in Georgia and falsely accused of plotting Lincoln's assassination. He spent almost a year imprisoned in one of the fort's casemates before he was released on a $100,000 bail bond, posted by such unlikely people as Northern journalist Horace Greeley and Commodore Vanderbilt.

Today at Fort Monroe, Davis's spartan cell is still displayed in the sod-roofed **Casemate Museum,** part of the original walled battlement. Also displayed are a series of exhibits on the history of the fort and the military presence in Hampton Roads. Across the street from the museum, the white verandah-wrapped residence that was once home to Robert E. Lee still exudes an antebellum charm. Nearby, **Quarters Number One,** an even more impressive antebellum home, is the fort's most prestigious residence. Both Lincoln and the Marquis de Lafayette slept here as official guests of the fort. If you exit the East Gate across the moat here, you will find yourself overlooking the Chesapeake Bay. The memorable stone Old Point Comfort Lighthouse still beckons to mariners from these banks, as it has since 1802.

■ OLD FORT WOOL

Offshore from Fort Monroe, Old Fort Wool is a compelling "ghost fort." Part of that series of early nineteenth-century coastal fortifications, it was designed to be Fort Monroe's counterpart. Together, the trained guns of the two were intended to block virtually any enemy from entering Hampton Roads. Initially named Fort

Calhoun, after John C. Calhoun, Secretary of War and Vice President, the fort was built on a shoal called the Rip Raps. Boulders dumped here raised the natural shoal and created a 15-acre man-made island. Enormous blocks of granite were floated in to form the casemates. The original plan called for a tower battery, with three tiers of casemates, topped by a barbette tier. The problem was the weight of just the lower level of casemates began to sink the artificial island. Engineer Robert E. Lee oversaw the dumping of more stone pilings during the sweltering summer of 1834, but even that didn't help. With the costs mounting, work temporarily halted on the project.

Nonetheless, the island, situated amid the gulls and sea breezes of Hampton Roads, provided a compelling getaway for Pres. Andrew Jackson, who used its quarters as a sort of informal summer White House. One of his successors, John Tyler, also sought Fort Calhoun's solitude after his wife died in 1842.

By the late 1850s, the island seemed to have stopped sinking. When war broke out soon thereafter, the half-complete fort was occupied by a naval brigade and saw some minor action. It also got a new name. Since John Calhoun was a Southerner, his name was dropped in favor of Wool, after Maj. Gen. John E. Wool, Union commander of the Department of Virginia.

At the turn of the century, the fort underwent another building phase as new batteries and emplacements were added to the existing ones. During both the World Wars, the fort was manned and on guard to protect the mouth of Hampton Roads, but by 1967, the army was ready to relinquish it to the state of Virginia. Now the city of Hampton's harbor cruise boats stop at the fort and give passengers a tour of the impressive granite casemates and the grounds of the old ghost fort.

■ NEWPORT NEWS

With apologies to this city, it suffers from the same malady that Gertrude Stein ascribed to her hometown of Oakland, California. There is simply "no there there." What used to be a thriving downtown in mid-century is now boarded up and virtually deserted. Even the town's nostalgic stone Victory Arch, through which so many World War II veterans marched, sits in the middle of a kind of nothingness. Newport News does have some very fine attractions; they are simply spread about a bit.

The town got its name from Christopher Newport, that intrepid seventeenth-century mariner who brought so many aspiring colonists across the Atlantic from Britain. Legend has it that when Newport tired of those endless sea voyages, he settled on the James River in the area that is now Newport News, and opened a small store. People would come here to hear the news. Hence the name, Newport News.

If Christopher Newport gave the town its name, it was railroad baron Collis Huntington who put it on the map. The self-made Huntington had visited the area when he was a teenage boy hawking watches and hardware up and down the East Coast. Hampton Roads apparently made a lasting impression on him, because he returned decades later with enterprise on his mind. He was looking for a terminus for an eastern railroad so that he could link his Pacific lines to Atlantic shipping channels. In the early 1880s, he opened the Chesapeake and Ohio Railroad through the Virginia Peninsula. A few years later, he also established the Newport News Shipbuilding and Dry Dock Company, to this day the mainstay of the city's economy.

Huntington was a man of many facets. A lover of poetry, he brought California poet Joaquin Miller to Newport News with him on one visit, and Miller penned this remembrance of the hard-working port:

> The palm, and the pine, and the sea sands brown
> The far sea songs of the pleasure crews
> The air like balm in this building town
> And that is the picture of Newport News.

As colorful as Collis Huntington was, he was outdone by his second wife, a Richmond beauty named Arabella. Though called Belle, she was not the classic Southern lady. Born of working class parents in post-Civil War Richmond, she carried on a quiet affair with Huntington for almost 20 years. When his first wife died, Huntington finally married Arabella. When he died 17 years later, Belle married Collis's nephew Henry and became one of the world's most renowned art collectors.

The poor Richmond girl found no difficulty in slipping into the role of dowager. One British acquaintance said of her, "Mrs. Huntington allows herself manners which even the Empress of Germany cannot afford." Nonetheless, she and her husband Henry endowed the world with California's renowned Huntington Library and Art Gallery.

In Newport News, too, the Huntington legacy lives on. Collis's shipyard, though it long ago passed from Huntington hands, has grown into the largest privately owned shipbuilding concern in the country. In the last half-century, it has produced the gargantuan Nimitz-class aircraft carriers, guided missile cruisers, and submarines, as well as the elegant luxury liner S.S. *United States.*

The end of the Cold War may spell hard times for this bastion of the military-industrial complex, with serious economic repercussions for the area. With 24,500 employees, the shipyard ranks as the largest private employer in the state, and its dry docks, berths, and piers claim two full miles (3.2 km) of the James River waterfront. Though no tours are given of the yards, you can get a glimpse of all this hardware from the James River Bridge and along the city's Huntington Avenue.

The Mariners' Museum is, in some ways, a more solidly enduring Huntington gift than the shipyard, with its fluctuating fortunes. Collis's son, philanthropist Archer Huntington, founded the museum in the early 1930s, spurred on by the shipyard's colorful president, Homer Ferguson. Both men recognized the need for a nautical museum "devoted to the culture of the sea." The museum has flourished ever since, and in 1990, it underwent major expansion and renovation. Its new low-slung, post-modern building overlooks the banks of tree-lined Lake Maury,

A couple of daytime seafarers test the waters of Chesapeake Bay.

A sailor experiments with windsurfing off Virginia Beach, circa 1940. (Underwood Photo Archives)

and its interior houses one of the finest "mariner" collections in the country.

The initial impact of the entrance gallery is enhanced by the romantic gleam of the old Cape Charles Lighthouse lens. The museum's other exhibits, covering 3,000 years of maritime history, cover such topics as the dying culture of bay watermen, the development of pleasure boats, and the reasoning behind those frequently bare-breasted figureheads on old ships. A dramatically darkened gallery exhibits the exquisite ship models produced by woodcarver August Crabtree. A collection of life-size craft—from Venetian gondolas to Brazilian balsa rafts—is housed on the museum grounds, and a brawny statue of that quintessential mariner, Leif Eriksson, designed by Alexander Stirling Calder, guards the museum entrance.

Adjacent to the Mariners' Museum is the **Peninsula Fine Arts Center,** an affiliate of the Virginia Museum in Richmond. The center's changing exhibits feature works by regional artists and craftspeople, as well as traveling exhibitions. Surrounding both museums are the pleasantly forested grounds of the **Mariners' Museum Park.** The five-mile (8-km) Noland trail leads through the park and down to the banks of the broad James. Take I-64, Exit 258A; the museum is located at 100 Museum Drive.

Virginia Living Museum, more a wildlife complex than a museum, houses an impressive array of native animal life. Its state-of-the-art indoor exhibits feature aquariums filled with bay and river critters, as well as woodpeckers, owls, and flying squirrels. A two-story, glass-enclosed aviary allows you to get a close-up look at songbirds, and a planetarium takes you to the stars. Outside, a boardwalk trail, cantilevered above a serene lake, leads past cages with larger fauna: raccoons, beavers, fox, bobcat, and even a bald eagle are housed here. Many of these animals were injured in the wild and brought to the museum for humane reasons, a fact which makes their captivity far more palatable. The museum is located at 524 J. Clyde Morris Boulevard, about a mile (1.6 km) west of Mariners' Museum.

The War Memorial Museum of Virginia takes an enlightened look at America's wars, from the Revolution to the present. Rather than simply celebrating battle, the museum and its 50,000 artifacts reveal the human impact of war—from its hardships and tragedies to its hyped-up propaganda. Perhaps the most interesting artifacts here are the war posters used to rouse public sentiment and support. There are a number of Axis- and Allied-nation propaganda posters on display, and they say something critical about how populations have been whipped into heated frenzies in order to "destroy the enemy." The museum grounds bristle with an array of weaponry—pre-World War I howitzers, tanks, anti-tanks, and more. The War Memorial Museum is located at 9285 Warwick Boulevard, on the north side of the James River Bridge.

The U. S. Army Transportation Museum lies, appropriately, on the grounds of Fort Eustis, headquarters for army transportation. Located off Route 60 at the northern edge of Newport News, not far from Williamsburg, the museum features impressive full-scale dioramas and artifacts that trace the history of army movement from horse-drawn Revolutionary wagons to what is billed as "the world's only captive flying saucer." The outdoor exhibits of actual vehicles include a variety of Jeeps, amphibious landing craft, railroad tank cars, and a forbidding armorplated Vietnam-era truck called "The Eve of Destruction."

■ NORTHERN AND MIDDLE NECKS

Virginians like to call their peninsulas "necks." Thus, the long arm of land bordered by the Potomac and Rappahanock rivers is affectionately known as the Northern Neck and the one below it, brushed by the Rappahanock and York rivers, is called the Middle Neck. Still flavorfully rural, these necks stretch away in corn and soy fields bordered by distant oak and evergreen forests. Along their coastlines, meandering creeks burrow in off the big rivers. Sailboats glide in and out of the marinas that dot their east ends where they jut into the bay, and little seafood houses, specializing in crabs, fish, oysters, and clams, nestle at the edges of inlets.

(following pages) Winter sunset at the small town of Saxis on the Chesapeake Bay.

In some ways, this land is as unspoiled and unpretentious as it was centuries ago when it was the birthplace of four of Virginia's most illustrious sons—George Washington, James Monroe, James Madison, and Robert E. Lee. All but Madison are from the Northern Neck's Westmoreland County, and Washington and Lee were actually born within 10 miles (16 km) of one another, about midway down the neck. Besides geography, destiny and even marriage link the two. Their kin mingled and meshed in some byzantinely Southern ways. The birthplaces of both are now sites pleasingly in keeping with the stature of these two great Virginians.

■ GEORGE WASHINGTON BIRTHPLACE NATIONAL MONUMENT

You know you have arrived when the farm fields of Route 204 abruptly end in a replica of the Washington Monument. Beyond the white granite obelisk, picturesque Popes Creek meanders past the elegant copse of red cedars that edges Washington's birthplace. Destroyed by fire in the Revolution, the old home is marked now by an outline of ground-up oyster shells. Behind it stands a "memorial" house, constructed in the 1930s. The one-and-a-half story central hall brick Colonial, spacious but not grand, is furnished with eighteenth-century antiques that give a good sense of the style in which a well-off planter's family would have lived in the mid-1700s.

Washington's roots in this area go back three generations. His great-grandfather John had come from England to Virginia in the mid-seventeenth century. In 1658 he had married Anne Pope, whose father Nathaniel owned much of the Popes Creek area. By the time Washington himself was born, his father, Augustine, was comfortably ensconced at Popes Creek Plantation with his second wife, Mary Ball. Washington was the couple's first child. When George was three-and-a-half, the family moved farther up the Potomac, to Augustine's Little Huntington farm. This is the property the world now knows as Mount Vernon. That stay, too, was short-lived, and Augustine soon resettled his family yet again, this time at Ferry Farm, on the Rappahanock below Fredericksburg.

Augustine died when George was 11, leaving behind his young family by Mary Ball and two older sons by his first wife. One of these, Augustine, Jr., inherited the Popes Creek land, while the other, Lawrence, became the squire of Little Huntington Creek. Young George spent time with both brothers, and so as an adolescent he became reacquainted with the languid, lazy charms of Popes Creek.

"Father I cannot tell a lie: I cut down the cherry tree." An 1889 engraving by John C. McRae depicts an apocryphal event held dear by generations of Americans. (Virginia State Library and Archives)

Today, the property again functions as a working colonial farm. Horses and cows graze behind quaint split rail fences, costumed "cooks" work in the tidy kitchen dependency beside the memorial house, and vegetables ripen on vines. A long, lovely country lane leads past Dancing Marsh and Dogwood Swamp back to the shaded, brick-walled family burial ground. The remains of more than a score of Washingtons reside here, including George's half-brother Augustine, his father, and great-grandfather.

■ STRATFORD HALL

As imposing as the family who lived here, Stratford Hall embodies the spirit of the Lees, one of Virginia's finest lineages. To reach it from George Washington's Birthplace get back on Route 3 and take it to Route 214, looking for signs to Stratford Hall. The unusual Georgian Great House, with its broad exterior staircase and dominant "chimney clusters," is now most famous as the birthplace of the South's enduring hero, Robert E. Lee. The Lees that preceded him were a striking lot, and their story is worth telling.

A Shropshire gentryman named Richard Lee arrived in Jamestown in the 1630s and established the family on American soil. His descendants would distinguish themselves as colonial officials, signers of the Declaration, military heroes, and mothers of presidents. (Zachary Taylor's mother was of the Lee line.) With what would prove to be a family talent for land acquisition, Richard Lee got the family off to a fine start, leaving his heirs several plantations, including one on the Northern Neck. It was Richard's grandson, Thomas, who built Stratford Hall.

Thomas had been raised on the Northern Neck on the family's Machodoc Plantation. For years, he apparently had been eyeing a nearby piece of land called the "Clifts" as a potential home site. In 1716 he purchased the land from the Pope family—the same family who had once owned the site of George Washington's birthplace. Early in the 1730s, his elegant new home was complete and he and his wife and numerous children moved in. A well-respected colonial official and a member of His Majesty's Council of Twelve (the upper house of the Virginia legislature), Lee went on to serve briefly as chief executive of Virginia during the royal governor's absence.

His sons continued in their distinguished father's footsteps. As conditions with Britain grew more strained, however, several of them became vocal proponents of

Roe Terry carves a duck decoy.

more freedom for the colonies. When the Continental Congress met in Philadelphia, it was Richard Henry Lee who introduced the resolution "That these United Colonies are, and of right ought to be, free and independent States . . . absolved from all allegiance to the British Crown." Several months later, Richard Henry and Francis Lightfoot Lee affixed their names to the Declaration of Independence, the only brothers to do so.

After a generation Stratford Hall passed to Thomas Lee's granddaughter, the "divine Mathilda." This is where the Lee story becomes ever more entangled. At the end of the Revolution, Mathilda married her second cousin, the dashing Revolutionary war hero, "Lighthorse Harry" Lee. He had earned his romantic sobriquet from his lightning quick raids on the British. A great compatriot of George Washington, he remained a public hero after the war and delivered Washington's famous eulogy, "First in war, first in peace, and first in the hearts of his countrymen . . . ."

If Lighthorse Harry had a talent for politics, he didn't have one for managing his private affairs. Under his guidance, or lack of it, Stratford Hall gradually fell into financial ruin. After only eight years of marriage, Mathilda died, leaving Lee with three children. Several years later, while serving as governor of Virginia, Lighthorse Harry took a second wife, Anne Hill Carter, a descendant of Virginia's

A country vegetable stand typical of rural Virginia.

land mogul, Robert "King" Carter. In January 1807 the couple's fifth child, Robert Edward, was born at Stratford Hall, but by the time the boy was learning to walk, his father had been sent to a nearby debtors prison. When Lighthorse Harry regained his freedom, he took his family to Alexandria, where family members were willing to lend assistance. And so Robert E. Lee left behind Stratford Hall before he had reached the age of four. Though he had been born here, the great home really belonged neither to his father nor his mother. And so it passed to his half-brother, Mathilda's son, Henry Lee. Sadly, this Henry, too, seemed star-crossed, and in the early 1800s, he sold the house out of the family.

Decades later, a disconsolate Robert E. Lee wrote his wife this letter from the battlefield. It was Christmas Day, 1863, and their house in Arlington, Virginia, was in the hands of the Union.

In the absence of a home, I wish I could purchase Stratford. That is the only other place I could go to, now accessible to us, that would inspire me with feelings of pleasure and love. . . . It is a poor place, but we could make enough cornbread and bacon for our support, and the girls could weave us clothes.

Happily, Stratford is no longer "a poor place." In the 1930s Mrs. Charles Lanier, inspired by a poem on Lee written by her famous father-in-law, Sydney Lanier, founded the Robert E. Lee Memorial Association. Through grass-roots efforts, the association raised the funds to restore the property. The Great House's large main floor rooms are now filled with eighteenth-century antiques, including the crib, daintily draped with mosquito-netting, once occupied by Robert E. Lee. Outside lie a boxwood garden, kitchen and office dependencies, and a working stone grist-mill. The gracious green grounds overlook the sweep of the Potomac River as it makes its way to the Chesapeake Bay.

■ CHRIST CHURCH

Near the small town of Irvington, Christ Church was constructed within a few years of Stratford Hall and has remained virtually unchanged since then. Robert "King" Carter, Virginia's colonial baron par excellence, donated the funds to build the elegant little church with its pagoda-like roof. Inside, the three-tier pulpit overlooks the original high-backed pews. Outside, Carter and members of his family rest in peace, having lost none of their prestige to time. Christ Church is located on Route 646, northeast of Irvington.

COLONIAL HEARTLAND

WHILE COLONIAL CHURCHES AND PLANTATIONS are scattered through Virginia's Tidewater, the spirit of the seventeenth and eighteenth century unquestionably hovers closest to the area known as the Colonial Triangle: Jamestown, Williamsburg, and Yorktown. Here, at about the middle of the Virginia Peninsula between the James and York Rivers, the state's history is preserved from the first settlement to Independence. A good bit of the historic landscape of Williamsburg and Yorktown and the stretch of plantations along the James is populated by real people who are careful to preserve the colonial character of their abodes. In the case of Colonial Williamsburg, where only lucky employees are allowed to live in the historic district houses, this carefulness is mandated. Cars are parked carefully out of view, and electric wires and all other signs of modernity are carefully buried underground or tucked into discrete green spaces. If one wants to live here, one has to live intimately with the past.

Frankly, the workings of the past on this area are less complex than the machinations of the present. Just who owns and operates these momentous sites today is a little confusing, but in brief it works this way: The National Park Service administers the Colonial National Historical Park, which includes Jamestown Island, the Yorktown Battlefield, and the lovely 23-mile (37-km) Colonial Parkway that travels through woods, rivers, and marshlands, linking the two sites and Williamsburg. From Richmond, take I-64 to the Colonial Williamsburg exit.

At both Yorktown and Jamestown, the Commonwealth of Virginia also operates separate interpretive areas, with museums and re-creations of colonial life. To complicate matters further, Williamsburg maintains a very distinct identity. The private Colonial Williamsburg Foundation owns, operates, guards, and translates the past in this extensive historic area.

The rich heritage of the colonial heartland extends along both sides of the James River as well, where a score of exceptionally fine old plantation manor houses still gild the sloping riverbanks. Many of these are open for public tours.

■ JAMESTOWN

To tour the colonial past, a first stop might be Jamestown, at the Colonial Parkway's western end. This little island looks almost the way it did when those three

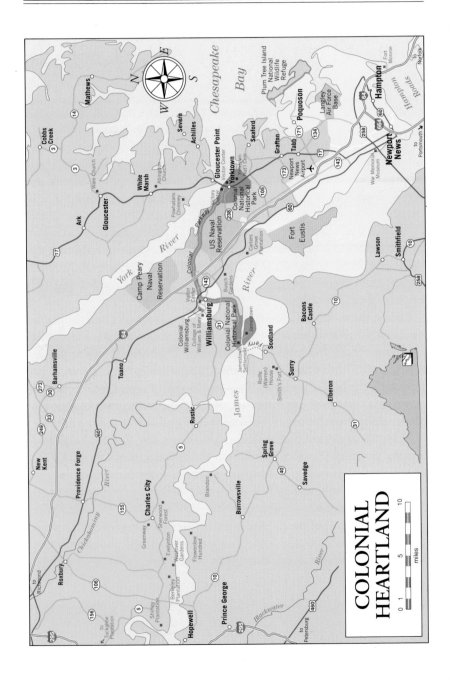

COLONIAL HEARTLAND

small ships landed in the new world. Herons strut through its marshes, and tall pines wave in the breeze off the river, mingling their resinous scent with the fresh smell of the James. A "figure-8" road loops through the forests on this almost deserted 1,500-acre island, and imagination must serve to resurrect life here in the early seventeenth century. The only human activity still left on the island is focused around the visitors center and the excavated site of the first capital. In the visitors center, exhibits explain the history of the settlement. An excellent film shown here makes no attempt to romanticize the hardships of Jamestown's early, ill-fated decades.

Behind the museum, the narrow streets of modest old James Cittie (Jamestown) are clearly visible, lined by the excavated foundations of the small homes that rose in an otherwise vast wilderness. The one historic structure still standing is the Old Church Tower, attached to the ruins of an old church. A rather pathetic statue of Pocahontas, erected decades ago and dressed in the garb of a Plains Indian, is a testament not so much to the Powhatan princess as to how far historical accuracy and interpretation have come in the last few decades. A blustering, heroic statue of Smith looks out across the grounds as well. The river, however, has long since

The Susan Constant *(reconstructed here) was one of the three sailing vessels which delivered Capt. John Smith and the first 105 colonists to Jamestown in 1607.*

VIRGINIA'S NATURAL INHABITANTS

*F*or their apparel they are sometimes covered with the skins of wild beasts, which in winter are dressed with the hair but in summer without. The better sort use large mantles of deerskins, not much differing in fashion from the Irish mantles—some embroidered with white beads, some with copper, others painted after their manner. But the common sort have scarce to cover their nakedness but with grass, the leaves of trees, or such like. We have seen some use mantles made of turkey feathers, so prettily wrought and woven with threads that nothing could be discerned but the feathers. But the women are always covered about their middle with a skin, and very shamefast to be seen bare.

They adorn themselves most with copper beads and paintings. Their women, some have their legs, hands, breasts, and face cunningly embroidered with diverse works, as beasts, serpents, artificially wrought into their flesh with black spots. In each ear commonly they have three great holes, whereat they hang chains, bracelets, or copper. Some of their men wear in those holes a small green and yellow colored snake near half a yard in length, which, crawling and lapping herself about his neck, oftentimes familiarly would kiss his lips. Others wear a dead rat tied by the tail. Some on their heads wear the wing of a bird or some large feather with a rattle. Those rattles are somewhat like the shape of a rapier but less, which they take from the tail of a snake. Many have the whole skin of a hawk or some strange fowl stuffed with wings abroad, others a broad piece of copper, and some the hand of their enemy dried. Their heads and shoulders are painted red with the root puccoon [bloodroot] brayed to powder, mixed with oil; this they hold in summer to preserve them from the heat, and in winter from the cold. Many other forms of paintings they use, but he is the most gallant that is the most monstrous to behold.

—Capt. John Smith, *History of Virginia,* 1608

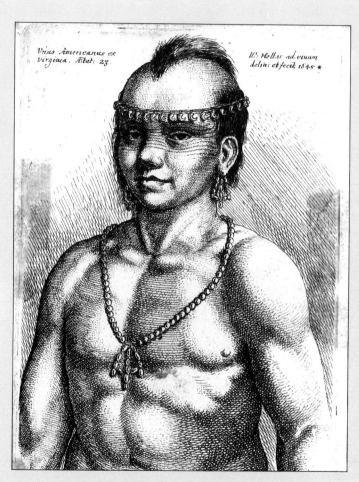

A Virginia Algonquian Indian, probably a Powhatan, sketched by Wenceslaus Hollar in 1645. (Virginia State Library and Archives)

Capt. John Smith, 1580–1631.
(Virginia State Library and Archives)

washed away the site of ill-fated Fort James, which lies submerged offshore. That could be seen as an act of grace on the part of the river, since so much pain must still echo through its stockaded walls.

Across the isthmus on the mainland, just before the bridge, is something a bit more corporeal— the **Jamestown Glasshouse.** Of the many products those early colonists tried to wrest from Virginia to make their settlement lucrative, glass, manufactured from river sand, proved one of the most viable. In the glasshouse today, skilled artisans in knee breeches and muslin shirts stoke the beehive kilns and blow glass the old way, twisting their blowpipes into the molten mass of glass, then blowing and turning the fiery gobs into shapely green vessels and vases. These latter-day artisans spend several years in apprenticeship, just as their colonial predecessors did.

Nearby, also on the Colonial Parkway, the state's **Jamestown Festival Park** brings the old settlement resoundingly to life. A fine museum explains the conditions in seventeenth-century England and Europe that forced the Elizabethans to look for new horizons beyond their cramped motherland. Exhibits here also do justice to the Powhatan culture and to the endurance of the early colonists. Outside, the park re-creates a Powhatan village, and leather-clad "natives" cook native foods, tend fires, and explain how the Powhatan hunter-gatherers and farmers lived off the abundance of Virginia's woodlands and rich river shores.

The Powhatans' simple but abundant life contrasts strikingly with the re-created, stockaded fort of the settlers. The fort seems tenuous and ill-conceived, its small, thatch-roofed, wattle-and-daub buildings dark and musty, exuding a kind of malarial malaise. It's easy to imagine all the dying from disease and starvation that would have gone on in a place like this.

Tethered down at the shoreline are replicas of those three original ships—the *Susan Constant,* the *Godspeed,* and the *Discovery.* Visitors are welcome aboard the 110-foot (34-m) *Susan Constant,* where latter-day "colonials" in knee-breeches are happy to explain what it was like to cross the Atlantic in the dark, breathless hold of such a ship, sharing quarters with too many other humans, not to mention a menagerie of livestock.

■ WILLIAMSBURG

When the Jamestown statehouse burned down in 1698, colonial officials finally decided, after 91 disease-ridden years, to move the capital off the miasmic island.

A blacksmith dressed in period costume at Jamestown.

Middle Plantation, a site on higher ground five miles (8 km) to the west, was chosen. Actually a small village, it had recently become home to the new College of William and Mary. Within a year, the new capital had been laid out and named for England's king, William III. The royal governor, Francis Nicholson, was probably the person most responsible for turning the small village into a well-proportioned village. Dominated by a central Market Square, the town centered around the mile-long Duke of Gloucester Street, buttressed at the east end by the College of William and Mary, and at the west by the impressive brick capitol building, which was completed in 1705.

The new capital village quickly established itself as the administrative and cultural focus of the colony. Small artisans' shops lined its streets and the gracious clapboard homes of well-placed Virginians clustered around Market Square and the elegant Governor's Palace. But as dissension grew in the colonies, Williamsburg became polarized. This, after all, was the seat of royal British government in Virginia and at the same time a hotbed of the popularly elected "revolutionaries"—Washington, Jefferson, Patrick Henry, Richard Henry Lee, and others. Only recently, they had sat in the House of Burgesses, decorously tending the king's business. But decorum had given way to treasonous speeches in the halls of the old capitol, including Patrick Henry's famous speech: "Caesar . . . had his Brutus, Charles the First his Cromwell, and George the Third may profit by their example. If this be treason, make the most of it." By 1774, the royal governor had been forced to dissolve the seditious burgesses, but they simply adjourned to nearby Raleigh Tavern and continued the business of government and revolution. Through the turmoil that ensued in the following years, Williamsburg remained the home of the colony's elected government and the meeting place for many of the Virginia patriots who would ultimately press the fledging colonies toward independence.

As the Revolution dragged on through the late 1770s, Williamsburg seemed less and less defensible. Finally, in 1780, then-governor Thomas Jefferson moved the capitol 50 miles (80.5 km) northwest, to more centrally located Richmond. By 1781, the war was upon Williamsburg, as colonial and French commanders headquartered themselves in the town's homes and from here launched the decisive siege of Yorktown.

After the war, the old colonial capital, like Jamestown before it, lost its preeminence. Unlike Jamestown, however, it did not lapse into a stilled and forgotten backwater. It had the College of William and Mary and the county seat to keep it

Patriot Patrick Henry regales the House of Burgesses with calls for revolution prior to its dissolution by the royal governor in 1774. (Virginia State Library and Archives)

alive. Over the course of the nineteenth century, it survived as a quiet farming hamlet and college town, albeit one with a rich architectural heritage. Many of its colonial structures remained, though dilapidated or Victorianized with porches and frills to the point of being virtually unrecognizable. Some served as service stations and small stores, others as homes. Still, the general layout and sense of the old eighteenth-century village prevailed into the early twentieth century, and visionaries who could imagine Williamsburg's past glory dreamed of a more promising future.

One of those visionaries was the Reverend W. A. R. Goodwin, rector of the town's prestigious Bruton Parish Church. Goodwin managed to convey his dreams to John D. Rockefeller, Jr., and found a receptive audience in the philanthropist. For 30 years, Rockefeller poured his money and enthusiasm into reconstructing and restoring the little country hamlet to its eighteenth-century grandeur. He and his family even maintained a home in gracious old Bassett Hall.

Today, Williamsburg has surely regained its preeminence—as the most elaborately restored and reconstructed colonial site in America. Just off I-64, and in the middle of the Colonial Parkway, the historic area now covers about 175 acres and preserves almost 90 restored colonial structures, as well as a number of reconstructions built on original foundations. All of this, as well as Carter's Grove Plantation eight miles (13 km) away on the James River, is under the aegis of the non-profit Colonial Williamsburg Foundation. More than a historic site, Williamsburg is sublimely genteel. Men in knee breeches and white stockings and wide-skirted dames, mob-capped and well-mannered, add a human dimension to the town's colonial-style shops, taverns, inns, and historic sites. "People of the past" are stationed throughout the town, offering up colorful impersonations of actual residents of old Williamsburg. Just wandering the historic area, even without having purchased an entry ticket to the buildings, will give you a taste of the past. Charming, faithfully restored clapboards are surrounded by eighteenth-century gardens and lived in by lucky Colonial Williamsburg staff. No noisome traffic is allowed to detract from the swish of long colonial gowns down Duke of Gloucester Street.

No traffic, that is, save that of the crowds. About a million visitors a year purchase tickets to Colonial Williamsburg, anxious to imbibe the ambiance and experience a little history along the way. Tricorner hats off to Williamsburg—it manages to teach history in an eminently palatable way, though it has definitely cleaned up the unpleasantries of the eighteenth-century past. Its streets are hardly a muddy morass scented by animals and sewage. Disease is no threat here, and sanitation no drawback. While the former Virginia capital may be bit too perfect now to authentically re-create colonial life, it does offer the best of both worlds—the picturesque romanticism of the past and the anesthetized, air-conditioned comforts of the present.

■ TOURING THE TOWN

The best way to do that is the old-fashioned way—on foot. Start at the visitors center, located outside the historic area. You can park here and purchase an inclusive ticket to all the sites. (The ticket also allows you to use the shuttle bus that runs from the visitors center and through the historic area.) While you're at the visitors center, take in the 35-minute docu-drama, *Williamsburg—The Story of a Patriot.* Once armed with that historical grounding, you're ready to attack the town itself.

At the east end of Duke of Gloucester Street, **the capitol,** scene of so much history, makes a good starting point. Actually, the brick building, with its uniquely rounded sides, is a reconstruction of the 1705 capitol, which burned down in 1747. (It was replaced in 1753, but that building, too, was destroyed by fire in 1832.) The distinctive H-shape of this reconstruction perfectly symbolizes the kind of bicameral government that typified Virginia in the eighteenth century. The royal governor and his twelve-man council of gentry, appointed for life by the king, were ensconced in the opulent quarters on the west side of the building. Here, they literally held court, presiding as justices over both civil and criminal cases, and serving as the upper house of the legislature. The lower house, of course, comprised the publicly elected burgesses. Their space, on the east side of the capitol, is decidedly less extravagant, with no whiff of royal trappings or even serious royal imprimatur. That difference in decor seems to sum up the contrast between America's spirit of informality and practicality and the entrenched, autocratic conventions of old England.

Apparently, the world of politics hasn't really changed too much in the past 300 years, because the immediate neighborhood surrounding the capitol is replete with taverns. To the east, on Waller Street, lies **Christiana Campbell's Tavern,** a favorite with George Washington and still a favorite with seafood lovers. To the west of the capitol, politicians and pooh-bahs had their choice of no less than four taverns in the first block of Duke of Gloucester Street, all now in service again today:

Shields, the **King's Arms**, **Wetherburn's**, and the famous **Raleigh Tavern**. Social and political center of the old capital, this hostelry witnessed many a historic moment, from the meetings of patriotic burgesses to an 1824 ball in honor of the Revolutionary hero, the Marquis de Lafayette. (Shields Tavern and the King's Arms continue to provide sustenance to hungry travelers, while Raleigh and Wetherburn are operated solely as historic sites.)

Also scattered along Duke of Gloucester Street is an array of colonial shops—a watchmaker, peruke-maker (wigmaker), milliner, book binder, scrivener, apothecary, harnessmaker, and more. Some of these establishments sell their wares, some are open free of charge and others require a general Williamsburg admission ticket.

Halfway down, Duke of Gloucester Street opens into Market Square. In the past, this greensward bustled with colonial farmers who came to hawk their produce to the wealthier urbanites of Williamsburg.

The small brick courthouse that served as the seat of government of James City County in the eighteenth and nineteenth century still stands on the square, as does the old guardhouse and the octagonal magazine. The magazine itself played a prominent role in the build-up to the Revolution. In April of 1775, Governor Dunmore ordered British troops to move in by night and stealthily remove the gunpowder from the magazine. When his deed was discovered, Virginians were outraged and mustered troops to move against the British. The governor backed down and paid for the purloined powder.

Once the most prestigious address in town, **Market Square** is faced by several fine colonial homes, including the sprawling clapboard abode of the distinguished Randolph family. Built in 1715 and expanded several times, the home still contains much of its original interior paneling. One of the home's residents, Peyton Randolph, presided over the First and Second Continental Congresses in Philadelphia.

Market Square's western side gives onto the Palace Green, at whose end rises the majestic **Governor's Palace**. Perhaps the most impressive piece of architecture in British colonial America, the original palace was completed in 1722 and housed seven royal governors, as well as Patrick Henry and Thomas Jefferson, the Commonwealth's first two governors. After the capital was moved to Richmond toward the end of the Revolution, the palace was turned into a hospital for colonial troops injured in the siege of Yorktown. On the night of December 22, 1781, fire took the building, burning it to the ground in three hours. The current palace is an

The Fife-and-Drum Corps of Williamsburg.

elaborate reconstruction of the old eighteenth-century structure. Its richly paneled entry hall contains a remarkable display of musketry and armaments arranged in swirling, decorative patterns on the walls. Predictably, the palace features an elegant supper room and ballroom and private quarters for the governors and their families. A labyrinthine series of walled and terraced gardens surrounds it, including a boxwood maze that remains a favorite with young palace visitors.

Two notable buildings front the Palace Green. One is the fine brick **manor house of George Wythe**—jurist, law professor, mentor to both Thomas Jefferson and John Marshall, a signer of the Declaration of Independence and generally acknowledged sage of Williamsburg (sadly poisoned to death by his own nephew). The other is **Bruton Parish Church,** a surviving colonial jewel. Its walled cemetery protects graves dating from the late seventeenth century, but the current brick cruciform-shaped church wasn't constructed until 1715. Its elegantly simple interior, with high enclosed box pews, clear glass windows, and a cantilevered pulpit, has been used continuously as a house of worship.

In the block beyond Bruton Parish, Duke of Gloucester suddenly rejoins the twentieth century. Boutiques and eateries cluster here around the **College of William and Mary** (at the end of Duke of Gloucester Street between Jamestown and Richmond roads), but when you enter the walled grounds of the Wren Yard, the historic area of the college, you quickly re-enter the past.

Chartered in 1693 by its namesakes, King William and Queen Mary, this college boasts the oldest structure in continuous academic use in the United States. Now called the Wren Building—after its reputed designer, prominent British architect Sir Christopher Wren—the stately brick building bristles with academic import. Partially burned and restored several times, the current building reflects the style of the early 1700s. Its well-proportioned interior houses bare, Colonial-style classrooms, an ornate chapel, and a Great Hall for dining. The piazza along the rear overlooks a sunken garden and a portion of the serene college campus. Flanking the front of the building are the Georgian brick President's House (1732) and the Brafferton (1723). Originally built as a school for Native Americans, the Brafferton was made possible by funds from the estate of eminent seventeenth-century English scientist Robert Boyle.

These days Williamsburg's second-most important thoroughfare is **Francis Street,** which parallels Duke of Gloucester on the south. Quieter and in that way more appealing, Francis features the elegant Williamsburg Inn and the pleasant

Williamsburg Lodge. It is also the site of a rather unusual museum concept. On the eve of the Revolution a **Public Hospital** for the mentally ill opened in Williamsburg, and a reconstruction of it now traces the history of mental health treatment from 1773 through the late nineteenth century. The reconstructed hospital also serves as a clever "historically correct" entrance to an entirely modern museum structure.

The **DeWitt Wallace Decorative Arts Gallery,** designed by noted architect Kevin Roche, is housed in a low-slung, partially underground structure that looks like a simple brick wall behind the hospital. It actually encompasses 26,000 square feet of exhibit space and displays one of the world's finest collections of seventeenth through early nineteenth-century British and American decorative arts. Among its masterworks are Charles Willson Peale's military portrait of George Washington; mid-seventeenth and eighteenth-century furniture, ceramics, silver, and pewter; and an extraordinary collection of historic prints. The gallery is named for benefactor DeWitt Wallace, who, with his wife, Lila Acheson Wallace, was co-founder of *Reader's Digest.*

The counterpoint to this gallery is the nearby **Abby Aldrich Rockefeller Folk Art Center,** one of the nation's premier folk art museums. Wife of John D., Jr., Abby Rockefeller was an ardent admirer of American folk art, and her collection of weathervanes, folk portraits, and wood carvings forms the core of this exceptional collection. Recently expanded, the museum's exquisite exhibit galleries also house textiles, ceramics, and a number of different versions of the Americana classic, "Peaceable Kingdom," by self-taught artist Edward Hicks. The museum is also home to the renowned folk art portrait "Baby In Red Chair." Turn down South England Street from Francis Street to find the museum.

■ MODERN WILLIAMSBURG

Banking on the notion that modern travelers might want to cut their colonialism with some late twentieth-century diversions, several enterprising concerns have set up in close proximity to the historic area. One of these is **Busch Gardens**—a theme amusement park three miles east of Williamsburg which, perhaps sensitive to its historic environs, calls itself the Old Country and tumbles across 360 precisely landscaped acres. Adding to this megamagic, Busch has also recently acquired nearby **Water Country,** a "water theme park" with 40 acres of waterslides, wave pools, and meandering streams.

On the other side of the historic area, along the old Richmond Road, strings of factory outlets interrupt the otherwise green countryside of Lightfoot. The granddaddy of all this consumer cravenness has to be the **Williamsburg Pottery Factory,** a mind-boggling complex of more than 30 warehouse-like structures filled to overflowing with glasswares, furnishings, foods, plants, etc. Don't be misled by the name of the place: This is no factory; this is a merchandising marathon.

■ YORKTOWN

Farther along the Colonial Parkway, 14 miles (22 km) southeast of Williamsburg, is Yorktown. Of the three pieces of the Colonial Triangle, Yorktown in some ways seems the most compelling, perhaps because much of it still functions as a real town. Now, as in much of its past, it drowses on high banks above the York River, while traffic arcs across the nearby Coleman Memorial Bridge, and ships come and go from the Naval Weapons Station upriver. Families still swim and picnic along its sandy strip of beach or visit the **"Cornwallis Cave."** Really just a hole in the red-clay bank, this is where British troops took cover while Revolutionary forces pummeled their position during the Siege of Yorktown. It is that 1781 siege, of course—and its consequences—that make Yorktown more than just another lazy little river hamlet. So what were the circumstances that led history to choose quiet Yorktown as the culminating spot of the Revolution?

By the time the Revolution came to Yorktown, Washington's men—ill-clothed, disease-plagued, underfed, underpaid, and undervalued by the Continental Congress—were on the verge of deserting. Victory rarely visited the Colonials, while the British had the men and resources to fight on forever. The one bright spot for Washington lay in the new French commitment to the cause. Though they had been sending money and supplies to the Americans, the French did not send troops until 1780. Fortified by this fresh infusion from a powerful ally, the success of the Revolution again seemed possible.

Late summer of 1780 found Washington's forces in New York, engaged in a futile campaign to drive the British out of New York City. To the south, Britain's daunting Lord Cornwallis had swept through Virginia, then, under orders from his superiors in New York, had fallen back to the sea, situating his 7,000 troops on the banks of the York River. Here, strategically near the mouth of the Chesapeake, he prepared a naval depot and waited for reinforcements by sea.

The French commander, Rochambeau, sensed something precarious in Cornwallis's position and persuaded Washington to move south and attack. In what has to be one of the great moments of military stealth, Washington secretly pulled his men out of New York and in a forced march, covered the 500 miles (804.5 km) to Virginia in four weeks. Perhaps believing that what was coming would spell ultimate victory or defeat, Washington himself made a detour on this march, and, after six long years of war, stopped at Mount Vernon to see his family.

Meanwhile, Rear Adm. Thomas Graves and his 19 British warships had set sail from New York to reinforce Cornwallis at Yorktown. Rounding the Virginia Capes on September 5, the fleet was taken by surprise by 24 French ships under Adm. Joseph Paul de Grasse. The Battle of the Capes sent the British limping back to New York and left Cornwallis unfortified, unsuspecting, and vulnerable, with his back to the sea in Yorktown.

By mid-September the combined allied force of some 17,600 men had reached Virginia, positioned themselves in Williamsburg, and were preparing to lay siege

"Storming a Redoubt at Yorktown" by Eugene Lami hangs in the Old Senate Chamber of the state capitol building in Richmond. The painting shows Revolutionary soldiers over-running British breastworks, leading to the surrender of Cornwallis. (Virginia State Library and Archives)

to Cornwallis's 8,300 men in nearby Yorktown. On September 28, the fighting began. In classic eighteenth-century tradition, redoubts were dug by both sides, and attacks were often waged to gain an inch of ground at a time. While this went on, the Revolutionary forces also kept up a perpetual bombardment of the British. After two weeks of this, Cornwallis realized he faced defeat. On October 14 he signaled his desire for a parley. The opposing parties met in the pleasant little clapboard Moore House and worked out the formal terms of surrender. On October 19, the troops of both armies gathered on what is now called Surrender Field to witness a ceremony that would ultimately lead to freedom for the 13 colonies.

Just another grassy meadow today, **Surrender Field,** a few miles south of town, rests quietly now, though at twilight white-tailed deer drift across it like Revolutionary ghosts. The ghosts of another war haunt the brick-walled **Yorktown National Cemetery.** Within its walls lie the Civil War soldiers killed during Union commander George McClellan's infamous Peninsula Campaign. McClellan spent a month here in a face-off with Confederate Gen. Joseph Johnston's far weaker forces. "No one but McClellan," Johnston said, "could have hesitated to attack." But hesitate he did, allowing Johnston time to slip away without terrible casualties.

Back at the **park visitors center,** the theme returns to the Revolution. Exhibits, including Washington's original field tent and a docu-drama, explain the decisive events that happened here. A lookout area atop the visitors center provides a good overview of the earthworks that still make serpentine scars across the old battlefield. The center is located on the Colonial Parkway, just southeast of town.

It's an easy walk from the visitors center to the townsite. At the edge of town, on the bluffs above the river, rises the **Victory Monument** (1884), a pedestal topped by a classical rendition of Victory, arms outstretched in hope. Yorktown's **Main Street** boasts a scattering of old colonial buildings, most built in the first half of the 1700s, when Yorktown was a prosperous tobacco port. By the time the war struck, the soil of surrounding plantations had been depleted and the port had lost its product. The grandest structure still standing from that period is the Georgian brick **Nelson House,** home of Thomas Nelson, Jr., a signer of the Declaration of Independence. Built in 1711 by Nelson's grandfather "Scotch Tom," the restored home re-creates the pleasantries of life in Yorktown before the war. During the war, the British were assumed to be headquartered here, and the house was ordered shelled by none other than Nelson himself, commander of the Virginia militia. That was not Nelson's only selfless act. He borrowed heavily against his own fortune to support the war effort and died a pauper as a result.

Rising across the street from the Nelson House is the oldest **customhouse** in the country, dating from the early 1700s and Yorktown's bustling days of commerce. Small and lovely **Grace Church** (1697) stands nearby on Church Street, its marl walls having endured both the Revolutionary and Civil wars. Its walled cemetery holds a number of historic graves, including those of Thomas Nelson, Jr., whose remains had lain unmarked until this century; and Nicholas Martiau, the first American ancestor of George Washington.

The Yorktown waterfront claims two non-colonial but critical landmarks. The **Watermen's Museum**, located at 309 Water Street, evokes the centuries-old and now dying culture of the Bay's oystermen, crabbers, and fishermen. Down the street, **Nick's Seafood Pavilion** cooks to perfection fresh catches from the bay in a setting of classical statuary.

Just northwest of the old historic area, at Route 238 and the Colonial Parkway, the state maintains its **Yorktown Victory Center,** both a museum and living history site where costumed guides work a Colonial-style farmsite and man a Revolution-ary-period military encampment. The center's film, *The Road to Yorktown,* offers a particularly good explanation of the area's history.

DIARY OF A PLANTATION OWNER, 1740

January 25

I rose about 6, read Hebrew and Greek. I prayed and had hominy. The weather was cold and clear, the wind southwest. The Doctor and Mr. Anderson went away. I read records and Latin till dinner when I ate sparerib. It snowed again a little till the evening, then danced because could not walk. At night talked with my people. Mrs. Byrd had the headache pretty much. I prayed.

January 26

I rose about 6, read Hebrew and Greek. I prayed and had sage tea. I danced. The weather was cold and clear, the wind northwest. My son was hurt in the eye with a snowball; God preserve him. I read records and Latin till dinner when I ate pork griskin. After dinner my man Peter ran here from above. I played billiards and danced. I had letters from England, and prayed.

January 27

I rose about 6, read Hebrew and Greek. I prayed and had tea. I danced. The weather was cold and cloudy, the wind west. I sent Peter up again with Bob. I put myself in order and sent Mr. Procter over the river. The boat came from the Falls, where all were well, thank God. Mr. B-r-n came and Mr. Ravenscroft and Mr. Wendey to dinner and I ate sparerib. After dinner we talked and had coffee. The company went away. In the evening I talked with my people and discoursed my family till 8, then retired and prayed.

—William Byrd, *Secret Diary,* 1740

GENTRY ON THE JAMES RIVER

Along the middle stretch of the James River, from roughly Williamsburg to Richmond, lies a virtual gold mine of colonial and Georgian manses. Virginia planters built these palaces in the plantation heyday, and the homes epitomize, to this day, the gentrified life. Most are still privately owned, some have remained in the same family since they were built. While they dot both sides of the river, the greatest concentration can be found in **Charles City County** near or along Route 5, the renowned Plantation Route (see "Colonial Heartland" map in this chapter). Several of the historic homes along this scenic, wooded lane now offer bed and breakfast hospitality; others are open for guided tours, and still others open their doors only during Historic Garden Week. The half-dozen below deserve special attention for their historic or architectural merit.

CARTER'S GROVE

Located eight miles (13 km) east of Williamsburg on Route 60, this stately mansion was built in 1750 by a grandson of Virginia's baronial Robert "King" Carter. (804) 220-7645.

The elegant entry hall of Carter's Grove Plantation House.

SHERWOOD FOREST

This stately home lays claim to being the only home owned by two U.S. presidents, William Henry Harrison (who owned it, but never lived there) and his running mate John Tyler, who later bought it from a Harrison relative. Tyler did live at Sherwood Forest, and at the behest of his young, second wife, he added the Greek Revival touches to this already elegant Georgian clapboard. Tyler's descendants still live in the home. (804) 829-5377.

BERKELEY PLANTATION

One of the oldest large brick houses in Virginia, this Georgian mansion is more memorable for its history and its boxwood gardens than its beauty. Benjamin Harrison, signer of the Declaration of Independence, built it, and his son, future president William Henry Harrison, was born here. (804) 829-6018.

WESTOVER

This elegantly proportioned Georgian manor house (c.1730) was built by William Byrd II, one of the Virginia colony's most prominent—and arrogant—gentlemen, and the man credited with founding Richmond. Though the house interior is open only during Historic Garden Week, the grounds themselves are well worth a visit. The striking facade of the home faces out on the James, fronted by a line of centuries-old poplars. (See excerpts from Byrd's love letters and diaries in this chapter.)

SHIRLEY PLANTATION

Virginia's oldest plantation, Shirley was established six years after the founding of Jamestown. Birthplace of Robert E. Lee's mother, Anne Carter Lee, it has been in the Carter family since 1723. A remarkable walnut staircase seems to rise unsupported for three stories through the center of the house. (804) 795-2385.

TUCKAHOE PLANTATION

The boyhood home of Thomas Jefferson, this H-shaped frame house with its outbuildings (c. 1714) are considered by preservationists to be classic eighteenth-century plantation buildings. Tuckahoe is located on the James River north and west of the houses listed above, seven miles (11 km) on the River Road above Richmond. (See the Piedmont map in the "PIEDMONT" chapter.)

For more information, check with the Metropolitan Richmond Convention and Visitors Center at (804) 649-3001.

A PLANTATION OWNER'S LOVE LETTERS

*T*o Brillante

I am as much astonisht at your being cross, as I shou'd have been at your being kind, the high opinion I have of you, makes the first surprizeing, as the low one I have of myself, wou'd do the last. For peace sake Madam, why do you put your self into all this fury. I'm sure you must be a Woman, by the unreasonableness of your resentment, and a marry'd woman, by your useing those the worst, that love you best. Allowing, that in the Frenzy of my passion for you, I might use a little more briskness than ordinary in my expression, yet it being with good manners, you ought to have imputed it to excess of Inclination, which dont use to create a quarrel betwixt a Lover and his Mistress . . . .

*T*o Rampana

Rampana has been beholden to Nature for such materials, as with a moderate improvement wou'd make her a finisht woman. And if it were not for a large mixture of laziness to keep her fine Qualitys under, Envy wou'd make her too many enimys of her own sex, and Love too many admirers of ours. Her understanding is capable of takeing the brightest polish: but her industry to improve her Mind, is discourag'd by too great a dependance on the beautys of her Body . . . .

*T*o Panthea

I had the honour of your enchanting letter, and I may very justly call it enchanting, because it pleas'd me at the same time, that it refus'd the dearest of my Inclinations. However I confess you are . . . mistress of the Art of pleaseing, and can dress up pain so delicately as to make it agreeable. But stil I cant forgive your ill-nature, tho I must commend your skil in setting it off . . . .

—William Byrd, *Secret Diary,* 1696–1726

Shirley Plantation is Virginia's oldest plantation. The birthplace of Robert E. Lee's mother, it has remained in the same family (the Hill-Carters) since it was built in 1723. On the roof, between the two chimneys, sits a huge carved pineapple, an ancient symbol of fertility that became a popular design element in seventeenth-century England and, in Virginia, came to symbolize hospitality. The design of the interior is just as interesting as that of the exterior. There is an extraordinary carved walnut staircase, and the three rooms on the first floor, the only ones open to the public, are furnished with museum-quality paintings and antiques. The plantation grounds boast views of the James River which surpass those of any other plantations in the area.

P I E D M O N T

ROLLING ACROSS THE CENTER OF THE STATE, Virginia's Piedmont sweeps through farm fields and pastureland and some of the most sought-after horse country in the nation. Punctuating all this ruralness are several of the Old Dominion's most winsome cities—places full of themselves and of their own histories. Many of the citizens of these cities preserve the essence of the *haute Virginia* style. Things are done to a "T" here, with old-school Virginia grace and refinement. While that style may seem passé to some, it's a dying art form well worth appreciating.

■ RICHMOND

All roads lead to Richmond, or at least the state's major highways—I-95, I-64, and U.S. 360—do. Which is fitting, because old Southerners like to call this city "the navel of the universe." Quixotic in every sense, Richmond is many things to many people: the industrial hub of Virginia; a cultural mecca rich in museums and historic sites; the place at which Patrick Henry proclaimed, "Give me liberty or give me death"; the benighted but beloved capital of the old Confederacy; and the current capital and headquarters of state officialdom. It has been home to John Marshall, Edgar Allan Poe, tap dancer Bill "Bojangles" Robinson, and Arthur Ashe. It is also a linchpin of the "New South" and host to better than a dozen Fortune 500 companies; the Tobacco Capital of the World; and the unrepentant heartland of the old Virginia aristocracy. A new city, an old city, a mild city, a harsh city. An enduring city. An endearing city.

Richmond's highrises thrust suddenly into view, startling to the senses, really, in a state with so few pockets of towering urbanism. Devoted mostly to state government, banking, and financial interests, the highrises cluster just above the downtown edge of the James River, and they leave a somewhat misleading first impression. Richmond, ultimately, is more horizontal than vertical. Its avenues spread out across seven hills through neighborhoods like Church Hill, the Fan, and the Boulevard, where restored Victorian rowhouses overlook shady streets. But Richmond's streets also lead into crime-ravaged inner city neighborhoods like Jackson Ward, a place that once had an illustrious history.

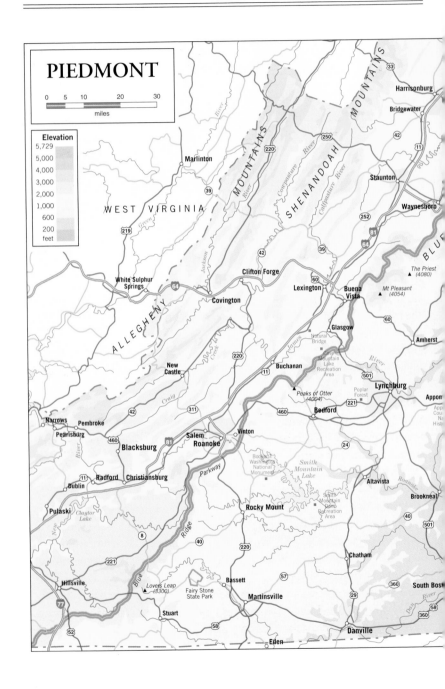

PIEDMONT

0 5 10   20   30
miles

Elevation
5,729
5,000
4,000
3,000
2,000
1,000
600
200
feet

WEST VIRGINIA

219

Marlinton

39

White Sulphur
Springs

ALLEGHENY

64

Covington

Clifton Forge

New
Castle

42

311

Narrows
Pembroke
Pearisburg
460   Blacksburg
81
Salem
Roanoke
Vinton

Dublin
11 Radford Christiansburg

Pulaski Claytor
Lake

8

221

Hillsville

77

52

Stuart

58

Eden

33

Harrisonburg
Bridgewater

MOUNTAINS

220

250

42

11

Staunton

Waynesboro

252

SHENANDOAH

81

64

39

Lexington

60

Buena
Vista

The Priest
▲ (4080)

Mt Pleasant
▲ (4054)

60

BLUE

Glasgow

Natural
Bridge

Mountain
Lake
Recreation
Area

Amherst

501

Buchanan

220

11

▲ Peaks of Otter
(4004)

Poplar
Forest

Lynchburg

Appom

221

460

Bedford

Appo
Cou
Na
Hist

24

Booker T
Washington
National
Monument

Smith
Mountain
Lake

Parkway

Altavista

Roanoke

Brookneal

Rocky Mount

Smith
Mountain
Dam
Recreation
Area

40

501

Ridge

40

220

Chatham

Bassett

57

360

South Bos

29

58

Martinsville

360

58

Danville

Lovers Leap
▲ (3300)

Fairy Stone
State Park

Blue

New
River

Craig
Creek

Jackson
River

Green

Compasture River

Coldpasture River

River

James

River

River

River

Dan
River

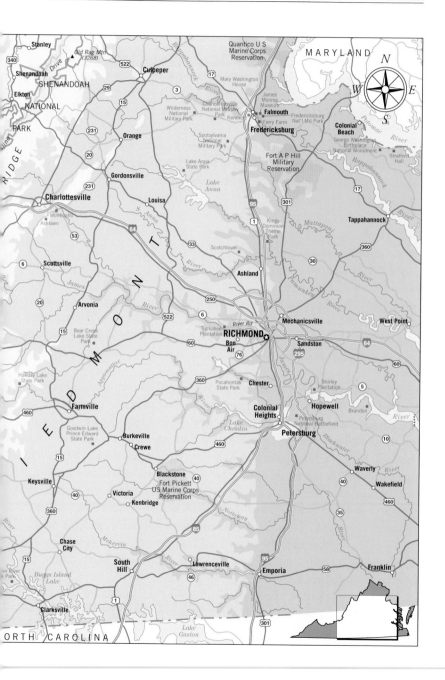

■ DOWNTOWN

Richmond, like any other city with a past, is a paradox, and it is paradox that gives this town its fascination. Richmond seems to have been in a perpetual battle for its own soul—whether to live securely in the past or to move forward into the future. Slowly and carefully, it is inching its way into the future, though it tends to build its future out of its past.

Take the tobacco industry. Richmond became a preeminent tobacco manufacturing town in the 1800s, and though in this century it gradually lost some of its older companies, it gained a monumental new one. Philip Morris has headquartered itself on the southern outskirts of town in a sprawling, state-of-the-art complex designed by renowned architect Gordon Bunshaft. The company ranks as the city's largest private employer, but the metropolitan area is also home to other major banking and industrial concerns: Sovran Bank, CSX, James River Corporation (a major paper producer), and Reynolds Metal—a company whose past reads like a history of corporate America. Reynolds, too, began as a tobacco manufacturing plant; the metals angle came in when it began producing foil liners for its cigarette packs, and gradually, aluminum replaced tobacco as the company's primary product. In recent years Reynolds has been taken over by R. J. R. Nabisco in a famous corporate battle that formed the basis of the movie *Barbarians at the Gate.*

In redefining itself, the city has come to understand the cosmetic value of its industrial past. The old **Shockoe Slip** and **Shockoe Bottom** tobacco warehouses on Cary Street down along the river are the new focus of revitalization. Slowly, the cavernous redbrick buildings are being trendified into upscale shops and restaurants. So far, the redevelopment has only reclaimed a block or two, but the city has high hopes. It also fosters some hopes for its old downtown commercial district along Broad Street. Once, it ranked as the most fashionable place in the South to shop, with classic department stores, like Thalheimer's and Miller & Rhoads. The latter's tea room featured models at lunchtime, and the dinging sound of those old department store call bells overlaid the place with a now lost aura of civility. Those stores are now boarded up, and Broad Street, despite city efforts, is a dilapidated has-been.

In these unpredictable economic times, anything can happen. In fact, a long-deserted part of the city has just been resurrected as a major new museum/history complex called **Valentine Riverside**. The innovative project, designed by the staff of the city's progressive Valentine Museum, is located on the site of the historic Tredegar Iron Works, one of the antebellum South's few industrial giants. Billed as an "urban history complex," the site, when complete, will encompass several buildings. Already the old Pattern Building has been turned into an indoor/outdoor museum. Its exterior walls serve as the screen for a larger-than-life laser show that features historic characters. Inside, a top-floor exhibit hall offers a 360-degree view of the industrialization of America. Out one set of windows, you can see the riffling fall line of the James, the very thing that provided power to Tredegar. Spanning the river is the railroad. The old black trestle still bridging the James was built of iron from this plant. On another side are the ruins of the James River-Kanawha Canal, which took people and cargo west into the Alleghenies. And in the complex's brick courtyard are monumental pieces of equipment from the age of industry. Shined up now, they look to the modern eye like great, gleaming works of art. Despite all this renovation, the site does not romanticize the past. You get a good idea of the booming, gritty cacophony that Tredegar meant to the workers who spent virtually their whole lives here.

In its day, Tredegar was a progressive employer that watched out for its workers. Many were slaves, either "owned" by the company or "rented" from other owners. Tredegar provided a hospital and housing, and in the mid-1800s, when white artisans demanded that blacks be removed from certain skilled jobs, the whites went and the blacks stayed.

Race relations have a complex past in this city. Long a hub of black culture, the city today is about 55 percent African American. In the antebellum era, house slaves apparently lived well here—if any human who is considered property can be said to live well. In any case, there was a strong social network among blacks, and even a kind of "downstairs" aristocracy that mirrored the city's white aristocracy. Some blacks were able to purchase their freedom and set up as artisans or small businessmen in the town. Still, this was a Southern town, and blacks were expected to "know their place," even into the mid-twentieth century.

One woman who seemed to understand how to negotiate her standing in this ambiguous color-coded world was **Maggie Walker.** Walker was the daughter of a former slave and assistant cook in the Church Hill mansion of Elizabeth Van Lew, a passionate abolitionist and Union spy. Despite her rather humble beginnings, Walker let neither social conditions nor her own physical handicap (she was a paraplegic the last years of her life) impede progress. Early in this century, she took

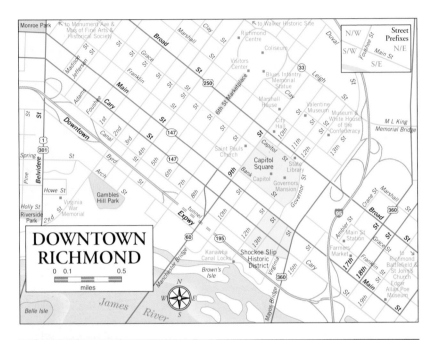

A storm brews in the sky over downtown Richmond.

a small fraternal society and turned it into a lucrative black business concern that owned a newspaper (for which she served as editor) and a bank (for which she served as president—the first woman bank president in the United States). Walker was also an early champion of civil rights and African American pride, and remained actively committed to improving educational opportunities, economic development, and racial cohesiveness in her community until her death in 1934.

Her substantial Victorian house, now a National Historic Site open to the public, stands amid the sad decay of the Jackson Ward neighborhood. Once a thriving black community filled with prospering businesses and famous for its jazz and ragtime, the area now reeks of inner city desolation. Even though a few of its rowhouses have been renovated, it's a far cry from the days when Bill "Bojangles" Robinson or Duke Ellington played its clubs.

While Richmond continues to sort through its race relations, its museums are now determined to tell the whole story of the city's history, both black and white. One of the best places to experience this is at the **Valentine Museum**, 1015 E. Clay Street, which has taken as its mission a "reinterpretation of the city's history" that locates "Richmond in the mainstream of American history." Its Wickham-Valentine House, an early nineteenth-century showcase of Federal-style architecture, goes a long way beyond the classic house museum/decorative arts approach. Dramatic recordings in several rooms of the house effectively capture conversations between house slaves working for the Wickham family and the members of the family themselves. It makes a memorable impression to hear the first group

Maggie Walker, daughter of a slave and the first woman to found a bank in the United States. (Maggie L. Walker National Historic Site)

whispering about a beating of one of their brethren out in the county, and then to hear the "white folk" enter the room, with their mindless social chatter.

John Wickham, a New York lawyer who moved to Richmond and became a prominent citizen, had the house built in 1812. Unique for its exquisite wall murals and spiral staircase, the townhouse bespeaks money, urbanity, and fine living—for Wickham, at least, if not necessarily for his slaves *or* his wife. She rarely went out, as she spent her time confined by 17 pregnancies.

After the progressive approach of the Valentine Museum, it's a study in contrasts to walk a block away to 1201 Clay street to the stuccoed, porticoed **White House of the Confederacy.** Here, Jefferson Davis had his brief reign as president of the Southern states. The house interior, decorated as it was in the Davis era, is truly something to see. Its brocaded, chandeliered, red-velvet bordello-esque decor is aptly characterized by some of its tour docents as "Gosh-awful Victorian." The decor notwithstanding, the docents do a good job tracing the poignant and tragic history of the Davis family here. In the same complex is the **Museum of the Confederacy,** with paintings, war memorabilia, and accurate, rather than heavy-handed, exhibits on the history of the Civil War.

A couple of blocks away at 818 Marshall Street stands the large, solid brick house of "The Great Chief Justice," **John Marshall.** Marshall became the country's third chief justice in 1801, taking the post somewhat reluctantly, as he believed the Supreme Court was a weak sister to the two other branches of government. In his 34-year tenure (the longest of any chief justice), Marshall decisively changed that, making the court an equal partner in a tripartite governmental system. Over the objections of his political nemesis, Thomas Jefferson (who also happened to be his cousin), he interpreted the Constitution in a way that firmly established the federal government's authority over individual states.

Marshall was not by nature an intellectual. Robust and athletic, he liked sports, and a set of quoits (horseshoes) still lie in the family parlor where he used to play. Even while serving as chief justice, Marshall lived here with his beloved wife, Polly, and their brood of children. In those days, the Supreme Court had no home of its own, and it often met nearby in the Virginia capitol. In fact, it was here that Marshall heard the famous treason case against Aaron Burr.

The suave, sophisticated Burr cut quite a figure when he came as a prisoner to Richmond in 1807. Even though he was accused of plotting the overthrow of the federal government in territories west and south of Virginia, society welcomed him. While awaiting trial, he was housed in a three-room prison suite, and his admiring public dispatched servants with daily notes and gifts of fruit. Legal sensibilities were apparently different in those days, as Burr attended a dinner party at the home of one of his attorneys, none other than John Wickham. The other dinner guests included members who were to sit on his jury and the chief justice himself.

During the trail, Marshall clearly favored Burr's cause, and ultimately, the dashing "traitor" was acquitted of the charges against him. A cynic might conclude that in Richmond, lack of charm was a far greater offense than treason. And Burr was a charming man.

The Hall of the House of Delegates, where Burr was tried, still occupies one side of the gracefully pillared **state capitol building,** designed by that consummate lover of the neo-classical, Thomas Jefferson. He modeled it after the Maison Carré, a temple that the conquering Romans built in Nîmes, France. The central core of the building has been in use since 1788, making it the "second oldest working capitol in the United States." Today it is filled with images of Virginia's favorite sons, including a statue of George Washington done from life by French sculptor Jean Antoine Houdon. Washington, looking somber and dignified, occupies the

An old view of Richmond—pictured here around 1850. (Library of Congress)

place of honor under the dome, and in the niches around him are busts of the seven other Virginia presidents, as well as one of the Revolutionary hero, the Marquis de Lafayette. As the guides explain it, Lafayette is merely a place holder, there only until the country elects its ninth Virginia-born president.

■ LEAVING DOWNTOWN

If you leave downtown and head west on wide and sedate **Monument Avenue,** you'll get a good sense of the fluid graciousness of this city's old neighborhoods. The avenue's circles sweep around heroic statues of those monuments that give the street its name. Almost all are Civil War heroes mounted astride their trusty steeds—Lee, Jackson, Jeb Stuart, Jefferson Davis (unmounted but gesticulating) and finally, Matthew Fontaine Maury, best known as the "Pathfinder of the Seven Seas" for his ground-breaking charts of Atlantic currents. Small side streets, rich in Victorian architecture, lead off the avenue to the southwest and the Fan district, so named because its streets "fan" out from the café/student scene at Virginia Commonwealth University.

Monument Avenue eventually intersects with yet another glorious thoroughfare—The Boulevard. This is where the city keeps much of its culture—at the acclaimed **Virginia Museum of Fine Arts,** at Boulevard and Grove Avenue. Endowed by such philanthropic giants as the Mellons, the rambling, elegant museum can hold its own with virtually any museum in the country. Founded in 1936, it boasts a collection that spans 5,000 years, from Egyptian, Roman, and Greek works, to twentieth-century decorative arts, impressionist and post-impressionist paintings, and an outstanding collection of Fabergé Easter eggs. The museum also supports an active program of performing arts in its auditorium.

A block away at 428 N. Boulevard stands the **Virginia Historical Society,** yet another example of the Richmond of paradoxes. On one side of the lobby is the Cheek Gallery, lined with towering murals depicting Southern heroism and struggles in the Civil War. Yet the rest of the building is devoted to imaginative, interactive exhibits that portray—not Southern gallantry—but the common man's history in the state.

Though it is hardly part of the common man's heritage, fantastical **Maymont** is worth a drive to the southwest side of the city. Occupying a sweeping knoll above the river, this turn-of-the-century estate glimmers with cascading Italian fountain gardens, Japanese gardens, a small farm, and a nature center. The austere, turreted

Alice Duesberry, tour guide to St. John's Church in Richmond.

stone house itself is remarkably intimate inside, the rooms decorated with the personal possessions of its original owners, May and James Dooley. May's feminine French furnishings vie with the dark German pieces of James's rooms. And May's boudoir is not to be missed. Her bed is designed as a swan, something she had created for the family country estate, Swannanoa (still standing in the Blue Ridge). Her dressing table is a Tiffany confection of sterling silver with posts and legs made of narwhal tusks. As environmentally incorrect as the thing is, it's still a work of art.

Not far from Maymont, you can find yourself in the whispering forests of **Hollywood Cemetery,** whose serene hillsides have been the favored burying place for a host of famous Virginians, including presidents Monroe, Tyler, and Davis (president, that is, of the Confederate States). One famous Virginian not buried here is Edgar Allan Poe, but he is celebrated at the **Edgar Allan Poe Museum,** at 1914 E. Main Street on the southeast edge of downtown.

Tortured and brilliant as an adult, Poe apparently spent a contented childhood in Richmond as the foster son of the Allan family. (His own mother, an acclaimed young actress, had died when he was two, and his father before that.) When Poe got to the University of Virginia, his relations with his foster father began to sour, and money became a growing problem—a problem that would haunt him the rest of his life. In order to continue his education, he enrolled at West Point, but the military milieu was crippling to his creativity, and so he deliberately got himself dismissed. After the academy, he spent some time with his aunt, Maria Clemm in Baltimore, and here he fell in love with his young—very young—cousin.

Poet Edgar Allan Poe (1809–1849), who spent a happy childhood in Richmond. (Library of Congress)

By then he had published three volumes of poetry, but his financial situation was deplorable. In 1834, he took a job back in his native Richmond as critic for the newly established *Southern Literary Messenger*. In his 18 months on the magazine, its circulation went from 500 to 3,500. It was during this time that the 26-year-old Poe married his 13-year-old cousin, Virginia. As much as he apparently loved his wife, the marriage did not settle Poe's situation. His bouts with depression and the bottle led to his dismissal from the magazine, and he and his wife left Richmond for the North.

Though Poe's literary reputation continued to flourish, his personal life did not. In 1842, his young wife suffered a ruptured blood vessel in the brain, and lingered as an invalid for five years. In 1849, the now-acclaimed writer made his final visit to Richmond and was warmly received. He wrote to his mother-in-law, "I have been invited out a great deal—but seldom go, on account of not having a dress coat." A few months later, he sailed for Baltimore, with plans to return to Richmond. He never did. He was found semiconscious and ill on the streets of Baltimore, and he died soon thereafter. The words of Poe's own poem, "Eldorado," seem to sum up his life:

> Gayly bedight,
> A gallant knight,
> In sunshine and in shadow,
> Had journeyed long,
> Singing a song,
> In search of Eldorado.
>
> But he grew old,
> This knight so bold,
> And o'er his heart a shadow
> Fell as he found
> No spot of ground
> That looked like Eldorado.

The museum complex to his memory holds his memorabilia, his writings, even architectural parts of Richmond buildings that he lived or worked in. The complex also holds a separate piece of history—the **Old Stone House,** built in the late 1730s and the oldest structure still standing in the city.

Poe's young actress mother rests a couple of blocks from his museum, at **St. John's Church,** located at 2401 E. Broad Street at 24th Street. The large clapboard building is probably better known as the site of Patrick Henry's famous "Give me liberty or give me death" speech. Beyond the church at 3215 E. Broad Street, on a high hill facing south, stands another artifact of the nation's psyche: **Chimborazo,** the old Confederate hospital that cared for some 76,000 wounded during the Civil War. Now the hospital serves as headquarters for the **Richmond National Battlefield Park,** which traces the long torturous history of the war here and the ultimate fall of Richmond.

After nearby Petersburg fell in April 1865, Lee sent word to Jefferson Davis that the North would be moving on the Confederate capital. Davis fled and the South set fire to tobacco warehouses along the riverfront to keep their contents out of Yankee hands. The fire spread, Richmond burned, and much of the white population fled in fear. Much of the black population secretly rejoiced that they would be free at last. By April 4, Abraham Lincoln entered the city, triumphant. Ten days later, Robert E. Lee rode into the city astride Traveller and defeat. He was going

Currier and Ives lithograph depicting the burning and evacuation of Richmond on the night of April 2, 1865. (Virginia State Library and Archives)

home to his wife and their temporary home at 707 East Franklin Street. The townhouse is still there, surrounded by—and a part of—modern Richmond. Its upper levels hold offices for architects now, but remember, this is a city that spins its present and its future from the past. The lower level of 707 East Franklin is a restaurant . . . . named (but of course) **Traveller.**

■ FREDERICKSBURG

Fredericksburg was built where it was because humans, opportunistic creatures that they are, like to situate themselves at river fall lines. Fifty-eight miles (93 km) north of Richmond on I-95 (and about an hour's drive south of Washington, D.C.), this little burg has rested beside the falls of the Rappahanock River, near its confluence with the Rapidan, for about 250 years. You couldn't really call it a river town today, but you could call it historically correct and, despite its proximity to the Washington, D.C. suburbs, decidedly Southern.

Small Colonial and Federal-style brick buildings, leftovers from the halcyon days of the eighteenth and nineteenth centuries, make the waterfront downtown a charming place. Now filled with antique and craft shops, sophisticated little restaurants, and galleries, the buildings bear witness to the resilience of this town, because, as every Virginian knows, Fredericksburg was ravaged during one of the worst battles of the Civil War. Though it took close to a hundred years to reclaim and rebuild itself, the town has achieved that now, and any visitor here is guaranteed to be pleased.

You can't walk more than a few feet along Fredericksburg's quaint streets before encountering the name Washington. George himself spent a good bit of his youth at **Ferry Farm,** a few miles south on the river, but it is his siblings that left an indelible mark on Fredericksburg. His brother Charles built an understated and pleasant frame house on Caroline Street in about 1760 and lived in it for 20 years. Still standing, the building now celebrates its early nineteenth-century days, when it served as a tavern. Nowadays, when you walk up onto the low-slung verandah of the **Rising Sun Tavern,** at 1306 Caroline Street, mob-capped serving "wenches" will greet you and take you on a memorable tour through the darkly inviting tavern rooms. Along the way, the wenches are quick to dispel any romantic notions you may have of the colonial past. Their descriptions of tavern life highlight the robust, less-than-genteel side of early America—like the way tavern diners passed along their dirty wooden plates to the next diner. Why bother washing dinnerware, after all, when everyone would be eating the same thing—whatever "pot luck" hung in the pot over the hearth. Baths were offered only in July and August, because, except during the hottest months, who needed them?

Things are a bit more genteel a few blocks away at the **Mary Washington House** at 1200 Charles Street. George purchased this colonial clapboard for his 64-year-old mother in 1772, "to make her more comfortable and free from care . . . ." He may have thought it a fine idea, but one wonders whether his brother-in-law, Fielding Lewis, liked the set-up. While George was a safe way down the Potomac at Mount Vernon, Fielding and his wife Betty lived a quick walk west of mother-in-law Mary in the town's finest manor house, **Kenmore**, at 1201 Washington Avenue.

Influential and respected, Fielding Lewis came from Tidewater gentry, settling in Fredericksburg in 1747. Commerce in the burgeoning rivertown quickly made him wealthy, and he began constructing a Georgian manor, in the style prevalent in his native Tidewater. At the time, Kenmore was at the heart of a 13,000-acre plantation on the edge of town. Today, it has been reduced to four acres of lawn, gardens, and shade trees in the midst of a pleasant old neighborhood. Decorated in period furnishings, the gracious, high-ceilinged rooms reflect life in Lewis's time. The home's most memorable feature is its ornate plasterwork on the ceilings. The craftsman responsible for this artistry also did work at Mount Vernon, but history, like the Washington family, remembers him simply as the "Stucco Man."

James Monroe, Jefferson's protégé and America's fifth president, practiced law as a young attorney at 908 Caroline Street. For decades the low-slung, dormered brick cottage there, now the **James Monroe Museum,** was believed to have been Monroe's law office. In fact, his twentieth-century descendants even saved it from the wrecking ball in the 1920s. But preservationists from Mary Washington College, also in Fredericksburg, have dated the building to the nineteenth century, decades after Monroe's stint in Fredericksburg. No matter, the museum is still filled with an impressive amount of Monroe memorabilia, including the Louis XVI desk on which he wrote the inaugural address that was to form the basis of his famous Monroe Doctrine. About the desk: Lawrence Hoes, Monroe's great-great-grandson and the man who founded the museum, grew up with the desk in his family home. Since boys will be boys, he managed as a young child to topple it. When the desk was taken to a local cabinetmaker for repair, a secret compartment was discovered, something fairly common in such old pieces. Only this one was still filled with Monroe's personal correspondence, 250 pieces of it, and some from the greatest thinkers of the day.

Time spreads out from the river in Fredericksburg, climbing away from the Colonial/Federal downtown and into the morass of the Civil War. The war visited Fredericksburg and the surrounding countryside—Chancellorsville, Spotsylvania, The Wilderness—twice, once in December 1862 and again in the spring of 1863. The four battlefields together make up the **Fredericksburg and Spotsylvania National Military Park,** all within 17 miles (27 km) of Fredericksburg. At the infamous **Marye's Heights** (pronounced Marie's), the now green hills terrace gently up to a national cemetery memorializing the 1862 Fredericksburg carnage. The Union boys fell in heaps that cold winter when they charged across open ground toward the Southerners entrenched on this hillside.

If you drive west out of town, past the sprawl of strip center malls that line Route 3, you'll suddenly return to the wood and pastureland that marks the historic **Chancellorsville Battlefield.** Here Grant, Lee, and Jackson squared off in 1863, and here Lee scored probably his most brilliant battle success. The battle, though, cost him dearly, because as every Civil War buff knows, this is where the mythic Stonewall stood his last. After a victorious day, Jackson was wounded by Southern men who mistook him for the enemy when he rode out on an evening reconnoiter.

The fallen general was taken to Guinea Station, a railroad crossing to the southeast, where he could be quickly transported to Richmond for medical treatment. Jackson outflanked the plans of even his own comrades. For almost a week, he lay in the small frame plantation office at Guinea Station, now the park service's **Stonewall Jackson Shrine** 15 miles (24 km) south of Fredericksburg. Here he fought his own wounds and the North. In his delirium, he called out battle instructions to his fellow officers. He also had cogent moments, when he knew that his wife was by his side. Pneumonia gradually gained on him, and on May 10, a Sunday, the devout Jackson calmly remarked, "I have always desired to die on Sunday." He lapsed briefly back into delirium, shouting final battle orders for Gen. A. P. Hill. Then he grew serene again. "Let us cross over the river," he said at the last, "and rest under the shade of the trees."

■ JEFFERSON COUNTRY

Albemarle County dips and rises in the lavish greenness of classic Virginia horse country, virtually in the center of the state, along the eastern flank of the Blue Ridge Mountains (take I-64 northwest from Richmond). Leggy Thoroughbreds graze its neatly fenced pastures, and the very rich and sometimes even the famous live at the end of tree-lined entrance lanes, in houses that have stood for a couple of centuries.

"Toney" best describes the ambiance in much of the county, and that mood leaches somewhat into the city of Charlottesville, which the county surrounds. Some of the high tone comes from the fact that this is Jefferson country, and early on he gave the county a sophisticated taste for the good life. Old-line Virginia gentry live here on estates whose families have a long pedigree, but they have been joined in recent decades by industrial barons and celebrities who like the low-key ambiance and intense beauty of the area. John Kluge, one of the richest men in the country, keeps a house here, as do Sissy Spacek, Jessica Lange and Sam Shephard, writers Peter Taylor, Rita Mae Brown, and Anne Beatty.

Subtlety is a cultural byword here, and hence celebrity stalking is frowned upon. Novelist William Faulkner, who spent two years in the 1950s as writer-in-residence at the University of Virginia, explained it this way: "I like Virginia, and I like Virginians. Because Virginians are all snobs, and I like snobs. A snob has to spend so much time being a snob that he has little left to meddle with you, and so it is very pleasant here."

Not all the county reeks of money and manners. There are pockets, particularly on the west side, of simple, rural Virginia, where musty, plank-floored general stores stand at crossroads and farmers keep modest herds of cattle or tend apple orchards. Down along the James, outside the little town of Scottsville (corner of routes 6 and 20), one of the few remaining hand-poled cable ferries in America still crosses the river. If you don't feel comfortable having the ferryman struggle to pole you across on the old **Hatton Ferry,** you can rent an oversize inner tube at the adjacent James River Runners, but mind the snakes the outfitters keep in cages on their porch. With a tube under you, you can float mindlessly downriver with your backside for ballast and the wooded shoreline of the James conjuring an image of an earlier, simpler time.

Fox Hunt at the Princess Anne Country Club.

VIRGINIA WINE

The wine-making tradition has deeper roots in the Old Dominion than anywhere else in the East. Those first Jamestown diehards managed to produce wine from native grapes within two years of their arrival. Problem was, it wasn't very drinkable. They kept trying, though, even importing French *vignerons* (winegrowers) to oversee vineyards planted in European stocks. But even the redoubtable French failed to make a successful Virginia wine.

Thomas Jefferson, a wine aesthete, tried his hand, too, at Monticello, but alas, Virginia winters were simply too harsh for the delicate European *viniferas*. Then in the 1830s, an American hybrid called the Norton Virginia gave Virginia an award-winning claret, sought after both on the Continent and in America.

Still, it took almost a century and a half and the pressures of late twentieth-century living to firmly establish a flock of Virginia winegrowers. In the 1970s, as wine fever spread across the country, a number of amateur Virginia vineyardists began experimenting, more or less in their own backyards. Many of them started their vineyards simply as a labor of love, but as the fever spread, retired professionals or professionals tired of the hassles of the workplace began to look to wine growing as an alternative lifestyle. They found that *vinifera* varietals and French hybrids did well in the sun and soil of the Commonwealth.

Today, there are about 40 wineries scattered through the state. While there are a few big-time operators among them, such as Ingleside and Prince Michel, most are small family-run farms that nonetheless produce some very respectable commercial wines. Big or small, Virginia's winemakers are a welcoming lot, happy to show visitors around their operations and offer them a taste of their chardonnays, rieslings, vidals, and cabernet sauvignons.

While wineries can be found throughout the state, the greatest concentration occurs in the Charlottesville/Culpeper area, and in the Middleburg/Front Royal area. Roadside markers, with a grape cluster logo, lead the way to vineyards, a list of which, with directions, can be found in "PRACTICAL INFORMATION." At gourmet and grocery stores and at state-run ABC (Alcoholic Beverage Commission) stores, shelves are well stocked with the Old Dominion's own vintages. (Author's personal favorite: Naked Mountain chardonnay.)

Naturally, since this is Virginia, that love of the past is never far away in Albemarle. In fact, it springs tellingly to life every Thanksgiving, when the horsey set don their riding pinks, collect their horses and hounds, and gather for the annual **blessing of the hounds** outside the hallowed stone walls of graceful **Grace Episcopal Church,** on the southern side of the county (on Route 231, 10 miles [16 km] east of Charlottesville).

Gracing a wooded glen, the old stone church is a noble structure at any time of year, and its graveyard is replete with Jefferson's kinsmen and the pooh-bahs of early Albemarle. On Thanksgiving, the sight of those horses, steam rising from their flanks into the autumn air, seems to epitomize Albemarle's centuries-old devotion to living well.

As does the county's most prominent feature—Jefferson's own remarkable "Little Mountain," **Monticello** (Route 53, southeast from Charlottesville). A lifework and a passion, this domed, columned manorhouse has become a living emblem of Jefferson—and a well-minted American symbol, appearing as it does on each and every nickel. Jefferson spent 40 years on Monticello, rethinking it, redesigning it, laying out and experimenting with its gardens. "Architecture," he said, "is my delight. And putting up and pulling down one of my favorite amusements."

■ M O N T I C E L L O

Though he was born in Albemarle when it was the edge of the frontier, Jefferson was no backwoodsman. His tastes ranged the globe, though he had a strong preference for things Roman or French. Yet, Jefferson as a man was eminently informal. While serving as the third President, he sometimes answered the door to the White House himself—and in slippered feet. A persistent rumor clings to him, suggesting that Sally Hemings, a slave at Monticello, was his longtime mistress. Most, though not all of his biographers, have debunked this. Given that no biographer has indicated that the situation was forced on Hemings, it seems that the issue, after 250 years, would be moot. Yet it gets raised now and then, like some kind of tasteless campaign muckraking.

Admittedly, Jefferson himself never hesitated to castigate his political enemies—of which he had a number. But politics, though his profession, was not his obsession. He clearly had the soul more of a philosopher than of a politician, and it was

(following pages) Thomas Jefferson's home of Monticello so impressed a visiting French nobleman that he declared Jefferson "the first American who has consulted the fine arts to know how he should shelter himself from the weather."

his philosophy—of democracy itself—that kept him in the political arena of the fledgling nation. He has been the hero to more than one of his presidential descendants. In 1992, Bill Clinton chose, literally, to follow in Jefferson's footsteps, beginning his trip to his inaugural from Monticello itself. Thirty years earlier Pres. John Kennedy, while addressing a group of Nobel Prize winners gathered at the White House, said that they were "the most extraordinary collection of talent, of human knowledge, that has ever gathered together at the White House—with the possible exception of when Thomas Jefferson dined alone."

All the sophistication and experience that informed Jefferson the man went into his home, Monticello. A French nobleman visiting Jefferson here was so impressed

TRUTHS SELF-EVIDENT

The Declaration of Independence was the result of a committee of the Second Continental Congress which included John Adams, Benjamin Franklin, Thomas Jefferson, Robert Livingston, and Roger Sherman. It was prepared by Jefferson, and despite minor changes, the final version was still largely Jefferson's.

*W*hen, in the course of human events, it becomes necessary for one people to dissolve the political bands which have connected them with another, and to assume, among the powers of the earth, the separate and equal station to which the laws of nature and of nature's God entitle them, a decent respect to the opinions of mankind requires that they should declare the causes which impel them to the separation.

We hold these truths to be self-evident, that all men are created equal, that they are endowed by their Creator with certain unalienable rights, that among these are life, liberty, and the pursuit of happiness. That, to secure these rights, governments are instituted among men, deriving their just powers from the consent of the governed. That, whenever any form of government becomes destructive of these ends, it is the right of the people to alter or to abolish it, and to institute new government, laying its foundation on such principles, and organizing its powers in such form, as to them shall seem most likely to effect their safety and happiness.

—Thomas Jefferson, *Declaration of Independence*, 1776

with the manor (and apparently so unimpressed with other American edifices) that he declared Jefferson to be "the first American who has consulted the fine arts to know how he should shelter himself from the weather." As elegant as the house is, it is nonetheless full of the quirky character of Mad Tom, as his political enemies called him. An inveterate tinkerer, Jefferson placed his gadgets throughout the house—like a seven-day clock, operated by weights that descended to the basement, and a holographic copier for making two written copies at once.

He also took his inventiveness into the garden. "No occupation," he once wrote, "is so delightful to me as the culture of the earth, and no culture comparable to that of the garden." He kept up a lively correspondence with horticulturists and friends concerning his experiments with vegetables, flowers, even wine grapes. Today, Monticello's grounds have become famous. Flowers of Jefferson's vintage line the "roundabout" on the West Lawn, and vegetables grow profusely in a terraced plot below the house.

So infectious was Jefferson's delight in the countryside here, that he persuaded his protégé James Monroe to build a home nearby. **Ashlawn-Highland,** a much simpler and decidedly more pedestrian place than Monticello, still stands today just a few miles away on Route 795.

Had Jefferson followed his private instincts, he might never have left his mountaintop to participate in the fray of politics. But his public instincts pushed him into the arena of nation-building and marked him forever as one of this country's Founding Fathers and its "Great Democrat." Ironically, he died on the half-century anniversary of the Declaration of Independence, the document he wrote. He is buried at Monticello on a quiet slope below the house. In predictable style, he penned his own epitaph, remembering himself to the world for three accomplishments: his authorship both of the Declaration and of Virginia's statute of religious freedom, and the founding of the University of Virginia.

■ UNIVERSITY OF VIRGINIA

From Monticello, Jefferson could look through a spyglass down on the town of Charlottesville and on the university that he had founded. This university was the love of his old age, and it proved a particularly difficult lover at that.

To this day the University of Virginia remains Mr. Jefferson's University and the centerpiece of the well-heeled yet progressive city of Charlottesville. Long the bastion of the Virginia gentlemen, the school can hardly be classed as an entrenched "gentlemen's" institution anymore. For one thing, it's been coed for a couple of decades, and for another, with close to 20,000 students, it's become an eclectic modern university. To be sure, the Greek tradition is alive and very well in the Rugby Road fraternity manses. But there are plenty of non-Greek pockets in the UVA populace now, and all told, the tenor on the "grounds" (never say campus here) feels like that at many burgeoning state institutions in the East. The forward-looking, eccentric Jefferson would probably feel more at home wandering the grounds today than he would have felt amid the button-down, "gentleman's B" (an A grade would be ungentlemanly) crowd that populated his university earlier in this century.

Happily, however, time and modernization have not much altered the famous "Academical Village" that Jefferson designed. Now a designated World Heritage Site, the buildings have also been proclaimed an outstanding achievement of American architecture by the American Institute of Architects. The "village" essentially comprises the university's elegant rotunda building, flanked on either side by two rows of colonnaded buildings holding spare, but charming student rooms. Two-story pavilions punctuate the colonnades, and these were intended by Jefferson to

The "grounds" (as opposed to "campus") of the University of Virginia in Charlottesville.

house professors, so that students would have easy access to their mentors. Today, faculty clubs and such take up the pavilion spaces. The small student rooms, however, remain in the hands of the school's top students. A room on the "Lawn," as it is called, is a cherished honor.

Beyond the Lawn's hallowed halls, the city of Charlottesville sweeps west toward the Blue Ridge and east toward a pleasant pedestrian-style downtown mall with a number of sophisticated restaurants and a few galleries and bookstores. Fine old neighborhoods still grace Charlottesville, and most of the strip-mall grotesquerie has been confined to the unsightly corridor along U.S. 29 N.

■ LYNCHBURG

About 66 miles (106 km) southwest from Charlottesville on U.S. 29 N, Lynchburg traces its lineage to eighteenth-century Quakers who settled here on the banks of the James. Though they stayed only a few decades before economic conditions and their anathema for slavery pushed them on, the aura of those gentlefolk still pervades this city. They must have also instilled in the town its religious bent, because today Lynchburg calls itself the "City of Churches." Up on Court House Hill, overlooking the river, steeples reach heavenward like a profusion of supplicating hands.

Even televangelist Jerry Falwell calls Lynchburg home, preaching from the pulpit of Thomas Road Baptist Church and operating his Liberty University on the outskirts of town. But Lynchburg is hardly dominated by the moral right. Falwell may be a nationally known figure, but here he is just another resident. His university is only one of six college-level institutions in the area. The others are Randolph-Macon Woman's College, Lynchburg College, Sweet Briar College, Central Virginia Community College, and Virginia Seminary and College.

The college scene doesn't really encroach much on the heart of the old downtown, which is in the process of being revitalized. The James runs right through here, and historically it has served as Lynchburg's life blood. These days, though, the riverfront languishes, run-down and uninteresting—except for a weekend in mid-June, when the city plays host to the **James River Batteau Festival.** Then, the James comes alive with an armada of re-created batteaux, those open, low-slung boats that navigated its eighteenth-century currents, carting goods upriver and down. From Lynchburg, the present-day batteaux head downriver on an eight-day journey to Richmond.

Court House Hill slopes up from the river, ornamented by Lynchburg's renowned **Monument Terrace**, a 139-step stone staircase set with soldierly statues. At its top rises the Old City Court House, a columned Greek Revival antique that now houses a local history museum. More vintage architecture crowns the **Diamond Hill Historic District**, a few blocks southeast. Resplendent Italianate, Georgian, and Victorian mansions from the city's tobacco heyday mix with fine little cottages. After some rough years in mid-century, Diamond Hill is being returned to its former grandeur.

If you head out 12th Street, you'll get into a neighborhood where the feel is decidedly less patrician, but where there stands nonetheless more than a passing inspiration. Poet **Anne Spencer**, a respected member of the Harlem Renaissance movement of the 1920s, lived at 1313 Pierce Street for much of this century. Though the surrounding neighborhood is pretty dilapidated, her shingle home is still a charming place with an illustrious past. Spencer entertained the likes of James Weldon Johnson, Marion Anderson, Paul Robeson, Martin Luther King, Jr., and many other luminaries here. Congressman Adam Clayton Powell even honeymooned in the house. Though the house is open now only by appointment, the walled garden behind it is accessible. Sitting out there in her studio cottage, Spencer took much of her inspiration from the intimate garden itself. "What is pain but happiness here," she wrote, "amid these green and wordless patterns . . . ."

■ POPLAR FOREST

An earlier Virginian also took inspiration from the green countryside surrounding Lynchburg. In 1806 Thomas Jefferson, then in his second term as President, turned his eyes in this direction, perhaps wistfully contemplating a life of rural privacy after his long public years. He knew he would never have much true privacy at Monticello, and so he began planning a villa, secreted on a tract of land a few miles southwest of Lynchburg.

Jefferson had inherited the Poplar Forest land long ago through his wife's estate, and now it seemed the ideal place to find the peace and quiet he had always coveted. Besides, there was nothing that gave him greater pleasure than designing and building. After years of architecting, the 63-year-old Jefferson knew exactly what he wanted and he proclaimed that Poplar Forest would be the "best dwelling house in the state, except that of Monticello. Perhaps preferable to that, as more proportioned to the faculties of a private citizen."

Bill "Bojangles" Robinson (on left), a native of Richmond, with Lena Horne and Cab Calloway in the film Stormy Weather *in 1943. (Virginia State Library and Archives)*

High on a knoll above dipping pastoral hills, the intimate octagonal villa is unquestionably stunningly proportioned, and seems almost an extension of Jefferson the private man. He entertained no one but family and neighbors here, so he planned the villa to his own quirky tastes. The columned, classical portico, characteristically Jeffersonian, opens onto a narrow front hall that leads back to the home's heart—a soaring two-story dining room, which in Jefferson's day was over-arched with one of those skylights of which he was so fond. According to his granddaughter, who often accompanied him here, the house was furnished "in the simplest manner, but had a very tasty air; there was nothing common or second rate about any part of the establishment."

Unfortunately, the "tasty air" of Poplar Forest quickly changed after Jefferson's death. In 1845 a fire damaged the house, and the Hutter family, who then owned it, took it as an opportunity to "modernize." Those "innovations" stood in place for a century, giving Poplar Forest the look of just another brick farmhouse. The Watts family, who bought the house in the 1940s, tried to redress some of the architectural wrongs, but it really wasn't until the last decade that serious scholars began to plumb the depths of this Jeffersonian jewel.

Now owned by a private non-profit corporation founded by concerned Lynchburg businessmen, Poplar Forest has become a cause célèbre among Jeffersonian scholars and preservationists. The scholars are in the process of gutting the house and are letting the public in on the process. You can actually tour the gutted house and get a true sense of the thinking of Jefferson the architect. What's more, you will not be asked to admire even one Chippendale chair or crystal chandelier on the whole tour. Instead, be sure to study the two outdoor privies that flank the mansion. Like the house, they are octagonal—just another example of Mad Tom's mind at work.

■ APPOMATTOX COURT HOUSE

Appomattox Court House is the East's most compelling ghost town. Its cluster of brick and log buildings appears unexpectedly in the middle of pastureland, along the old dirt stage road that once ran between Richmond and Lynchburg. Plenty of living and breathing people come here every day, either out of curiosity or respect, but it is the dead, not the living, that populate this place.

To most Americans the name Appomattox symbolizes the end of a gruesome, fratricidal war, an end in which all the players acted with dignity and humanity. The events that culminated here had been years, even centuries, in the making. One could say that as far back as the 1600s, the North and the South had begun to develop separate cultures, separate expectations—that the Mason-Dixon line was a kind of political fault line waiting to quake and pull apart. Appomattox was the place where the knitting back together of the fault began.

In the spring of 1865, Lee's Army of Northern Virginia was a bedraggled, starving mass of men who somehow had managed to endure 10 months under siege in Petersburg. By early April, they could endure no more, and Petersburg finally gave way. Without Petersburg as a buffer, Richmond itself could not hold, and soon the Confederate capital was a chaos of fleeing bodies, fire, rioting, and looting. Meanwhile, Lee, desperate for fresh supplies, marched his army southwest toward Amelia Court House, expecting to find rations waiting there. Through some bureaucratic mix-up, there were none. Out of food and out of will, the Confederates had to spend a precious day foraging for rations while Grant drew the net ever tighter.

The Union army was quickly closing in on the South. Yet one of the North's army heroes, Joshua Chamberlin, recalled that "We could not help admiring the courage and pluck of these poor fellows, now so broken and hopeless." On April 6, at Sailor's Creek, the Federal advance forces overtook the Confederate rear and left them in such disarray that Lee, watching in disbelief, lamented, "My God, has the army been dissolved?"

Time raced against the war-ravaged Rebel army as it staggered toward the railroad junction called Appomattox Station and the hope of new supplies. By nightfall of April 8, it was clear that that hope, too, was futile. As Lee camped with his advisers in the forest outside Appomattox Court House, they could see the fires of the Union army twinkling a dozen miles (19 km) in the distance around Appomattox Station. Grant sent a dispatch to Lee broaching surrender, and Lee replied simply, asking Grant's terms. There was only one: That Lee's men would be "disqualified for taking up arms against the Government of the United States . . . ."

Reenactment of a Civil War battle takes place at the Petersburg National Battlefield.

IDEALIST OR TRAITOR?

Elizabeth Van Lew, born to a prosperous Richmond family, was sent north to Philadelphia to school, where she became convinced that slavery was evil and that she had no other recourse than to vigorously oppose it. On returning to Richmond, she arranged to have several of her slaves sent north for schooling. One of these slaves she later placed as a servant in the home of Jefferson Davis, president of the Confederacy. This servant passed important information about the movements of Confederate troops to Elizabeth Van Lew, who in turn sent it north to an "uncle" who passed it on to Gen. Ulysses S. Grant. When Union troops marched into Richmond, Elizabeth Van Lew raised the Union flag above her house and opened it to wounded Union soldiers.

Reviled by her neighbors, whose own sons and husbands had died at the hands of the Union, she became increasingly embittered. Nevertheless, she served as Postmaster of Richmond from 1869 to 1877 under the Grant administration, and she acted as Third Assistant Postmaster General of the United States from 1883 to 1887. It's interesting to note that one of Elizabeth Van Lew's slaves—her cook— was the mother of Richmond banker Maggie Walker. In the later twentieth century, when the Van Lew home was condemned to make way for a highrise, no one stepped in to suggest it be saved as a landmark.

—Kit Duane

(Virginia State Library and Archives)

Late on the night of April 8, Lee wrote again, asking that the two generals meet the following day to discuss terms for the "restoration of peace." Though Lee never used the word surrender, he dressed for it as dawn broke. There in the woods, as a heavy spring fog clung to the trees, he put on a new uniform with an embroidered red sash and attached golden spurs to his well-polished boots. One wonders whether he had saved this finery for the moment of victory or defeat.

The South made one more futile attempt to break out of the Northern stronghold, but that quickly failed. Lee recognized the end, as did his officers. Many of them urged him to disperse the army, letting them make their own way home, rather than surrender. Lee was set against that, believing that the starving, disaffected men would wreak havoc through the Southern countryside. He would ride to meet Grant, Lee declared, though he knew history would judge him harshly. "They will not understand how we were overwhelmed by numbers," he admitted to a dissenting officer. "But that is not the question, Colonel: The question is, is it right to surrender this army. If it is right, then I will take all the responsibility."

He sent his aide, Col. Charles Marshall, into Appomattox Court House to make arrangements for the meeting. It was Palm Sunday, and the village was shut up tight. The first resident he encountered was Wilmer McLean. McLean took him to a locked-up home in such disarray that Marshall found it unsuitable for the surrender. McLean then offered his own home. Lee, accompanied by a fellow officer, rode forward to wait for Grant in the McLean parlor.

Grant, meanwhile, made his way to the village. General Sheridan (who had marched on the Shenandoah) and General Ord were anxiously awaiting him, to warn him that the whole surrender scheme was a ploy on the part of the Confederates so that they could slip away. Grant waved them off and rode on to meet Lee.

Dusty, disheveled, wearing a slouch hat, and with his soldier's shirt unbuttoned, Grant arrived in the McLean parlor and greeted Lee. The two men chose a common ground to oil their meeting; they discussed the Mexican War and army life. Then Lee brought the pleasantries up short, asking Grant to name the terms of surrender and then to write them out. Grant sat quietly at a small desk and wrote. The short paragraph he handed Lee required Confederate "arms, artillery, and public property to be parked, stacked and turned over . . . ." When that was done, the Southern men could go home.

Lee recognized how generous the terms were, but he raised one more issue: Could the men take their horses with them, to help them replant and replenish their land? Grant agreed. Before they parted, Grant also offered to send through rations to Lee's starving army.

Lee, astride the gray bulk of Traveller, rode through the ranks of men who had gathered to salute him. "Men," he said, "we have fought the war together, and I have done the best I could for you . . . . Goodbye."

Later, Grant recalled that he "felt like anything rather than rejoicing at the downfall of a foe who had fought so long and valiantly." When his troops tried to set off cannons to celebrate, Grant halted them, saying, "The Rebels are our countrymen again," and the Union troops therefore should "abstain from all demonstrations in the field."

On April 12, the Confederate army marched forward to lay down its arms in a formal ceremony of surrender. Maine's Joshua Chamberlin, who presided over the event, remembered the Southern men as "thin, worn, and famished, but standing erect, and with eyes looking level into ours . . . . was not such manhood to be welcomed back into a Union so tested and assured." Chamberlin ordered his army to salute the vanquished, and the South returned the salute. As the last arms were stacked, the Union army once again saluted the South, this time with a spontaneous three cheers that rose from within the ranks.

Interior of the Hanover County Courthouse, north of Richmond in the town of Ashland, reflects early American values of simplicity and dignity.

Appomattox was the finest moment in the nation's long, arduous road to recovery and healing. It was no more than a moment. Almost immediately, assassination, factional politics, and greed intervened to make Reconstruction a nightmare. As to the small court house village itself, it lapsed back into rural quietude. In 1892, the brick court house burned down, and the county seat was moved to Appomattox Station. Still the commercial hub of the area, it's now cluttered with small malls and fast food franchises. Which is good, because historic Appomattox has been saved from all this.

In 1935, Congress passed a bill turning the virtually deserted village into the **Appomattox Court House National Monument.** Since then, the park service has been busy restoring the site's 13 original buildings and reconstructing such historic edifices as the old court house itself and the McLean home. To get there from Lynchburg take U.S. 460 20 miles (32 km) east to Route 24.

A substantial though simple two-story brick house fronted by a verandah, the McLean home is full of ironies. Its owner was dogged by a war he tried his best to avoid. At the beginning of the conflict, Wilmer McLean and his family were living in Manassas. Twice battles raged around their home, and so in 1863, Wilmer moved his family here, to this quiet village out of harm's way. He purchased a house that had originally been built as a tavern in 1848, and he continued his talent for trade, speculating in sugar during the war. But the war hunted him down and brought its two commanders into his very parlor.

As soon as the surrender meeting ended, the McLean house itself was virtually attacked, as souvenir-hunting Union soldiers descended on its parlor, carrying off, among other things, the two chairs the generals had sat in. Four years later the McLeans moved to Alexandria. In 1893, their old home was dismantled brick by brick by a speculator who hoped to reconstruct it for display at the Columbia Exposition in Chicago. When the necessary funds for this project weren't found, the bricks were left in a heap in Appomattox, easy prey for relic-hunters. Thanks to careful drawings done at the time, though, the park service has precisely reconstructed the house and the historic parlor.

The entire National Monument site rambles over almost 1,700 acres, but the core is focused around the village. At the old **Clover Hill Tavern,** you can see the rooms where the Confederate paroles were hastily printed, and the Southern men were, at last, granted official leave to go home.

CIVIL WAR IN THE VIRGINIA PSYCHE

To a seasoned Virginian—black, white, male, female, liberal, conservative, old, but maybe not too young—the Civil War still somehow rages in the psyche. For some, the war has become a lifelong entertainment, something that adds color and romance to an overly sterilized, homogenized world. For others, it is the cause célèbre, Virginia's finest hour, in spite of defeat. For the author of this book, a self-professed liberal in her 40s, that war never seems to have resolution. Like a picture out of focus, I can never quite adjust it into a sharp black-and-white, or even a blue-and-gray, image.

Against all my intellectual leanings, I find myself always rooting for the South. Surely not because I believe in any of its causes—not states' rights and obviously not slavery of human beings. Had the South won, humankind at large would have lost. And yet . . . and yet who can deny the remarkable valor with which the Confederacy fought. Or that its heroes—Lee, Jackson, Longstreet, Mosby—did it with such élan, even to the end. They went into the war with nothing they needed to wage it, not even a true cause, and they came out of it with less than nothing. It was, as Walt Whitman said, "a strange sad war," and it left behind more American dead than both World Wars together. It also left behind monumental heroes, men who would otherwise have lived all their lives as farmers, college professors, doctors.

Had I grown up in New England, I'm sure my heroes would have been different, and I could have rested easy, knowing that *our* side had fought the good fight and won. But I grew up in Virginia, where the smoke of defeat still lingers in the air, and the ghost heroes still ride through the dusk, reminding you not to forget, never to forget, that they were brave and gallant men, and that in an ironic way, they are the true survivors of that "strange sad war."

—K. M. Kostyal

A movie theater in Richmond celebrates Lincoln's birthday with a display of the Stars and Bars; circa 1950. (The Chrysler Museum)

NORTHERN VIRGINIA

IT'S NOT UNCOMMON TO HEAR OLD-LINE VIRGINIANS point a finger north and proclaim that they "should never have let those Yanks come across the Potomac into Virginia territory." They're not referring to troop movements so much as to urban encroachments. In truth, northern Virginia shares more, by way of attitude, politics, and lifestyle, with its neighbor, Washington, D.C., than it does with the rest of the state. For one thing, it tends to be one of the few jurisdictions in the state that consistently votes Democratic in national elections. And of course, it also tends either to go boom or bust with the fickle fiscal policies of Congress. Money coming out of the national capital has always oiled the economy of northern Virginia, though in recent years the area has begun to attract non-government businesses, and its cities and counties now like to proclaim themselves more than merely "bedroom communities." Maybe. But they remain at least satellites, pulled by the gravity of their world-class neighbor across the river.

Still, northern Virginia *does* belong to the past—and present—of the Old Dominion. All you have to do is cross the District line from Washington into, say, Old Town, Alexandria, and you can sense the pace slowing down and the vowels drawling out just a shade. As in the rest of the state, history curls around the area as surely as the wide Potomac curves around its edges. In some ways, it's the best of Virginia: Its roots are as long and deep as any place in the state; it's got all the cultural offerings of an urban center; and it's become a robust and dynamic melting pot where Asian, African, and Middle Eastern immigrants add a tantalizing new spice to the old Virginia mix.

■ OLD TOWN ALEXANDRIA

Tree-lined, brick-paved, and charming, Old Town looks much as it did 200 years ago, when this was a rowdy little tobacco port on the middle Potomac. Now more genteel than rowdy, Old Town is a mix of carefully tended eighteenth- and nineteenth-century homes radiating out from a vibrant café-style commercial district, with galleries, craft shops, and veritable bouquets of boutiques. Old Town also boasts some truly monumental ghosts—among them George (Washington)

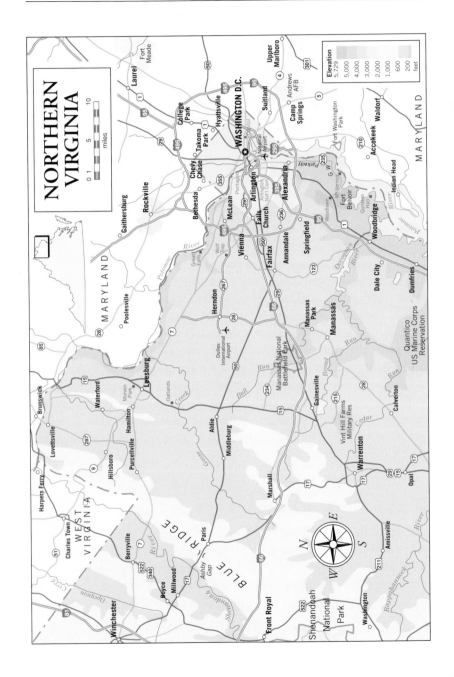

and Uncle Robert (E. Lee). Both heroes "slept here," as it were, and left their ineluctable marks on the little town. To get there, take the George Washington Parkway, which becomes Washington Street.

You have to admire Old Town's equanimity. The place has had its ups and downs over the course of two and a half centuries, but its basic character has remained remarkably solid. It traces its beginnings back to a scattering of tobacco warehouses on the Potomac in the 1730s. This "last and best Virginia anchorage for ocean vessels before the Potomac Falls" served the planters whose tobacco farms dotted the countryside. For some reason, the new spot on the northern frontier also attracted a number of Scottish merchants, whose bonny brawn can still be whiffed in the town's character.

In 1749 the state honored a petition jointly submitted by the planters and merchants to found a town on a 60-acre plot along the river. Since the land was then owned by the Alexander family, the town, naturally enough, was to be called Alexandria. In the best eighteenth-century style, the site was laid out in a precise grid pattern, and, on what was probably a hot July day in 1749, a public auction was held to sell the half-acre lots. The savvy town planners wanted residents, merchants, real people in Alexandria—people who had the desire to turn a gridded riverfront into a town, and so they limited land speculators from buying up large parcels. The planners got what they wanted. Old Town grew up quickly, its waterfront lined with shipyards and tobacco wharves and taverns, and its streets fronted by modest brick and clapboard homes, as well as by the imposing Georgian townhouses belonging to such Virginia "royalty" as the Fairfax family.

A quarter century later, the Revolution struck, and native son George Washington, who had a small townhouse in Alexandria and a large plantation home just downriver, became a national figure. The town itself managed to stay out of the direct line of fire. Only once did the British sail up the Potomac, fire a few shots at the seaport, and then leave.

The aftermath of war, however, and the making of America struck the town with full force. In 1789, Virginia hospitably ceded the town of Alexandria to the nation, to be part of the new diamond-shaped federal capital on the banks of the Potomac. With Washington not much more than farmland and marsh, Alexandria became almost overnight a boomtown catering to the politicians and pundits who quickly congregated around the federal district. There was a problem for the burgeoning seaport, though. Congress passed an amendment prohibiting the building of any government structures on the Virginia side of the Potomac. Historians believe that Washington, ever mindful of his integrity, was behind the amendment: He owned land in Alexandria and didn't want to appear to be capitalizing, as it were, on the situation.

Slowly, as Washington became a true city and other seaports captured more and more of Alexandria's trade, the town's promising boom went bust. By 1846, it was ready to return to Virginia, and Congress graciously retroceded the struggling little burg back to the state. And there, happily, it has remained ever since.

■ EXPLORING OLD TOWN

Walking is the best way to see Old Town. You can poke around the commercial shops, then detour off into residential streets where the architecture is intriguingly varied. The Alexandria citizenry, by the way, take inordinate pride in their small but perfectly tended gardens and in the posted plaques that officially declare their residences of historic merit.

King Street, as the name suggests, acts as the city's main commercial row, stretching west in a mile-long string of shops that lead from the low-lying Potomac shoreline all the way uphill to the town's towering Masonic Memorial. The foot of King is home to the trendiest shops and restaurants, as well as the city's famous **Torpedo Factory.** Though the building now sports a brightly painted exterior and cheery banners, it really *was* built as a torpedo-casings factory in 1918. In the 1970s clever urban renovators eyed the cavernous, unused space and realized they could turn it into shops and studios for artists and craftsmen. It now houses about 150 artists.

Two blocks up King, the twentieth century fades and the past comes into focus at the **Ramsay House visitors center** at 221 King Street. The north end of this colonial clapboard cottage lays claim to being the oldest structure in Old Town, though it was built elsewhere and moved here soon after the town was established. Another early building, the **Stabler-Leadbeater Apothecary,** one block south on Fairfax has been returned to its late eighteenth-century appearance, and now gleams with glass bottles and other paraphernalia it housed when it served as a major dispenser of pharmaceuticals.

If you keep walking down Fairfax and turn left onto Prince Street, you'll find yourself in **Gentry Row,** where stately eighteenth-century Georgian homes bristle with refinement. (Two of George Washington's physicians lived at nos. 209 and 211.)

If this block is a bit formal for your taste, wander down to the next one, locally known as **Captains' Row**. Here, there's a decided seaport feel to the way the small but winsome old cottages press against a street still lined with cobblestones. The cobblestones, by the way, probably came from across the Atlantic, serving as ballast in the holds of ships.

The sternly simple **Old Presbyterian Meeting House** at 321 South Fairfax has roots that go back to 1772, when Alexandria's burgeoning Scottish population founded it. The church's hour of glory came in the winter of 1799, at George Washington's death. A winter storm raged, so with "the walking being bad to the Episcopal Church," where Washington normally worshipped, the former President's funeral service was held here. For four days, the bell in the church tower pealed out its mourning. In 1835 the old church was struck by lightning and virtually destroyed, but its solid congregation quickly rebuilt it. Today, its unpretentious clapboard uprightness continues to attract a devout following. The plain but compelling interior is open weekdays, and services are held every Sunday.

The meetinghouse graveyard holds the stones of several prominent colonial Scotsmen, including the church's builder and local entrepreneur, John Carlyle. Beyond the graveyard stands the old manse, notable for both its age—it was built in 1787—and its peculiarly vernacular Alexandria-style architecture. This sort of "half house" is called a flounder because of its flat, windowless high side. About a score of these early nineteenth-century flounder houses are scattered through Old Town.

The best place to get a taste of what socializing was like in early Alexandria is **Gadsby's Tavern**, at 134 N. Royal Street. In the early days of Washington politics—before there was really much of a Washington, for that matter—this public house was popular with the movers and shakers of government, including Washington, Adams, and Jefferson. Its rooms re-create that early period, and you can get a sense here of what it was like to play a gentlemen's game of whist of an evening or attend a minuet gala in the large upstairs ballroom. On the third floor, things are decidedly less lustrous. Here, overnight guests who wanted simple lodgings got them—as long as they were willing to share one of the small beds with a stranger or two.

The imposing Georgian facade of the **Carlyle House**, at 121 N. Fairfax Street, proves what a hard-working immigrant can attain. One of those early Scots merchants, John Carlyle came to Alexandria as a tobacco agent for an English concern, but he soon established his own business. Obviously no fool, he made a good marriage—to Sarah Fairfax, the daughter of one of Virginia's most respected families. By 1753, he was able to build himself the showiest house in town. The freestanding stone mansion clearly attracted attention, because in 1755 Gen. Edward Braddock held the now famous Governor's Council here, at which he exhorted five colonial governors to back the British in their fight against the French and Indians.

Today, Carlyle House is restored to its colonial look, and boasts a particularly lovely garden. The commodious but rather unpretentious interior of the mansion brings home the fact that in the mid-eighteenth century even the wealthy of Alexandria were still living on the edge of the frontier.

The Lyceum betokened the coming of "culture" to Alexandria. Built in the late 1830s as a lecture hall-cum-museum-cum-library, the columned Greek Revival building once thundered with the oratory of such speechifiers as Daniel Webster. It continues to serve as a museum, with well-executed exhibits on state and local history. The Lyceum is located at 201 S. Washington Street.

Tobacco has played a large part in the fortunes of Virginians past and present. Here a farmer waits to sell his tobacco at auction in 1940. (The Chrysler Museum)

Shell racing on the Potomac River near Alexandria.

The serene, walled grounds of historic **Christ Church** (1773) offer a welcome break from the hustle of Washington Street. Located on the corner of N. Washington and Cameron streets, the beautifully proportioned little church, with its pepper-pot steeple and hourglass pulpit, is modeled after eighteenth-century English country churches. Washington worshiped here (and Lee was confirmed here), and every year, on the Sunday closest to Washington's birthday, the current President comes across the Potomac to sit in the First President's original pew and attend a service.

Alexandria also celebrates Washington's birthday with a big parade, but Old Town's most festive moment unquestionably comes during its annual **Scottish Christmas Walk.** Held the first Saturday in December and very Scottish in character, the day starts with a merry fife-and-drum and bagpipe parade. After the parade is over, the musicians wander the streets, serenading as they go. The shops and restaurants get into the Christmas spirit, as do the historic sites, and, with no cars allowed on many streets, the little town truly does take on the feel of colonial merrymaking.

■ ALEXANDRIA'S LEE CONNECTION

As history, in its intricately flowing design, would have it, a few years after Virginia's first great hero, Washington, died, the state's second great hero was born. Robert E. Lee was himself the son of a Revolutionary hero, "Lighthorse" Harry Lee, but by the time Robert was born, his father was an older man with a tarnished reputation. He was also on the verge of bankruptcy. In 1811 he moved his family from the Northern Neck of Virginia to an Alexandria townhouse at 611 Cameron Street. A year later, he moved them again, to a nearby house owned by his wife's relatives. And there, if the blunt truth be told, he left them.

Ostensibly on a trip to recover his health, Harry sailed for Barbados and died away from home. At six, Robert became the man of the house, and the chief care giver for his arthritic mother. **Robert E. Lee's boyhood home,** a gracious old Federal townhouse, still stands at 607 Oronoco Street and its rooms are open for public tours, as long as no special event is going on at the house. Its lovely walled garden has inspired a local tale that, even if apocryphal, is worth the telling. The story goes that some time after the Civil War, the owner of the house was sitting in

his garden, when a distinguished, white-bearded head peered over the garden wall. It was Lee. "I just wanted to see if my mother's snowball bush was in bloom," the old general explained.

Lee's relatives owned so many homes in this vicinity that the corner of Oronoco and Washington streets was called "Lee Corners." Part of this legacy, the **Lee-Fendall House** (614 Oronoco Street), is open for tours and decorated in fine early nineteenth-century antiques. Ironically, it was also the home of labor czar John L. Lewis from 1937 to 1969.

Robert E. Lee shortly after his surrender to Grant in 1865. (Library of Congress)

■ MOUNT VERNON

If you follow the shaded and scenic George Washington Memorial Parkway south along the Potomac from Old Town, in about eight miles (13 km) it will deposit you at the gates to one of America's favorite shrines, George Washington's Mount Vernon. Close to a million people a year make a pilgrimage to this pleasant knoll above the river, not because the columned and cupolaed red-roof farmhouse itself ranks as an exceptional architectural landmark, but because it was the beloved home of the beloved "father of our country."

After two hundred and fifty years Washington has become more monumental than mortal. Whoever and whatever he was as a person seems to have become inconsequential in the face of that marbleized and immortal national hero. Coming here to his home does seem to rehumanize him, transform him back into what he was at heart—a practical, hard-working planter who considered farming "the most delectable occupation."

Washington was not technically to this manor born. He spent a few young years here after his family had established the fledgling farm, but most of his childhood occurred on another small farm east of Fredericksburg. When George was 11, his father died. Exposed to little formal education, the boy could have grown up to be another unsophisticated colonial frontiersman had not his elder half-brother, Lawrence, intervened.

Mount Vernon was actually Lawrence's plantation, deeded to him through his father, and young George spent increasing amounts of time there. It was through Lawrence, who had married into the planter aristocracy, that George was introduced to Virginia society. Upon Lawrence's death, the 20-year-old George leased the farm from his sister-in-law, then proceeded to distinguish himself in the French and Indian War. Returning victorious, the young man conquered the heart of an extremely wealthy young Tidewater widow, Martha Dandridge Custis, already the mother of two young children. About that marriage historians have often disagreed. It seems certain that young George had suffered a serious infatuation for Sally Fairfax, the wife of his good friend, George Fairfax. That love was obviously doomed, even though romantic letters from Washington to Sally were uncovered after her death in England. Whatever his deeper longings, George apparently treated Martha, a woman several years his senior, with affectionate respect. Though the couple never had children of their own, Washington raised his step-children and his step-grandchildren as though they were his own. Contrary to his reputation as a womanizer, he seems to have been a dedicated family man. At the end of his life he was often able to escape back here to the role that seemed to please him above all others, being the squire of Mount Vernon.

Just as in Washington's day, Mount Vernon is hardly a quiet place. A steady flood of visitors stream through its rooms, admiring the ornate wall paneling and marble mantels and furnishings and walking out on the mansion's trademark piazza overlooking the river. Probably the most moving place is the master bedchamber, where the great man finally succumbed in 1799. After a miserable winter day overseeing outdoor work, Washington came down with a serious throat inflammation called quinsy. His doctors bled him with leeches and tried other remedies, but the 67-year-old hero could not recover. "I die hard," he whispered, "but I am not afraid to go."

George and Martha now lie side by side in marble sarcophagi out in the family burial grounds above the river. Washington would likely be pleased with the shape his estate is in. The parterred gardens are well-tended, and the score of small dependencies—a laundry room, smokehouse, greenhouse, and the like—are freshly

An aerial view of George Washington's home, Mount Vernon, where he lived with his wife and two step-children.

painted and in good working order. And on the bowling green fronting the house some of the tulip poplars that Washington planted himself wave luxuriantly in the breezes off the river.

Woodlawn represents a compelling coda to Mount Vernon. Only three miles (5 km) west off Route 235, this estate was a wedding gift from Washington to his step-granddaughter, Nelly. Considered an exceptionally accomplished young woman, Nelly had actually been raised at Mount Vernon and had met her husband, Lawrence Lewis, a nephew of Washington, there.

Both Lawrence and Nelly appear to have shared a fine aesthetic sense and a love of good living. Their Georgian brick home was designed by a prominent Washington architect, Dr. William Thornton, and is still decorated with many of their own tasteful furnishings. Apparently, though, the couple lived their lives shadowed by their great ancestor. They tried, perhaps too hard, to keep up Washington's high standards, but they lacked his business sense and were perpetually in debt.

The estate grounds, overlooking the Potomac, are renowned for their boxwood hedges and rose garden. The National Trust for Historic Preservation now owns the property, which explains why you can find an unexpected architectural jewel nestled in the woods behind Woodlawn. The unpretentious yet remarkable **Pope-Leighey House** was architect Frank Lloyd Wright's answer to affordable but well-designed housing for the middle class. He called this his Usonian style, and the simple, L-shaped house reflects the way Wright blended functionalism and aesthetics. He built it in 1941 for a northern Virginia journalist named Loren Pope. But Pope's four-person family found the house a bit too precious to live in, and so sold it to the Leigheys. In 1964, they donated it to the National Trust, which had it moved here from its original site in nearby Falls Church.

■ GUNSTON HALL

Another eighteenth-century manor house in this area, Gunston Hall was home to Washington's friend and compatriot, George Mason. A brilliant thinker and statesman, Mason tends now to be overlooked when Virginia's greats are listed. That's unfortunate, because he deserves to be admired as one of the "pens" of the Revolution. Anyone will recognize his language in the Virginia Declaration of Rights, written in May 1776: "That all men are by nature created free and independent and have certain inherent rights . . . the enjoyment of life and liberty . . .

and pursuing and obtaining happiness." Two months later, similar sentiments found their way into the Declaration of Independence, written by Mason's younger friend and admirer, Thomas Jefferson.

Perhaps Mason's relative obscurity is a holdover from his own lifetime. A private man who abhorred the fray of politics, Mason used his influence quietly through his writings and in behind-the-scenes conversations with friends. He refused to take a more active public role in part because of his devotion to his nine children who had been left motherless when his wife died at a fairly young age. And so Mason let his authority radiate out from Gunston Hall, his dignified brick manor house. Mason must have taken great pride in the home, because to this day it is quite a showplace. Its elaborate wood paneling is the work of an indentured servant who arrived in the colonies in 1755 and apparently attempted to prove his talent by lining Mason's walls with exquisite woodwork. One wonders if Mason had a gardener with similar ambitions, because the grounds are impressive, particularly their centuries-old boxwood allée and their Magnolia Avenue, a double line of cedars and magnolias flanking the carriage entrance to the house. Gunston Hall is located 15 miles (24 km) south of Alexandria off I-95. Take Exit 55 and look for signs.

■ ARLINGTON

Though Arlington and Alexandria are close neighbors, they have very different characters and very different pasts. They do have in common the fact that they were both part of the original national capital tract. In fact, what is now Arlington was part of the County of Alexandria from 1846, when the whole parcel was retroceded to Virginia, until 1870. At that time the Virginia General Assembly passed a rather unique law that confuses all non-Virginians. It decreed that any city with a population of 5,000 or above would constitute a separate jurisdiction, completely independent of a county affiliation. And so Alexandria parted company with its rural northwestern half. It eventually became Arlington County, named in honor of its most obvious landmark, Arlington House, Robert E. Lee's home.

Throughout most of the nineteenth century, Arlington remained a rural, farming community, but with the coming of World War I, its old farming fields became fertile ground for war offices and "bedroom commuters." The county's population growth through the twentieth century has been quickly and steadily upward. Yet Arlington still has a friendly, unpretentious feel to it. Fine old neighborhoods grace the northern side of the county, while high-rise condominiums are scattered across its eastern half. In recent decades south Arlington has become a favored relocation spot for Hispanic and Asian immigrants, and consequently, the county now has a fine offering of ethnic restaurants.

The city has recently decided to bill itself as "the Virginia Side of the Nation's Capital," and its riverfront, threaded by the George Washington Memorial Parkway, does boast two national landmarks—the Pentagon and Arlington Cemetery.

Formidable five-sided fortress of the military establishment, the **Pentagon** sprawls beside the river like an enormous beached starfish. Except for its location, there is nothing charming about this gargantuan, low-slung structure, but its statistics are intriguing. The largest single-structure office building in the world, it covers 6.5 million square feet, each of its five sides is larger than the U.S. Capitol, and it was completed in just 16 months in 1941.

Guided tours of its interior are given weekdays by spit-and-polish enlisted men and women, but make sure you bring a photo ID or you'll be summarily rejected. The tours pass offices and display areas in this labyrinthine maze, whose design is formed by five concentric circles radiating out from a central courtyard. Though your straight-faced tour guide will never admit it, to the some 20,000 employees working here, that courtyard is gruesomely known as "ground zero." To get there take the Pentagon exit off of I-395, southwest of Washington, D.C. For information about tours call (703) 695-1776.

Arlington National Cemetery stands within sight of the Pentagon, directly in front of Memorial Bridge, a reminder, one hopes, of the human cost of war. For all the tragedies it recalls, the 612-acre cemetery, with its row after row of plain white headstones lined up and down grassy slopes, is an affective, even beautiful place. More than 200,000 military personnel and their dependents are buried here, as are Robert Kennedy and John Fitzgerald Kennedy, whose simple grave is watched over by an eternal flame. Smart-stepping soldiers guard the cemetery's Tomb of the Unknown Soldier, which inters the remains of four unidentified soldiers—one from each of the world wars, one from Korea and one from Vietnam. The more recently erected Challenger Space Shuttle Memorial honors the memory of that lost crew.

Now solemn and honorable, Arlington National Cemetery actually got its start through an act of vengeance. Early in the Civil War, the Union took control of Lee's Arlington estate, and the Quartermaster General, Montgomery Meigs decided that it would make a perfect burial ground for Union troops. He planted the first

ALL QUIET ALONG THE POTOMAC TO-NIGHT

First printed in Harper's Weekly *in November 1861, this poem was reprinted a year later in a Southern newspaper, which claimed it was found on the body of a dead soldier. Later transformed into a Confederate song by John Hill Hewitt, and credited by Southerners to various Southern poets, "All Quiet" was actually written by Ethel Lynn Beers, a New York poet. Two stanzas of the poem follow here.*

All quiet along the Potomac to-night,
 Where the soldiers lie peacefully dreaming,
Their tents in the rays of the clear autumn moon,
 And the light of their watch-fires are gleaming.
A tremulous sigh, as the gentle night wind
 Through the forest leaves softly is creeping,
While the stars up above, with their glittering eyes,
 Keep guard, for the army is sleeping.

There's only the sound of the lone sentry's tread,
 As he tramps from the rock to the fountain,
And thinks of the two on the low trundle bed,
 Far away in the cot on the mountain.
His musket falls slack—his face, dark and grim,
 Grows gentle with memories tender,
As he mutters a prayer for the children asleep,
 And their mother—"may Heaven defend her."

—Ethel Lynn Beers, 1861

graves virtually in Lee's yard, to make certain that the Southern rebel would never feel comfortable inhabiting his home again.

Lee never did return here, but **Arlington House** still stands in the middle of the cemetery, atop a bluff overlooking Washington. Though this was really his wife's estate, Lee loved it, declaring that at Arlington House, his "affections and attachments are more strongly placed than at any other place in the world." Sadly, he spent precious little time here. After his marriage to Mary Custis, the great-granddaughter of George Washington, the couple spent 30 years at the different posts to which the aspiring young army engineer was sent. But they thought of Arlington House as their true home and managed to spend some winters in the imposing Greek Revival mansion that Mary's father had built.

And it was to Arlington House that they repaired in April 1861, when war had become a certainty. Lee was still a U.S. officer at that time, eminently respected for his skills. On April 20, Lee was called across the river to a meeting at Blair House and offered the command of Union forces. He returned to Arlington House torn and tormented. A fervent patriot, he nonetheless couldn't bring himself to fight against his home state. And so with regret he resigned his commission. Two days

Arlington National Cemetery, where the nation buries those who died serving their country in war.

HOME ALONE IN WARTIME

Alexandria, May 4, 1861.—I am too nervous, too wretched to-day to write in my diary, but that the employment will while away a few moments of this trying time. Our friends and neighbors have left us. Every thing is broken up. The Theological Seminary is closed; the High School dismissed. Scarcely any one is left of the many families which surrounded us. The homes all look desolate; and yet this beautiful country is looking more peaceful, more lovely than ever, as if to rebuke the tumult of passion and the fanaticism of man. We are left lonely indeed; our children are all gone—the girls to Clarke, where they may be safer, and farther from the exciting scenes which may too soon surround us; and the boys, the dear, dear boys, to the camp, to be drilled and prepared to meet any emergency. Can it be that our country is to be carried on and on to the horrors of civil war? . . .

I shut my eyes and hold my breath when the thought of what may come upon us obtrudes itself; and yet I cannot believe it. It will, I know the breach will be healed without the effusion of blood. The taking of Sumter without bloodshed has somewhat soothed my fears, though I am told by those who are wiser than I, that men must fall on both sides by the score, by the hundred, and even by the thousand. But it is not my habit to look on the dark side, so I try to employ myself, and hope for the best. To-day our house seems so deserted, that I feel more sad than usual, for on this morning we took leave of our whole household. Mr. McGuire and myself are now the sole occupants of the house, which usually teems with life.

I go from room to room, looking at first one thing and then another, so full of sad associations. The closed piano, the locked bookcase, the nicely-arranged tables, the formally-placed chairs, ottomans and sofas in the parlor! Oh for some one to put them out of order! and then the dinner-table, which has always been so well surrounded, so social, so cheerful, looked so cheerless to-day, as we seated ourselves one at the head, the other at the foot, with one friend,—but one,— at the side. I could scarcely restrain my tears, and but for the presence of that one friend, I believe I should have cried outright. After dinner, I did not mean to do it, but I could not help going into the girls' room . . . . I heard my own footsteps so plainly, that I was startled by the absence of all other sounds. There the furniture looked so quiet, the beds so fixed and smooth, the wardrobes and bureaux so tightly locked, and the whole so lifeless! But the writing-desks, work-boxes, and the numberless things so familiar to my eyes! Where were they? I paused, to ask myself what it all meant. Why did we think it necessary to send off all that was so dear to us from our own home? I threw open the shutters, and the answer came at once, so mournfully! I heard distinctly the drums beating in Washington. The evening was so still that I seemed to hear nothing else. As I looked at the Capitol in the distance, I could scarcely believe my senses. That Capitol of which I had always been so proud! Can it be possible that it is no longer *our* Capitol? And are our countrymen, under its very eaves, making mighty preparations to drain our hearts' blood? And must this Union, which I was taught to revere, be rent asunder?

—Judith Brockenbrough McGuire, *Diary,* 1861

later, he was on his way to Richmond to become commander of the Virginia forces. It would be another year before the South would give him the kind of sweeping command that he had turned down from the North. One has to wonder how the course of war would have gone had Robert E. Lee commanded the Union army instead of the Army of the Confederacy.

Today, Arlington House holds Lee memorabilia and poignant traces of the man's private life—rooms with his children's toys in them, his portrait as a dashing young officer and one of his young wife. The mansion's wide portico with its Doric columns now overlooks the sweep of Washington and, just across the Potomac, the Lincoln Memorial. The view is not cruel coincidence. The Memorial Bridge between Arlington House and the memorial was intended as a symbolic link, bridging the gulf for all time between the two great leaders, and consequently, between North and South.

Arlington has one other unexpected inhabitant. Not only are Union soldiers buried in Lee's yard, but so is the capital's star-crossed designer—**Pierre L'Enfant.** This eighteenth-century Frenchman came to America to fight for the Revolutionary cause, then stayed on after the battle was won. George Washington, impressed with his skills, hired him to lay out the new federal city, and L'Enfant set about designing an urban center on a sweeping scale, full of monuments, parks, broad avenues, and circles.

It is largely owing to L'Enfant that the capital is the beautiful city we see today, though the Frenchman got little credit in his own lifetime. Obstreperous and arrogant, he offended the wrong people and was quickly removed from authority. His plans, however, remained. The Frenchman spent the rest of his life railing against his ill-treatment. Finally, in 1909, L'Enfant got his just deserts, when his body was moved here and topped with a marble plaque, incised with his city plan. He now enjoys a commanding view of his "City of Magnificent Distances."

Just north of Arlington Cemetery, on Marshall Drive, the marines are immortalized in bronze in the famous **Iwo Jima Memorial,** which shows four soldiers bravely planting the American flag. Rising near it is the 49-bell **Netherlands Carillon,** a gift from that country to the U.S. in recognition of our efforts in World War I. On Saturday afternoons and evenings in spring and summer, the carillon peals out a concert across the riverfront.

Down by the Potomac lies another memorial to a great man. **Theodore Roosevelt Island,** a surprisingly sylvan little spot linked by a footbridge to the Virginia side of the river, serves as a monument to that nature-loving "bully boy." It's laced with pleasant forest paths that lead to views of Washington's Kennedy Center and Georgetown. In its heart lies a large, fountained plaza where a statue of Roosevelt stands, hand upraised as though he were enthusiastically exhorting visitors to enjoy the forests, birds, and marshes of his little island.

The wide Potomac sweeps placidly by the island, but it takes on a very different character farther upstream at **Great Falls Park.** Hurtling along a boulder-strewn course, the river roars between high rock banks in a rare display of muscle for an East Coast watercourse. The drive to the park is, in itself, pleasant. Just follow the George Washington Memorial Parkway north along the river to Route 193 west. Then take 193 through a shopping district of suburban McLean and turn right on Old Dominion Drive (Route 123). Follow it past the pretentious, latter-day mansions of McLean, and it will lead directly to the park entrance.

■ VAST UNCHARTED SUBURBS

As in most American places, the riverfront in northern Virginia got developed before anything else. That left much of the rest of the area wide open to accommodate the invidious sprawl of late twentieth-century suburbia.

A Fourth of July fireworks display backlights the Iwo Jima Memorial while brightening the Washington Monument and the Capitol building in the background.

Shopping malls, strip malls, outlet malls, housing developments, condominiums, and a generally unmitigated miasma of clutter now pave the Virginia hills south and west of the Potomac. If you like to shop, you're in luck. Otherwise, the only serious attraction to consider here is **Wolf Trap Farm Park for the Performing Arts.** This complex of buildings lays claim to being "the only national park site dedicated solely to the performing arts." It got its start in 1966, when Catherine Filene Shouse offered to donate part of her farmland to the government and help fund a performance center. The park now encompasses three performance areas: the Theater-in-the-Woods, the Concert Shell, and the Filene Center, an open-air auditorium, where guests have an option of sitting in covered seats or out on the lawn. Its 65 x 70-foot (20 x 21-meter) stage is one of the largest in America and attracts world-class performers. To get there take Route 66 west to the Dulles Toll Road and look for the Wolf Trap Farm Park exit.

■ LOUDOUN COUNTY

A pastoral idyll of country estates, picturesque hamlets, and winding country lanes, Loudoun occupies the northeastern tip of the state (take Route 7 north or 50 west). Its rolling Blue Ridge foothills make it classic Virginia horse country, and the local population takes its equine amusement seriously. Here, they still anoint a master of the hunt and honor the "sport of queens," with a glamorous steeplechase season. Most steeplechase and point-to-point races are open to the public, and you can bring a picnic lunch and spend a fine afternoon watching Thoroughbreds leap over fences and lunge across green pastures. Or you can simply observe the way the horsey set socializes. Most of them set up "tailgate" parties, with fine food and drink filling, literally, their open tailgates.

Loudoun actually has several distinct faces. **Dulles Airport,** Danish architect Eero Saarinen's wonderwork, dominates the county's southeast corner and creates a kind of "break in the dam," letting urban sprawl seep through. Happily, though, it hasn't yet become a flood, and once you get beyond the Dulles "corridor," the new bedroom community developments become more scattered, giving way at last to fields that have been cultivated for centuries. They roll on and on, right up to the edge of the Blue Ridge.

The little city of **Leesburg** (at the intersection of routes 7 and 15), Loudoun's county seat, is a mix of the trendy and the traditional. Quaint eighteenth-century stone homes dot the historic core of town, and King Street, the main drag, offers several nouvelle colonial restaurants. The place still maintains a neighborly, distinctly Southern charm, and the turreted brick courthouse is guarded by an ever vigilant copper Confederate soldier.

A well-stocked **visitors center** occupies part of the old train-station-turned-mall, and here you can find information on the plethora of truly sybaritic bed and breakfasts around the county. Some are old estate cottages, others are right in historic homes, and almost all are uniquely charming. You can also pick up information on the fine restaurants that are scattered through the county's burgs and byways. Most important, you can get a map to the scenic byways themselves. Loudoun's narrow lanes bob and weave across some of the loveliest hill country in Virginia, past Thoroughbreds sunning themselves and sheep grazing in green pastures. It's a county made for easy-going, unplanned driving trips. Its rural simplicity appeals to all sorts of worldly characters. Like Russell Baker, for example. That famous chronicler of growing up in America and now host of *Masterpiece Theater*, apparently finds Leesburg compelling, because he has a home here. And Gen. George Marshall, war hero and author of the Marshall Plan, chose the peace of Leesburg to retire to after the fray of fighting and of then reconstructing Europe. His low-key but charming **Dodona Manor** lies on a shady side street. Recently renovated, it's open for public tours.

A more splendid edifice, **Morven Park**, the turn-of-the-century estate of Virginia's popular reform governor, Westmoreland Davis, rises on the northern outskirts of Leesburg, off Route 698. Its rolling hills and rich green grounds, now housing an equestrian center and horse museum, are still dominated by the boldly columned manor house.

The manor's rooms are filled with ornate tapestries and imported European bibelots in the high style. It looks like a movie set, waiting for a couple in riding pinks and British accents to enter the scene.

The county likes to boast of one other celebrity who settled here—Arthur Godfrey. He had an estate not far from the little burg of **Waterford**. Though Godfrey is gone, Waterford remains, like a lovely lingering shadow from the past. An almost unbelievably quaint collection of eighteenth-century stone cottages, the town originally grew up around an old grist mill that Amos Janney, a Quaker who had migrated down from Pennsylvania, built here about 1740. In 1755, Amos's son gridded the current townsite into lots, and Waterford soon became a strangely eclectic community. The Quaker reputation for tolerance attracted a number of

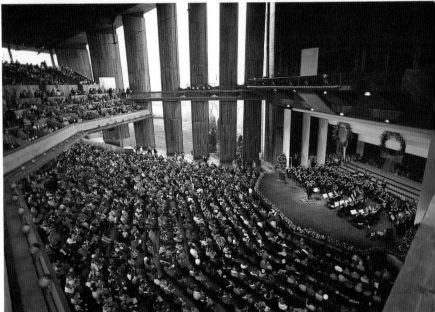

Dulles International Airport, 15 miles northwest of D.C. in Loudoun County, was considered innovative in design (Danish architect Eero Saarinen) when it was constructed between 1958–1962 (top). The Wolf Trap Farm Park for the Performing Arts lays claim to being the only national park site dedicated solely to the performing arts (bottom).

freed blacks and other Pennsylvanians with unorthodox religious views. These days Waterford still claims a rather unorthodox citizenry—those who want to preserve the grace and humanism of the eighteenth century from the cacophony and inhumanism of the twentieth.

The Quakers of Loudoun County are hardly a thing of the past. If you drive southwest from Waterford to Purcellville (on Route 7), then head due south on Route 722, you'll find yourself in the little crossroads of Lincoln, where the old stone **Goose Creek Meetinghouse** (1765) stands right across the street from the current brick meetinghouse (1817). Quaker living history, as it were, can be found in the adjacent general store, where Asa Moore Janney, a colorful and collateral descendant of Waterford's Amos Janney, sits at a desk in the rear. With a Quaker penchant for history, Janney serves as one of Loudoun's local historians.

From Lincoln, a fine webbing of Loudoun country lanes twist and bend south, through the toniest part of the county, and finally into the unofficial capital of Virginia hunt country—**Middleburg** (or take Route 50). Truly burgish, this small cluster of upscale shops with horsey themes serves an impressive clientele. Paul Mellon, for example, has a training farm not far away, and Mercedes seem to be the preferred vehicle on Middleburg streets. The town's imposing stone **Red Fox**

Loudoun County countryside—Blue Ridge foothills and Virginia horse country.

Tavern—located at 2 E. Washington Street, (703) 687-6301—has victualled travelers since 1728, making it the second oldest tavern in the U.S. The **Aldie Mill**, a few miles east of town on Route 50, has also withstood the test of time. Built in the early nineteenth century, the two-wheel grist mill still churns over the waters of Little River.

The rich and famous discovered the good life of Loudoun long before this century. President Monroe built his **Oak Hill** estate here in 1820, presumably consulting his friend Thomas Jefferson on its architecture. The Classical Revival manor house still stands along Route 15.

A few miles north of it, also on Route 15, a tree-lined country lane leads into **Oatlands,** a memorable example of a Federal-style Virginia country estate. Now owned by the National Trust for Historic Preservation, the stuccoed white home was built in the early 1800s by George Carter, a great-grandson of Virginia's major land baron, Robert "King" Carter. An enormous columned portico, elaborate plasterwork, and sweeping stairways leave no doubt that this is a house in the grand style. Surprisingly, George Carter was a bachelor at the time he built this monumental place. Perhaps the thought of rattling around in it to the end of his days became more than he could bear, because at the age of 59, he took a wife. Thirty-nine and widowed, Elizabeth was apparently, to put it gently, strong-willed. Her obituary described her as "a lady seldom, if ever, erring from her first judgment." In any case, the couple managed to produce four children. Their son, George, was left with the sad task of shepherding the large estate through the hard times of the Civil War and Reconstruction. In order to keep the property afloat, he and his wife began operating it as a country inn after the war, and such luminaries as Phoebe Apperson Hearst, California philanthropist and mother of William Randolph Hearst, were regulars here.

Today, Oatlands has regained its dignity, and its terraced gardens rank as some of the loveliest in Virginia, thanks to their landscaper, Alfredo Siani. Born and educated in Italy, Siani was directed by his father away from a career in horticulture and toward something more "practical and lucrative." After working for Alitalia in New York for 20 years, Siani finally chose love over pragmatism and enrolled himself in college-level horticultural courses. He was "discovered" by local gentry while working at a nursery in Middleburg. They recommended him to the National Trust, and Siani's talents finally have been put to proper use in restoring the Oatlands gardens to their intended English character—with just a hint of Italian on the side.

One other Loudoun note: **White's Ferry,** the only cable-guided ferry on the East Coast, plies the Potomac a few miles north of Leesburg, taking cars and passengers back and forth between the Virginia and Maryland shorelines. A ferry line has operated here since 1828.

■ THE GRAY GHOST

Loudoun's favorite ghost is its gray one, Confederate major John Singleton Mosby. A legend in his own time, Mosby and his Partisan Rangers patrolled Loudoun and its environs so well that the area became known as "Mosby's Confederacy." With Loudoun's proximity to the North, it was constantly crisscrossed by both armies

Maj. John Singleton Mosby, the "Gray Ghost" of Loudoun County. (Library of Congress)

and experienced terrible looting as a result. As one chronicler claimed, Loudoun "probably suffered more real hardships and deprivations than any other community of like size in the Southland." Though Mosby couldn't protect the population against this, he did manage to deal the North payment in kind. For several years, he and his small band of Rangers harassed and humiliated Union forces passing through their territory. Mosby's stated goal was "to destroy supply trains, to break up the means of conveying intelligence . . . and to diminish this aggressive power of the army of the Potomac, by compelling it to keep a large force on the defensive."

Fleet of foot and virtually invisible, the Gray Ghost and his men were constantly on the move and frequently scattered to keep their whereabouts unknown. But they could "gather at my call," Mosby claimed, "like Children of the Mist."

And, like Children of the Mist, after the war they evaporated. Though the North feared that independent raiders like Mosby's band would insist on fighting even after the surrender, Mosby responded to their fears in his characteristically cavalier style. "We are soldiers," he disdained, "not highwaymen."

Laying aside his trademark red-lined cape and ostrich plumed hat, Mosby went back to the practice of law—and on to serve his country. He eventually was appointed U.S. Consul to Hong Kong and an assistant attorney for the Justice Department.

■ MANASSAS NATIONAL BATTLEFIELD PARK

It's strange how remarkably peaceful old battlefields are. Somehow, the more lives lost on them, the quieter they become. Manassas seems almost hushed, as if embarrassed by the frivolous gaiety with which it began. After all, these smooth green hills and clustered forests, watered by a little creek called Bull Run, witnessed the first real battle of the Civil War. In fact, it was at this site that a naive populace became convinced that the war was real. So certain was Washington society that the battle here would provide them with simple, lighthearted entertainment, that they packed up picnics and drove out to watch it on a late July morning in 1861. They must have come to regret their choice of picnic spots, because when the smoke cleared, their men had suffered 2,700 casualties, and the South 2,000.

How did the two armies come to face off for the first time on this particular

(previous pages) At the Battle of Manassas, also known as the Battle of Bull Run, Washingtonians traveled out to view the action. (Virginia State Library and Archives)

piece of ground? As with most things in war, it had to do first with politics. Anxious for an early victory, Lincoln, in the summer of 1861, pressed his general Irvin McDowell to engage the Southerners and work toward Richmond. McDowell argued against it, knowing that his men, most "90-day volunteers," were woefully untrained and untested. "You are green," Lincoln admitted, "but they are green, also; you are all green alike." And so McDowell marched forward with 35,000 men, heading first to the railroad junction of Manassas, and its guard of 20,000 Southern troops. But Confederate spies in Washington had warned of the attack in time for a Southern contingent of 18,000 men under Joe Johnston to move stealthily up from nearby Winchester and reinforce the Confederates. On July 21, McDowell struck the Southern line at a weak spot near its rear. By noon, rebels were being driven south to Henry Hill. The North, already claiming victory, stopped to regroup at the base of the hill. When they resumed their charge up the hill a couple of hours later, the South was ready for them. Johnston's first brigade, under Thomas J. Jackson, had formed a defensive line out of sight of the North. Seeing their solid ranks, Confederate general Barnard Bee had yelled, "There stands Jackson like a stone wall. Rally behind the Virginians!"

By late afternoon the Union was in retreat, awarding the Confederacy a great victory, at least of morale. But the South, too, had suffered heavy losses and exhaustion, and consequently, Johnston did not pursue the retreating enemy.

Perhaps if he had, the Second Battle of Manassas (also known as the Second Battle of Bull Run) would not have happened 13 months later. By then "Stonewall" Jackson had waged his brilliant Valley Campaign against the North in the Shenandoah, and he was the prize that the North most wanted to take. When he and his men raided the Manassas supply base, by then in the hands of the North, Union general John Pope gleefully ordered his army to "bag" Jackson. But Jackson outwitted them, as he usually did, by hiding, and by the time he came out to fight, he was reinforced by Lee's army of 50,000. By nightfall of August 30, 1862, in an eerie déjà-vu, the Union was again in retreat toward Washington. No picnickers had come to this battle. By now everyone understood that the war was in deadly earnest.

Today, the park's visitors center has interpretive displays and a slide show explaining just what happened here—and just how it came to happen twice. The battlefield is located on Route 234 between Route 15 and I-66. For more information call (703) 361-1339.

VIRGINIA'S EIGHT PRESIDENTS

GEORGE WASHINGTON
FIRST PRESIDENT (1789–1797)

The "Father of Our Country" was born in Westmoreland County in 1732 and spent his early years as a surveyor, a craft that took him into many corners of the Commonwealth and gave him a keen overview of Virginia's vast potential. He distinguished himself as a soldier and natural leader during the French and Indian War, and when the Revolution came, he was chosen as commander of the Continental army. Despite overwhelming odds, he led the Colonials to victory. When the Constitutional Convention convened, he was its chairman. And when the confederated states needed their first President, he was the obvious choice. More a leader than a politician, Washington worked as president to reconcile hostile political factions in the fledging nation and to keep the nation out of further wars. In 1799, two years after his presidency ended, he died at Mount Vernon. **Virginia Sites:** Mount Vernon (on the Potomac, south of Alexandria), George Washington Birthplace National Monument (Westmoreland County), Ferry Farm (Fredericksburg vicinity), George Washington Masonic National Memorial (Alexandria), and George Washington's Office Museum (Winchester).

THOMAS JEFFERSON
THIRD PRESIDENT (1801–1809)

Philosopher, populist, architect, aesthete, inventor, gardener, and politician, Jefferson was the consummate Renaissance Man. And yet he abhorred class snobbery and spent his political life trying to establish the rights of the individual. These views, and especially his views on state's rights, earned him powerful political enemies, but Jefferson understood the political game and played it well. During his presidency, he also became a realtor, negotiating the

Louisiana Purchase with the help of his protégé James Monroe. Of his many accomplishments, the "Great Democrat" was most proudest of having written the Declaration of Independence and the Virginia statute for religious freedom, and of having established the University of Virginia. He died at Monticello on July 4, 1826. **Virginia sites:** Monticello (Albemarle County), Poplar Forest (southwest of Lynchburg), Tuckahoe Farm (his boyhood home on the James, seven miles (11 km) west of Richmond).

JAMES MADISON
FOURTH PRESIDENT (1809–1817)

Born in Port Conway, Virginia, this small, modest, soft-spoken man hardly cut the classic image of a politician. Yet his erudition was much respected and put to good use in the U.S. Constitution, which he fathered. Following his mentor, Jefferson, into the White House, Madison was president during the War of 1812, an event that cost him public popularity. He died at Montpelier in 1836. **Virginia Site:** Montpelier (Orange County).

JAMES MONROE
FIFTH PRESIDENT (1817–1825)

Handsome and urbane, Monroe gave to the nation its Era of Good Feeling. With Europe worn thin by the Napoleonic Wars, Monroe seized the day to establish America's place among nations. His Monroe Doctrine warned Europe against further attempts to establish new colonies anywhere in the Americas. He also oversaw the Missouri Compromise, which allowed Missouri into the Union as a slave state, but prohibited slavery north of the Mason-Dixon Line. Monroe died in 1831, in New York City. **Virginia Sites:** James Monroe Museum (Fredericksburg), Ashlawn-Highland (Albemarle County), Oak Hill (Loudoun County).

WILLIAM HENRY HARRISON
NINTH PRESIDENT (1841)

The son of Benjamin Harrison, a signer of the Declaration of Independence, William Henry was born at Berkeley Plantation on the James. Yet when he ran as a candidate on the Whig ticket, he was pictured as a man of the West and his symbol was a log cabin. (Harrison had spent years in Ohio and Indiana, but he was hardly of pioneer stock.) The oldest man ever to run for President, the 68-year-old Harrison died after a month in office. **Virginia Sites:** Berkeley Plantation (Charles City County), Sherwood Forest Plantation (also Charles City County, owned but not lived in by Harrison).

JOHN TYLER
TENTH PRESIDENT (1841–1845)

When President Harrison died, Tyler, as his vice-president, succeeded to the presidency. Called "Honest John," he refused to play party politics and alienated his own Whig colleagues. Tyler did not run for a second term. He died in Richmond in 1862. **Virginia Sites:** Sherwood Forest Plantation (Charles City County) and Greenway (not open to the public, also Charles City County).

ZACHARY TAYLOR
TWELFTH PRESIDENT (1849–1850)

Born in Orange County in 1784, "Old Rough and Ready" was a military man all his life, and it was his heroism in the Mexican War that catapulted him to the presidency. This, too, he tended to view as yet another military post. But in spite of his political naiveté, he stood up to Southern congressmen who wanted to thwart the admission of California to the Union as a free state. Taylor died unexpectedly midway through his term. **Virginia Site:** Only a historical highway marker in Orange County, to indicate the site of his birthplace.

WOODROW WILSON
TWENTY-EIGHTH PRESIDENT (1913–1921)

A scholar and president of Princeton University, Wilson imbued the presidency with his social philosophy. He also kept the U.S. out of World War I until 1917, when German aggression led him to commit American forces, "to make," as he put it, "the world safe for democracy." After the war, Wilson worked tirelessly to establish the League of Nations. While the European powers signed the League's Covenant, the U.S. Congress rejected it. Wilson died in Washington in 1924. **Virginia Site:** Woodrow Wilson Birthplace (Staunton).

S H E N A N D O A H

SHENANDOAH, VALLEY OF THE DAUGHTER OF THE STARS, the native peoples are said to have called it—a romantic name for what must have been, even then, a romantic place. From the Blue Ridge vantage above the valley, you can look down on the Shenandoah's broad, flat fertility and conjure the herds of buffalo that grazed here centuries ago. Long after them came the Europeans—eighteenth-century Irish, Scots, Germans—who knew a fertile field when they saw one.

Unquestionably, this long swatch of northwestern Virginia was, and still is, fertile. Watered by the Shenandoah River and the many brooks that weep their way out of the mountains, the valley smells like a farm, with the mixed aroma of fresh-mowed fields, turned earth, and pungent manure. While the Blue Ridge defines the Shenandoah's eastern extent and the higher, rougher Allegheny Mountains rise to its west, its north-south endpoints are a matter of some debate—but then North and South have never rested easy together here.

In general, the valley begins somewhere in the vicinity of Winchester, Virginia, and ends somewhere below the initials George Washington carved in the impressively arching rock known as Natural Bridge. If the exact space the valley occupies is in dispute, its temperament is not. Like Don Quixote, the Shenandoah clings to the chivalry of the past as if it were a life raft able to buoy one above the irreverences, and irrelevances, of the twentieth century.

Strung north to south along I-81 and U.S. 11, Winchester, Staunton, Edinburgh, Lexington, and all the other valley towns wear their manners and their antebellum histories like badges of courage. True, burger chains and strip shopping centers encircle many of their downtowns. But these enemy armies have been able to advance only so far. The center lines have held, and the main streets have kept their soda fountain-style drugstores, their homegrown restaurants, and their antique shops with the consoling mustiness of memories. Here and there old stone mills by the river have been gentrified into restaurants or shops, but their proprietors still greet you as if you were a kissing cousin whose citified ways they're willing to forgive.

White church steeples reach into blue heavens here, and local residents, living amid such smalltown grace, confer their own blessings on you. Pass a stranger on the street, and they almost always bestow a heartfelt "How you today?" They

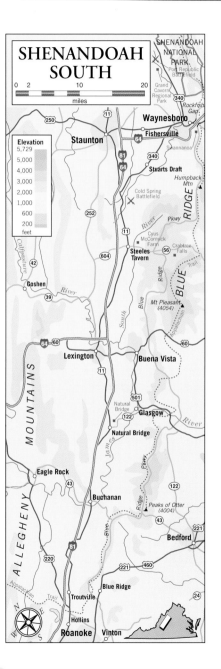

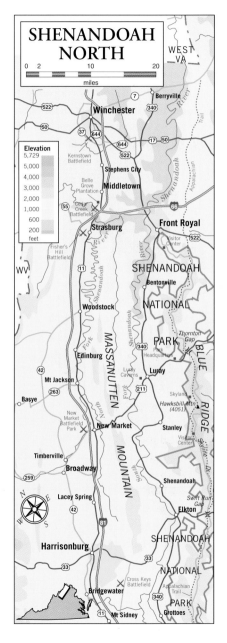

could be college people (the valley is full of small, well-heeled colleges); they could be farmers, merchants, horse-breeders, fiddle-players, or Mennonites (there are pockets of them living around Stuart's Draft and Harrisonburg). The valley and the hovering Blue Ridge have them all.

And it has memories still painful to the touch. Maybe more than any place in the nation, this swatch of earth was beaten and bruised beyond recognition during the Civil War. You can follow the trail of battlefields right through the valley, though only a few of them are marked by anything more than a roadside plaque (see "Civil War in the Shenandoah," following). Except for those markers, the valley today bears few visible scars of that era. In spring it is petalled with dogwood and apple trees above the pale green of new grass. Summers, it drowses to the drone of cicadas and frogs and sun-slowed cows complaining in distant pastures.

Then there is fall, when the sounds become more insistent, and the land seems to rouse itself for a grand finale before the inevitability of winter. Autumn is a good time to head for the hills of the Blue Ridge. The apples are ripe for picking then, and at roadside stands lean-faced men in overalls sell mounded baskets of them, as well as gallons of sweet cider, jars of honey, homemade pickles, and relishes. Almost any road you take will lead in the right direction, into the heart of a legendary Virginia.

Admittedly, you can also shoot through the entire Shenandoah in a matter of hours if you go nonstop on I-81. This old wagon route is still the main thoroughfare for the valley, and as such it's popular with multi-ton semis that shoulder down the road two abreast. Oddly enough, even the interstate has its upside. The valley fans out from it, banked on the west by the Alleghenies and dissolving on the east into the soft, melancholy folds of the Blue Ridge. With a little imagination, you might believe that the Almighty had painted that long, low smear of gray-blue on the horizon—to keep the the blended colors of Confederate and Union flying above this old battleground forever.

■ CIVIL WAR IN THE SHENANDOAH

Throughout the course of the Civil War, the Shenandoah Valley was trampled and trod and fought over perhaps more than any other piece of ground in the country (see crossed-sword symbols on map of Shenandoah for battle sites). For the North, it meant two things: a back door into Virginia and the Confederate capital in Richmond; and the fertile "Breadbasket of the Confederacy," something to be destroyed. And so, time and again Northern troops shoved into the Valley of Virginia. And time and again, they were shoved out of it by the South.

This shoving began in earnest early in the war, with Confederate general "Stonewall" Jackson's Valley Campaign in the spring of 1862. The summer before, Jackson's sang-froid at the First Battle of Manassas (or Bull Run) had earned him his famous sobriquet "Stonewall." Beyond

A rare youthful photograph of the Confederacy's great general, Thomas Jonathan "Stonewall" Jackson, conveys his personal charisma. (Library of Congress)

that designation, he remained another obscure Southern officer, headquartered in Winchester with a force of only 8,000 men under him. It was events unfolding in Washington that would bring Jackson his undying fame. There, Union commander George McClellan was preparing to march a huge force up the Virginia Peninsula to attack Richmond. Lincoln had reluctantly agreed to the plan to take the capital of the Confederacy. Once McClellan and his forces left Washington, the President became increasingly anxious about the federal capital being too exposed. So he ordered additional forces into the outlying areas, into Fredericksburg and the Shenandoah.

Stonewall's position at the north end of the valley put him square in the path of history. On March 23 he tangled with Gen. James Shields at the **First Battle of Kernstown,** and there he suffered a tactical defeat. Still, he managed to shake the Union's confidence and apparently build his own. His brilliant Valley Campaign was underway.

▪ CIVIL WAR TIMELINE ▪

1861 APRIL: Virginia secedes from the Union (following South Carolina, Mississippi, Florida, Alabama, Georgia, Louisiana, and Texas). Western counties of state remain loyal to Union and form West Virginia.

▪ Col. Robert E. Lee, offered command of Union forces, resigns his commission in order to serve the South.

MAY: Richmond, Virginia becomes the capital of the Confederacy.

JULY: Union forces are defeated at Battle of Manassas (Bull Run).

1862 MARCH: Ironclads—Union's *Monitor* and Confederate's *Virginia (Merrimac)* —duel at Hampton Roads.

▪ Confederate general "Stonewall" Jackson is defeated at Kernstown.

MAY: Jackson wins at Kernstown, beginning the Shenandoah Valley Campaign. Confederates evacuate the Norfolk base, destroying the ironclad *Virginia* to prevent its capture.

AUGUST: General Lee is victorious at Second Battle of Manassas (Bull Run).

SEPTEMBER: Union army under McClellan halts Lee's attack on Washington in the Battle of Antietam, the bloodiest day of the war.

DECEMBER: Burnside's drive on Richmond fails at Fredericksburg

1863 MARCH: Independent cavalry leader John Singleton Mosby captures Union General Stoughton at Fairfax Courthouse.

MAY: Lee defeats Hooker at Chancellorsville, and Jackson mortally wounded by his own men.

1864 MARCH: Union general Ulysses S. Grant named commander-in-chief of Union forces.

MAY-JUNE: Grant pushes Lee's Army of Northern Virginia back toward Richmond in the Wilderness campaign. In an attempted surprise attack at Petersburg, command delays deny Grant victory, and the siege of Petersburg begins.

1865 JANUARY: U.S. House of Representatives passes the Thirteenth Amendment, abolishing slavery.

APRIL: Confederates evacuate and burn Richmond.

▪ Lee surrenders army to Grant at Appomattox.

▪ President Lincoln shot dead at Ford's Theatre in Washington.

MAY: President Andrew Johnson proclaims amnesty for citizens of the South.

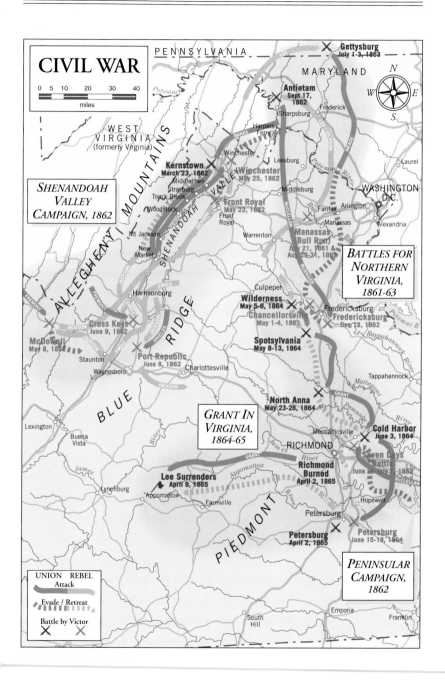

CIVIL WAR

0 5 10   20   30   40
miles

PENNSYLVANIA

MARYLAND

Gettysburg
July 1-3, 1863

Antietam
Sept 17,
1862

Sharpsburg

Frederick

Potomac

WEST
VIRGINIA
(formerly Virginia)

Harpers
Ferry

Winchester

Leesburg

Laurel

**SHENANDOAH
VALLEY
CAMPAIGN, 1862**

Kernstown
March 23, 1862

Winchester
May 25, 1862

Middletown

Strasburg

Tom's Brook

Front Royal
May 23, 1862

Middleburg

WASHINGTON
D.C.

Woodstock

Front
Royal

Fairfax

Arlington

Alexandria

Mt Jackson

Warrenton

Manassas

New
Market

Manassas
(Bull Run)
July 21, 1861 &
Aug 29-31, 1862

**BATTLES FOR
NORTHERN
VIRGINIA,
1861-63**

Harrisonburg

Culpeper

Wilderness
May 5-6, 1864

Chancellorsville
May 1-4, 1863

Fredericksburg

Fredericksburg
Dec 13, 1862

Rappahannock
River

Cross Keys
June 9, 1862

McDowell
May 8, 1862

Staunton

Port Republic
June 8, 1862

Spotsylvania
May 8-13, 1864

Charlottesville

Waynesboro

Tappahannock

North Anna
May 23-26, 1864

**GRANT IN
VIRGINIA,
1864-65**

Mechanicsville

Cold Harbor
June 3, 1864

Lexington

Buena
Vista

RICHMOND

Richmond
Burned
April 2, 1865

Seven Days
Battle
June 26-July 1, 1862

Lee Surrenders
April 9, 1865

Appomattox

Farmville

Lynchburg

PIEDMONT

Petersburg

Hopewell

Petersburg
April 2, 1865

Petersburg
June 15-18, 1864

**PENINSULAR
CAMPAIGN,
1862**

UNION REBEL
Attack

Evade / Retreat

Battle by Victor

Emporia

Franklin

South
Hill

The second engagement came in May. Now reinforced with more men, Stonewall moved against a large enemy contingent under Frémont, headed into the valley from the west. The Southern victory here at the **Battle of McDowell** forced the Yankees south down the valley. A couple of weeks later, the Stonewall Brigade thrust through a gap in Massanutten Mountain and surprised a Federal garrison at **Front Royal.** Two days later, it overtook the fleeing Yankee forces at **Winchester.**

By now, Lincoln was convinced that the capital was at risk, and he poured reinforcements into the valley. But to no avail. In early June, Jackson eluded three Union columns at **Strasburg,** while his compatriot, Gen. Richard Ewell, successfully took on General Frémont again, this time at **Cross Keys.** A day later, Jackson had also defeated Shields's men at **Port Republic,** and the Valley Campaign was at an end.

In just over two months of fighting, Jackson had pushed his self-proclaimed "foot cavalry" across 350 miles (563 km). Using the local gaps, ridges, and backroads to tactical advantage, he had bamboozled and surprised far superior Union forces for two months. His 18,500 men had defeated twice that number and had kept some 50,000 Federal troops occupied and unable to reinforce McClellan in his attack on Richmond.

A year later, Lee's second corps passed through the valley on its way to the debacle at Gettysburg. The South won a handy victory at the **Second Battle of Winchester,** and throughout the rest of 1863 and into the spring of 1864, the valley lay blessedly quiet. Then in May of 1864, the Union returned to the valley, intent on disrupting Confederate supply lines. The first engagement, at the **Battle of New Market,** proved yet another Southern victory. Several weeks later, the North's luck turned, when an overpowering Union division of 12,000 men routed a Confederate force of half that size, who were defending the depot at Staunton.

By the summer Rebel general Jubal Early was in the valley, winning battles at **Cool Spring** and **Kernstown.** His victories were only a sad prelude to defeat. In Washington Grant was now in charge, and at last Lincoln seemed to have a commander who knew how to win. Grant eyed the breadbasket of the Confederacy, then sent Philip Sheridan against it, telling him to "make of it a wasteland, so that even crows flying over will have to carry their own provender." Sheridan moved cautiously into the valley, knowing Jubal Early's men, though small in number, were war-hardened veterans. He managed to repulse them in the conflagration known as **Third Winchester,** although the fighting cost him 5,000 casualties. Troops sent in pursuit of the fleeing Early caught him three days later at Fisher's

Hill, and again the Rebels suffered defeat. When Confederate cavalry struck back at Tom's Brook, the Federals smashed them and sent them reeling south.

Now the valley lay open to Sheridan's devastating march. Though guerilla fighters, including the daring Gray Ghost (John Mosby) harrassed them, the Yankees burned barns, houses, mills, whatever lay in their path. By mid-October, Sheridan's army had proceeded as far as **Cedar Creek,** about 20 miles (32 km) south of Winchester. Sheridan had headquartered himself at **Belle Grove Plantation,** and feeling that the situation was well in hand, he made a brief visit to Washington. On his way back, he spent the night in Winchester. The following morning, with Sheridan absent, Early launched a surprise attack on the sleeping Yankee army. The tactic appeared to work brilliantly, and by mid-day the bluecoats were in disorganized retreat. But Sheridan was on the way, dashing madly from Winchester to Cedar Creek. As he met his fleeing men on the road, he forced them back into battle. By late afternoon, the tables had turned, and the North had snatched a decisive victory from near defeat. Early's mauled army never recovered. And Sheridan was free to continue his march through the Shenandoah, leaving in his wake wounds that have yet to heal.

■ WINCHESTER

Located at the northern end of the Shenandoah Valley and noted for something as innocent as apple blossoms, Winchester feels like old Virginia: Not overly stuffy, overly colonial, or unduly pretentious—just the Virginia of, say, 50 years ago, when the simple beauty of apple blossoms was something to celebrate. Unquestionably, Winchester, located west of I-81 in the northwestern wedge of the state, sits in conservative country—once the home ground for Virginia's own Kingfisher politician, Harry Flood Byrd, and his all-powerful Byrd machine. But the Byrd hegemony died with Harry a couple of decades ago, leaving the town to evolve on its own. Byrd was only one of Winchester's luminaries. Writer Willa Cather came from Winchester, though she made her reputation describing the broad Nebraska prairie. Country singer Patsy Cline, too, was born and buried here. Her gravesite and a memorial to her lie out on Route 644, south of town.

The town's roots go far deeper than this, actually, back to the Shawnee peoples and then to the first whites, Pennsylvania Quakers, who settled in the area in the mid-1700s. Today, the town is a mix of many eras—from colonial past to post-yuppie present. Small charming streets twist by old eighteenth-century stone structures, gracious antebellum ones, antique stores, and colonial-style restaurants. One small stone cabin at 32 W. Cork Street, now a little museum, served as **George Washington's office** when, as a young man, he was surveying and guarding Virginia's western frontier.

Stonewall Jackson also headquartered himself in this town during the winter of 1861–62, just before he began his Valley Campaign. The old Victorian house he lived in sits a few blocks away at 415 N. Braddock Street. Jackson alternately suffered defeats and victories while here, and his departure did not ensure Winchester peace. Throughout the war, this area at the head of the Shenandoah Valley was an endless battleground. Proof of that can be found in the 8,000-some bodies that lie in peace off Boscawen Street. About half are Confederate boys, taking their rest in Stonewall Cemetery, and the other half Union men, buried across Woodstock Lane in the National Cemetery.

Twenty miles (32 km) south of Winchester on Route 11, **Belle Grove Plantation** sits in the middle of a rolling field. Now a National Trust property, the columned old house served as Union headquarters for Gen. Phil Sheridan at the

A foggy morning in the Shenandoah Valley.

PATSY CLINE

1932–1963

Though her stardom lasted only three years, Patsy Cline left an indelible impression on country music. Known for her exceptionally clear voice and hauntingly personal delivery, she was famous for such songs as *Walkin' After Midnight* and *I Fall to Pieces.*

Born Virginia Hensley in Winchester, Virginia, she won a tap dancing contest at the age of four, marking the beginning of her focus on entertainment. Family financial difficulties forced her to quit high school and work as a drugstore clerk, but Virginia sang whenever and wherever she could, her experiences somehow adding a tone of a hard life to the cadence of her music.

At the age of 21, she married Gerald Cline, and adopted the professional name Patsy Cline. She sought out every opportunity she could to perform, appearing on such regional radio and television shows as the *Louisiana Hayride,* the *Ozark Jubilee,* and the *Jimmy Dean Show* in Washington, D.C. In 1955 she got a recording contract with Four Star Records, but her big break came when she won the nationally televised "Arthur Godfrey's Talent Scouts" competition with *Walkin' After Midnight.* The song was released immediately, and sold a million copies, going to number three on the *Billboard* country music charts.

At that point Patsy's career slowed. Her next recordings weren't as magical. She divorced her first husband, and married Charlie Dick in 1957, then went into semi-retirement for two years following the birth of her daughter. But in 1960 she accepted a spot as a regular on the *Grand Ole Opry* in Nashville, and signed a record contract with Decca. Her first Decca release, Hank Cochran's *I Fall to Pieces,* became her first hit to reach number one on the charts.

From that point Patsy Cline became one of the biggest names in country music. Her version of Willie Nelson's *Crazy* was a major hit, and was followed by *She's Got You, Leavin' on Your Mind, Imagine That,* and others. She was named top female vocalist in country music by trade publications, ending more than a decade of dominance by "The Queen of Country Music," Kitty Wells, and clearly marking Patsy's arrival at the top.

Then, in March of 1963, on the way back to Nashville from a benefit concert in Kansas City, she was killed in a plane crash along with fellow Nashville stars Hawkshaw Hawkins and Cowboy Copas. If her career ended there, her influence and popularity continue. As one of the first major country female singers to perform independently—not as a member of a group or duo—she had a profound effect on the likes of Loretta Lynn, Reba MacIntyre, and k.d. lang. Elected posthumously into the Country Music Hall of Fame in 1973, she was the first female solo artist to receive that honor, and remains one of the best-loved country singers of our time.

—Jessica Fisher

beginning of his slash-and-burn march through the valley in 1864. And it witnessed Sheridan's decisive victory at the Battle of Cedar Creek.

Before the war raged, the home knew better times. Built at the end of the eighteenth century, it was the home of Maj. Isaac Hite, Jr., the brother-in-law of James Madison. In fact, Madison is said to have enlisted the aid of his friend, Tom Jefferson, in helping Hite with the design of his home. You can see Jeffersonian touches in Belle Grove's pavilions and its hidden staircase. And considering that the valley was barely settled when this fine old manor was built, you can see why it would have been considered "the most splendid building west of the Blue Ridge."

■ NEW MARKET BATTLEFIELD

In some very strange ways, the Civil War still rages on in the Valley of Virginia. Local buffs argue over exactly where battles took place, exactly who won them, and exactly who the true heroes were. One modern battleground is New Market Battlefield, south and west of Winchester on I-81. For years, the Virginia Military Institute (VMI) has maintained the New Market Battlefield Park and a Hall of Valor, which among other things extols the heroic contribution of its cadets to the 1864 Battle of New Market. In recent years, however, a new museum has opened nearby on Route 305 (just off I-81)—the New Market Battlefield Military Museum. This columned roadside edifice, replicating Lee's Arlington House, displays some 1,500 artifacts from the Civil War to the present, and it takes a somewhat different approach to the Battle of New Market. Its founder contends that the battle did not take place on the VMI-designated site, and he hints that perhaps the role of the 247 teenage cadets in the battle has been somewhat overplayed.

You can take a look at both museums and decide for yourself who is winning the new battle about the old battle of New Market. Most historians do agree on these facts—that Confederate troops reinforced by VMI cadets bested Yankee forces that had entered the valley to disrupt Confederate supply and communication lines.

The battlefield park, now graced in green and set off by split rail fences, also features the old white clapboard Bushong farmhouse and nine re-created dependencies. A portrait of pastoralism most of the time, the farmstead and the surrounding battlefield are the scene of renewed fighting every May when latter-day Rebels and Yankees face off again in a reenactment of the 1864 fray.

■ LURAY CAVERNS

Of the many caverns that riddle central Virginia, this is the granddaddy of them all—and also the most commercialized. Its 64 underground acres of drip-castle stalactites, stalagmites, draperies, and flowstones do make for an awesome spectacle and have earned the caverns a National Landmark designation.

On the northeast side of the Blue Ridge off U.S. 211, the caverns actually are buried in a separate little pocket of land between the Blue Ridge and Massanutten Mountain. The latter, a wedge at the north end of the valley, cleaves the Shenandoah River into its North and South forks. Coming to Luray from either the east or west on U.S. 211, you have some mountain roads to negotiate.

The story of Luray's discovery bears all the hope and heartache of post-Civil War Virginia. In 1878, an itinerant photographer named Benton Stebbins arrived in Luray with his family and began soliciting locals for business. Apparently a frustrated but smart man, Stebbins was always looking for entrepreneurial ventures. He learned from locals about an old cave in the area, and he immediately saw it as

a possible business opportunity. But the cave had been vandalized and chipped at over time, and Stebbins turned his attention elsewhere. With the help of three local "partners," he set about exploring sinkholes in the region. After weeks of searching to no avail, the Phantom Chasers, as locals called them, discovered a large sinkhole with promise. Clearing the debris out of it, they could feel a stream of cool air blowing up from underground. Lowering themselves into it, they entered the subterranean wonderland now called Luray Caverns. Recognizing the import of their discovery, the group kept quiet, and a month later acquired the cave land through auction.

Several months later, the caverns opened for business, and they are proud to proclaim that they have offered guided tours every day since. It's too bad, though, that the caverns aren't like they were when the Phantom Chasers lowered themselves down that sinkhole. Now a paved walkway interrupts the natural beauty, and glowing electric lights illuminate such spectacles as the Wishing Well, where coins sparkle with the magic of money.

A wall of stalactites has even been turned into pipes for the cavern's famous Great Stalactite Organ—admittedly a fascinating contraption. In fact, the *1988 Guinness Book of Records* called it the "World's Largest Natural Musical Instrument." It doesn't exactly emit a rich Baroque sound, but it has worked well enough to provide the music for a number of subterranean weddings. The guide on your tour may stop and serenade your group with a few notes.

About the guides: Most all are natives of the town of Luray, and they grew up hoping—even expecting—to work here. Luray is, after all, a company town, and the caverns are that company. As the largest and most popular caverns in the East, they pull in about half a million visitors a year.

■ STAUNTON

Staunton (pronounced Stan-ton)—set along I-81 west of Charlottesville and north of Lexington—is a pretty little place that doesn't try to define itself too narrowly. Traditionally a farm town at the heart of agrarian Augusta County, its streets boast plenty of cap-wearing farmers driving pick-up trucks. The townsfolk here are particularly proud of a bunch of local boys who made good, the country music Statler Brothers. And the brothers seem proud of the town. For years, the

Churning applebutter at the Westview United Methodist Church in Staunton.

Statlers have treated their neighbors to a free Fourth of July country music extravaganza, "to repay the townsfolk for helping us out in the beginning." To investigate the Statler Brothers further, visit the **Statler Brothers' Mini-Museum** at 501 Thornrose Avenue.

Staunton wears several hats besides its farmer's cap. Something of an "institution town," it houses the barbed-wire, high-walled architecture of a state prison, as well as several state hospitals. But all this institutionalism dissolves around the old center of town. Here, the hills are lined with gracious Victorian homes and the creamy stuccoed charm of **Mary Baldwin College,** a Southern girls school in the haute tradition.

Across the street from the college sits a buttoned-down white manse that ranks as the birthplace of yet another Virginia-born President. If you had to guess *which* President, just looking at its starched exterior, you might guess right. The precise, intellectual—some have even said effete—Woodrow Wilson was born here in 1856. The son of a Presbyterian minister, Wilson spent only a few years in these genteel surroundings before his father was called to a church in Georgia. Nonetheless, Virginia seems to have held some claim to Wilson's soul. When he married his second wife, he chose to honeymoon at the Old Dominion's premiere resort—the lavish Homestead. As he pulled up to its doors, the normally reserved Wilson could be heard singing "Oh, you beautiful doll" to his new bride.

The Museum of American Frontier Culture, on the outskirts of town, is a stellar example of real—not sanitized history—brought to life. On its rambling grounds the state has re-created the life on the farmsteads of the Scotch-Irish, American, German, and English souls who settled the Shenandoah Valley. In a scholarly tour de force rarely seen in these financial times, the museum did not reproduce these buildings, but actually transplanted them here, piece by piece—three from Europe and one from the valley itself. Wandering through them, you get an unromanticized feel for the often harsh realities of life on the frontier. While the thatch-roofed, whitewashed Scotch-Irish cottage may look quaint, consider sharing its quarters with your livestock. Or consider the winter drafts that must have blown through the log house of a traditional American farm. The museum is located southeast of Staunton off I-81, Exit 222 to U.S. 250.

■ SWANNANOA

As incongruous as it may seem, there are pockets of new age awareness scattered around and above the valley. Most of these retreats operate quietly and judiciously, knowing that their message may not appeal to the local populace. Swannanoa, however, has never been afraid to flaunt its mission. This imposing Italianate Renaissance "palace" stands on a mountaintop above Skyline Drive and proclaims itself the headquarters for the University of Science and Philosophy, which teaches its followers how to claim their own divine power. To reach Swannanoa, go to Rockfish Gap, which is at the intersection of Route 250, I-64, the Blue Ridge Parkway, and Skyline Drive, then look for signs to Swannanoa (up the mountain).

What is particularly fascinating about this place is the perspicacity of its deceased founder, Walter Russell. Decades ago, Russell was using the term "new age" and teaching many of its now well-known tenets. Russell was, in his lifetime, a successful businessman, sculptor, figure skater, and spiritual leader. When Russell was 77, he and his second wife, Lao, also a "cosmic messenger," bought this abandoned and collapsing estate and set about repairing it with their own hands, believing that it was a Sacred Mountaintop from which they could expound their Message.

When Walter died, Lao continued their joint work. She has been dead now for years, and the estate today is slipping again into disrepair. Adherents of the Russells' message now give tours through ground-floor rooms, adorned by many of Russell's works of art. The guides tend to refer to the great couple in reverential whispers, explaining their genius and philosophy. There is an Addams Family quality to Swannanoa today that probably doesn't do justice to Walter's original intent. Still, it's a refreshing departure from the typical Virginia "historic house" motif, and the serenity of the Sacred Mountaintop is admittedly an inspiring thing.

Farther south, standing in the shadow of the Blue Ridge, lies the small **McCormick Farm** (also known as Walnut Grove Farm), an unpretentious little place that revolutionized agriculture. In 1831, a 22-year-old valley boy named Cyrus Hall McCormick, maybe tired of the laborious process of hand-reaping grain, figured out how to do it mechanically. McCormick's design for a horse-drawn mechanical reaper soon spread beyond the Valley of Virginia, opening up the country's vast western frontier with its simple technology.

A quiet, pleasing place, Walnut Grove Farm still holds the log workshop where young Cyrus tinkered. Beside it, the big overshot wheel of the family's stone mill turns picturesquely, and green fields stretch off around it. Though they are no longer harvested by Cyrus's simple reaper, his idea was the beginning of a farm technology that continues to this day. McCormick Farm is located on Route 606, near Raphine. From the parkway, take Steeles Tavern exit; from I-81, take Raphine exit.

■ LEXINGTON

Of all Virginia's towns, this, in the end, may be the loveliest. Located on I-81 south of Staunton, Lexington is small and intimate, winding along a classic Main Street filled with the cafés, haberdasheries, and bookstores typical of a university town. Up on the low hill two redoubtable Virginia institutions overlook the town—Washington and Lee University and the Virginia Military Institute (VMI), both as interwoven with the state's identity as the dogwood blossom.

Washington and Lee University stands with perfectly articulated gentility beneath an arbor of stately oaks. Begun as a men's school called Augusta Academy in 1749, it was endowed by George Washington, whose name it now bears—along with that of its most famous president, Robert E. Lee. Things have decidedly changed since Lee's time, because the school is now coed and the campus crawls with students that look like those at any other campus. Lee, the father of four daughters, no doubt would have approved.

Fall scene along the Maury River in Rockbridge County near Lexington.

Typical Shenandoah mountain farmstead.

Lee came here at war's end and never left. He is buried—and celebrated—in the campus's Victorian brick Lee Chapel. His office remains intact here, chairs still drawn up around a small conference table, and it's not hard to imagine the dignified, elderly Lee interviewing his students, explaining to them his simple code of behavior. "We have but one rule here," Lee liked to say, "and it is that every student must be a gentleman." Down the hall from his office Lee's remains are entombed in a family crypt with those of his wife, Mary. The chapel also holds the famous Peale portrait of a young George Washington in uniform and the Pine portrait of Lee.

Behind the chapel sanctuary is a small round room enshrining the famous recumbent statue of Lee by sculptor Edward Valentine. Uncle Robert, as his troops called him, lies with one hand on his chest, his features tranquil but ravaged, like the terrain of an old battlefield. Buried outside the chapel are the remains of Lee's trusted horse, Traveller. In a classic gesture of Southern noblesse, the university reinterred Traveller's remains here in 1971.

This college was Lee's final home, when he had no other. He and his family came here, virtually with nothing, and for the last five years of his life he served as president. Those were taxing but apparently satisfying years. From here he exhorted his fellow Southerners to forget the past, become Americans again, and rebuild their dreams. He himself did that, turning this poor small college into a prestigious institution. Yet, throughout those years Lee knew that at any moment he could be arrested and tried for treason.

Instead, he was left in peace, and at age 63 he died of cerebral thrombosis in his home. It's still there on the campus—columned, dignified, like the man himself.

Virginia Military Institute butts right up against Washington and Lee, and its sudden, distinctly martial milieu causes an almost surreal shift in reality. Cadets, chins tucked in and shoulders back, quickstep across the broad Parade Grounds in the shadow of turreted, military Gothic buildings that look like a child's Lego castle. This bastion of soldierly male traditionalism, founded in 1839, lays claim to being the first state military college in the country. These days, however, VMI feels a bit out of step with the times, as it fights what some consider the battle of its life. For a couple of years now the enemy—that is aspiring female candidates—have been knocking at its gates, and the courts may eventually force the diehard institution to let go its male guard. At this moment, however, it remains a macho place.

As such, it's a place that honors its heroes. Two of these rate special attention: VMI's **George C. Marshall Museum** traces the considerable contributions of this former cadet and Nobel Peace Prize winner toward creating a more congenial world, with his post-World War II Marshall Plan. The other hero, Thomas Jonathan Jackson, was one of the school's nineteenth-century professors. Intensely private, devout, and so eccentric that his students called him "Tom Fool" Jackson, this unlikely soldier is commemorated by a well-positioned statue. Stonewall stands forever surveying the comings and goings of present-day cadets across the Parade Grounds. For more information about the institute or museum, call (703) 463-7103.

Jackson's home, a simple brick townhouse, also stands nearby on 8 E. Washington Street, mirroring in its modest but somewhat severe facade the tastes of the man himself. In the 1850s Jackson spent a happy interlude here, content to pre-pare his lectures on "natural philosophy," read his Bible, dabble a bit in business, and listen to his wife Mary Anna play the piano in the parlor. The rooms today are pleasant, homey, filled with Victorian furnishings and personal possessions that paint a softer, more intimate portrait of a man who, in war, was a formidable martinet.

Jackson was 37 when he joined the Confederate cause. After his instant fame at the First Battle of Manassas, the newly christened Stonewall gradually became Lee's right hand. In his celebrated Valley Campaign, Jackson moved like no stone wall. Time and again he used daring, speed, and his knowledge of the terrain to re-pulse Union troops that far outnumbered him.

Jackson never lived to see the end of the war, dying in 1863 of complications suffered from a wound inadvertently inflicted by his own men. Even today, they say in the valley that if Stonewall had not fallen in the Battle of Chancellorsville, the war might have gone another way.

Stonewall lives on at Lexington's well-regarded **Lime Kiln Theatre,** where every summer season includes a replay of its "Stonewall Country." The theatre also pre-sents other fine dramas in an appealing outdoor setting. The thick stone walls of the open-air, earthen-floored theatre are the remains of an old lime kiln, and the setting makes for a dramatic experience.

Natural Bridge (Routes 11 and 130, about 15 miles [24 km] south of Lexington) has been called many things: the "Bridge of God," by the Monocan Indians; one of the Seven Wonders of the Natural World (who picks these wonders, anyway?); and "the most sublime of nature's works," by Thomas Jefferson. So impressed was he by

The approach to Natural Bridge is scarred by graffiti and roadside souvenir stands today, yet down below it still retains some of the sylvan beauty reflected in this nineteenth-century etching. (Library of Congress)

this arc of rock measuring 215 feet (66 m) high and 90 feet (27 m) across that he purchased it as his own, patenting the surrounding 157 acres "for twenty shillings of good and lawful money." But even before Jefferson had fallen in love with it, George Washington had surveyed it. Times being what they were (man conquering nature and so forth), he carved his initials in it.

The bridge still rises sublimely above wooded Cedar Creek, its top traversed by Route 11. Still privately owned—though not by Jefferson descendants—the bridge is operated as a public attraction. In other words, you have to pay a fee now to worship at the Bridge of the Gods.

THE NIGHT I STAYED TOO LATE

*W*here Tinker Creek flows under the sycamore log bridge to the tear-shaped island, it is slow and shallow, fringed thinly in cattail marsh. At this spot an astonishing bloom of life supports vast breeding populations of insects, fish, reptiles, birds, and mammals. On windless summer evenings I stalk along the creek bank or straddle the sycamore log in absolute stillness, watching for muskrats. The night I stayed too late I was hunched on the log staring spellbound at spreading, reflected stains of lilac on the water. A cloud in the sky suddenly lighted as if turned on by a switch; its reflection just as suddenly materialized on the water upstream, flat and floating, so that I couldn't see the creek bottom, or life in the water under the cloud. Downstream, away from the cloud on the water, water turtles smooth as beans were gliding down with the current in a series of easy, weightless push-offs, as men bound on the moon. I didn't know whether to trace the progress of one turtle I was sure of, risking sticking my face in one of the bridge's spider webs made invisible by the gathering dark, or take a chance on seeing the carp, or scan the mudbank in hope of seeing a muskrat, or follow the last of the swallows who caught at my heart and trailed it after them like streamers as they appeared from directly below, under the log, flying upstream with their tails forked, so fast.

—Annie Dillard, *Pilgrim at Tinker Creek,* 1974

■ SHENANDOAH NATIONAL PARK AND SKYLINE DRIVE

One of America's most popular parks, the Shenandoah is a gentle place, draped across the top of the Blue Ridge off of I-81 (from Richmond take I-64 W; from Washington D.C., I-66 W). Its quiet forests and deer-dotted meadows lie along the deservedly famous Skyline Drive. Meandering across the crest of the Blue Ridge, the drive runs from Front Royal south for 105 miles (168 km), with ample places to pull over and gaze down on the serpentine course of the Shenandoah River or across a precipice into an intriguing mountain hollow.

The hollows are unpeopled today, but it was not always so. Before the Civilian Conservation Corps began building the Skyline Drive in the 1930s, this now accessible mountain terrain was wild, remote, the home of mountaineers. Many made a hardscrabble living off the area's abundant chestnut trees, but the chestnut blight of the 1920s put an end to that, and change soon followed.

It came first with an entrepreneur named George Pollock. He took a mountaintop he had inherited near Luray, and turned it into Skyland, a resort frequented by statesmen and presidents. The way up to Pollock's Skyland was rough in those days and the accommodations rustic, but that apparently was part of the appeal. Nightly entertainment centered around a campfire where live snakes were exhibited and Pollock showed off his marksmanship. Away from the fire, off in the shadows of the night, mountaineers, too, would gather to see the spectacle. Pollock's showmanship brought fame to the area, and in 1926, Congress authorized the establishment of the Shenandoah National Park. Ten years later, Roosevelt sent the Civilian Conservation Corps in to build the Skyline Drive and to restore the overfarmed, overgrazed land to its natural beauty.

Today, the park is mostly pristine mountain land again, though it does have several developed areas with visitor facilities and accommodations. One of these is an updated version of Pollock's Skyland (entertainment is considerably milder than back in his showmanship days). Many of the park's trails follow the old mountain thoroughfares that used to be the main "highways" through these gaps and hollows. Some of them are now part of the **Appalachian Trail,** that hikers' highway that runs from Maine to Georgia, cutting straight through the park along its way.

You can still find traces of the mountaineers' handiwork here and there. Close by a streambed, you may discover an old homestead, marked now only by a neatly chinked chimney or a stone fence. If you look closely, you're likely to see an apple tree or two at its edges and maybe the shoots of a hardy iris, planted who knows how long ago.

On a fine fall day, you can feel something of what the mountaineers had here in the Blue Ridge. Around you, invisible choruses of crickets ring out their year-end swan song; streams shush across moss-draped stones and past dark hemlock groves; and any light breeze will set a blizzard of colored leaves falling. Above the canopy of trees, crows croak reassuringly, and wide-winged turkey buzzards wheel and dip in their incessant dirge to death. If you move quietly, you might see a deer or two gazing warily in your direction, their coats so blended with the forest that they recall poet Vachel Lindsay's "phantom deer . . ." who arise with "all lost, wild America . . . shining in their eyes."

Old Rag rears up on the far east edge of Shenandoah National Park, a rough and rugged peak with a lot of character. Its rock-riven 3,268-foot (996-m) summit offers all kinds of opportunities to negotiate chimneys and crevices and other geologic spectacles rarely found in the conformation of Old Dominion earth. The hike to the summit totals about seven miles (11 km) and requires no overwhelming stamina,

Mr. Brown, postmaster of Old Rag in the Shenandoah, photographed by a Farm Security Administration photographer in 1935. (The Chrysler Museum)

with the earlier part weaving up forested slopes. However, the higher elevations make you work, taking you over, under, and through pitching rock formations. At the summit, the views sweep back along the Piedmont and up into the Blue Ridge. For more information on the park and park facilities, call (703) 999-2266.

■ BLUE RIDGE PARKWAY

The Blue Ridge Parkway picks up where the Skyline Drive leaves off. From Rockfish Gap, it follows the crest of the Blue Ridge through southwestern Virginia for a long, lovely 355 miles (568 km). Crossing the border into North Carolina, it picks up the Black Mountains and keeps going for another 114 miles (182 km). As part of the national park system, it offers the typical interpretive sites, lodges and campgrounds, all done in classic park service style—professional but slightly homogenized. Still, hike a half-mile off the road and the terrain is alive with 'possums, black bears, deers, thickets of mountain laurel, and stands of oak and hemlock. The Appalachian Trail is usually no more than a few miles from the parkway, so if you'd prefer to walk the Blue Ridge, rather than drive it, that is an option.

The scenic parkway is not the fast road to anywhere. The speed limit rarely reaches 45 mph (72 kmh), and it's frequently considerably below that. Since you can get on and off the parkway at various points, many drivers choose to do a sort of Sunday drive along the parkway, then return to the flatlands when they need to make time.

The Virginia part of the parkway has several sites worth a stop. At **Humpback Rocks** (Mile 6) a re-created mountain farmstead features a windowless one-room log cabin, a weasel-proof chicken house, a barn, and the other small outbuildings which were moved here from old farms in the area. As the park service points out, they represent a hard-fought pioneer way of life that was still being lived in these hills less than a hundred years ago.

The irony surrounding a site like this is unavoidable. These days the park service and the state are intent on re-creating little roadside farmsteads. Yet, 50 years ago, it was they and their thirst for "progress" that helped destroy the mountaineer culture.

Just down the road from the farmstead rise The Rocks themselves—3,080-foot (939-m) Humpback Rocks. Jutting up above the forests, this outcrop was long a landmark along the old Howardsville Turnpike, a wagon trail that ran through the mountains. Now, the rocks serve as a hikers' landmark. Twisting through pleasant

(previous pages) The Blue Ridge Parkway follows the crest of the Blue Ridge Mountains, affording spectacular views along the way.

forests, the popular trail up to the rocks climbs about 700 feet (213 m) in just under a mile. School groups, young families, and fit seniors huff up the trail in determined hordes on any pretty weekend. At the top they're rewarded with a hawk's-eye view of the Shenandoah Valley to the west and the lower ranges rolling down into the Piedmont to the east. Even with the madding crowd, the sun-warmed slabs of rock make a fine place to lie back and enjoy the Virginia mountains.

Another 57 miles (91 km) down the parkway, the character of the land changes briefly where the **James River** passes through. Trees stand statuesquely along grassy banks, while the river passes in a sedate swirl on its way from the Appalachian hinterland to Tidewater and the Chesapeake Bay. As placid as the river looks, the James proved a cantankerous foe to the nineteenth-century canal builders who tried to tame it through here.

An old restored lock still stands just below the parkway, a remnant of the battle fought to make this river behave in accord with man's commercial whims. Naturally, it was George Washington, the Great Canal Builder, who pressed for a canal system along the James to link the coast to the lucrative lands of the West. By the turn of the nineteenth century, the James River Canal had conquered the falls at Richmond, but the going was slow after that. Funds were hard to come by and control over what had become known as the James River and Kanawha Canal

The James River Canal near the mouth of the North River was built by slaves and Irish immigrants. (The New York Historical Society)

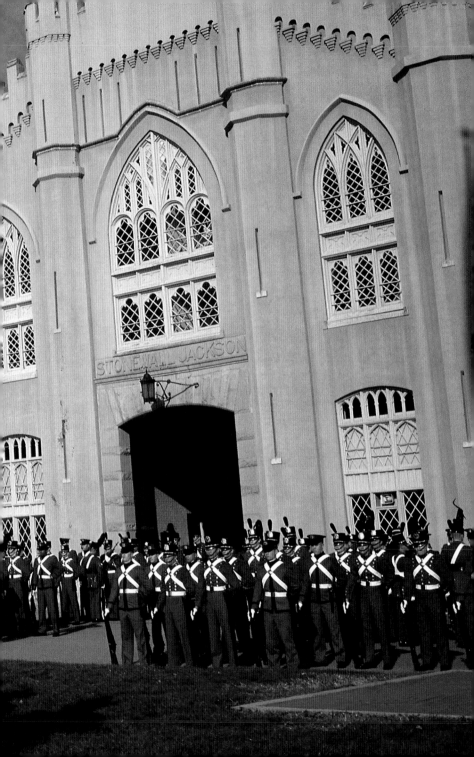

(after the Kanawha River in what is now West Virginia) passed back and forth between private ownership and the state. The work of cutting a canal through mountain wilderness was backbreaking. Slave owners hired out their men for some of the work, but by the mid-1830s, two-thirds of the workers were Irish immigrants.

Not until 1851 did the canal finally slice through the Blue Ridge, connecting Lynchburg with Buchanan. (It was, by the way, John Marshall, chief justice of the U.S. Supreme Court, who served as head of the project in the early part of the nineteenth century.) After Buchanan, the builders pressed on, hoping to complete the system far into the West, where it would link with the Kanawha River, and thus the whole Ohio River system. But that never happened. Mountain terrain, a monumental war, and the coming of the Iron Horse brought a slow death to the canal concept. By the 1880s, the James River and Kanawha Canal had become another relic of Virginia history.

From the James, one of the lowest elevations on the parkway, the road quickly climbs to its highest. At 3,950 feet (1204 m), this elevation is not exactly startling by world standards, but then the Blue Ridge is made up of old soft-sloping mountains, worn by time into a kind of gentled agedness. You can sense their time-taught patience particularly around the **Peaks of Otter,** about 20 miles (32 km) farther along the parkway. This is a park service developed area, with a pleasant lakeside lodge and campground—a place weekenders drive up to for a "mountain experience." The peaks themselves rise above Abbott Lake on three sides, though it would be unforgivable hyperbole to say they "hem it in."

In any case, the most famous of the peaks, **Sharp Top,** projects a stony crown into the sky, and busloads of tourists take the shuttle that winds to its summit. From here you can, as the song says, "see for miles and miles and miles and miles." The 360-degree view even takes in the distant Alleghenies, pressed like shadows against the western horizon.

Flat Top, at 4,004 feet (1,220 m) the highest of the Peaks of Otter, is accessible by trail only, with an elevation gain of 1,600 feet (488 m) in 4.4 miles (7.1 km). The final of the three peaks, Harkening Hill, also requires hiking, and its trail bears a designation of "steep and strenuous."

The classic Virginia town of **Bedford** is nestled in the hills just below the peaks. If you're ready to get off the parkway, you can take Route 43 for 10 miles (16 km) from the Peaks entrance down into this steepled, gracious little place.

(previous pages) The Virginia Military Institute was founded in 1839 as the first state military college in the country.

VIRGINIA HOSPITALITY AND FAVORITE DISHES

Jollity, the offspring
of wisdom and good living!
— Raleigh Tavern Motto

Virginians consider hospitality an art form, requiring a well-developed sense of the aesthetic. They will welcome you with heartfelt cordiality and a generous spirit, and some of them, particularly in the coastal and piedmont belt, will treat you to a taste of the fine old Virginia traditions—traditions that, sadly, are quickly passing into oblivion. After all, polishing heirloom silver and ironing heirloom linen (with little rolling irons so the hand-embroidery won't tear) are labor-intensive jobs. It's doubtful that such niceties will survive the post-historic, high-tech world of the coming century. So, for posterity, herewith are a few of the traditions that have made Virginia hospitality legendary.

First, the pineapple: These ancient symbols of fertility became popular design elements in seventeenth-century Britain, and in the Virginia colony the fruit came to symbolize hospitality. Its image was carved over doorways and furniture and hung outside inns. At Christmas, the fruit still makes a comeback, serving as a decorative centerpiece on tables. Christmas, being a season of both traditions and hospitality, is generally celebrated in high style. Pine garlands drape staircases, and magnolia, holly, boxwood, and cedar adorn doorways and mantles. Smithfield hams (raised and cured only in Smithfield, Virginia) become the highlight of linen-draped buffet tables—the red, prosciutto-like meat carved into paper-thin pieces and mounded inside beaten biscuits. Polished pewter Jefferson cups (small, stemless, and handle-less things) gleam on sideboards, and punch bowls hold frothy, fumingly potent eggnogs. Oysters, too, scalloped or in thick, white stews steam in bowls—though Virginia's native oysters have been depleted by blight in recent years. Little dishes of salted Virginia peanuts are set about to keep appetites whetted and to dilute the effects of the before-dinner "bourbon and branch." (This last word derives from branch water. The name sticks, though these days Virginians do take the water from the tap, rather than the stream, or branch, out back.) After dinner, guests can expect classic Southern desserts—pecan or mincemeat pie and plum pudding.

continues

In spring and summer, life becomes more casual and Virginians look to the bay to supply the provender for fish fries, clam bakes, and crab feasts. That exceptional gourmet treat, the small, sweet-fleshed Chesapeake Bay blue crab, is best when picked hot from the shell, dipped in butter, and eaten immediately by the picker. There are other ways to enjoy crab: as fat, succulent crabcakes; as stuffed, spicy deviled crab; as crab imperial; and as delicately sautéed soft crab. As to fish, there are flounder, spot, croaker, and in the fall, huge blues and rock fish. (By then, the drink of choice is a "stone fence"—fresh-pressed cider and bourbon.) The fish usually also come accompanied by homemade cornbread or custardy spoonbread, sliced tomatoes, cucumbers marinated in sugared vinegar, deviled eggs, fried okra, and robust potato salads.

Cookbooks abound with Virginia recipes, and even a non-Virginian can now attempt the culinary creations for which the state is justly famous. A few family favorites:

❧ CORNBREAD ❧

The secret to good cornbread is an iron skillet. So . . . preheat your oven to 450 degrees and coat an iron skillet with 2 tsp. of vegetable oil (Though this is hardly traditional, canola oil works very well.) Put the skillet in the oven and let the oil heat as you continue.

Mix 2 eggs with 2 cups non-fat buttermilk and a pinch, literally, of baking soda. Blend in 2 cups white, self-rising cornmeal and salt to taste. Pour batter into hot pan and bake about 20 minutes, until the top is slightly brown.

❧ CRAB IMPERIAL ❧

Pick through and remove any stray shells from 1 lb. of crab meat (backfin preferable). Beat 2 eggs with 1 1/2 cups mayonnaise, 1 tsp. Worcestershire sauce, salt and red and black pepper to taste.

Gently fold the crab into this mixture along with about 1 1/2 T. of capers (more if you are a capers fan).

Pour into a buttered baking dish and bake in a preheated 400 degree oven for 25 minutes or until top is golden brown.

❧ EGGNOG—FOR THE SPIRITED ❧

Separate 6 eggs. Whip the yolks and slowly add to them 6 T. rum and 6 T. sugar. Set aside.

Whip 1/2 pint whipping cream until it forms soft peaks and set aside. Whip the 6 egg whites until stiff. Gently fold first the whipped cream, then the egg whites into the egg yolk mixture. Add to this 1/2 cup whiskey of your choice, and about 1 pint of milk, to the desired consistency. Pour into a punch bowl and sprinkle the top with nutmeg.

One warning: If you worry about eating raw eggs, this may not be the beverage for you.

High Tea is served in the drawing room at the Martha Washington Inn in Abingdon. Virginia's top hotels are famous for their hospitality and elegance.

INTO MIDGET

*I*n the first year of their marriage, Ida Rebecca produced a son. In the next ten years she produced nine more, including twin boys. In 1897 . . . an eleventh son was born. He was to become my father . . . .

The line didn't stop there, though. Two years later there was, at last, a daughter; and five years after her, a twelfth son. Thirteen children was not a record for the neighborhood, nor even very remarkable. One family close by produced children in such volume that the parents ran out of names and began giving them numbers. One of their sons, whom I particularly envied for his heroic biceps, was named Eleven.

How big my father's family might have become eventually is hard to say, for Grandfather George suffered a stroke in 1907 and died at home, at the still fruitful age of fifty-two. There was a family mystery about his dying words. These, according to Ida Rebecca, were "into midget and out of midget." . . . Ida Rebecca never knew if this was exactly what he was trying to say or, if it was, what he meant by it. Nor did she ask him. He belonged to the Order of Red Men, one of those lodge brotherhoods common at the turn of the century which cherished secret handshakes and mumbo-jumbo passwords. Ida Rebecca hesitated to ask him what he meant by "into midget and out of midget" for fear she might be delving improperly into the sacred mysteries of the lodge.

—Russell Baker, *Growing Up*, 1982

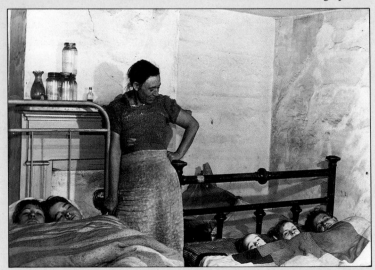

"A mother and some of her children." Photo by John Vachon for Farm Security Administration, 1941. (The Chrysler Museum)

WEST BY SOUTHWEST

FROM THE ROUGH SCARP OF THE ALLEGHENIES along Virginia's western flank to the Blue Ridge Highlands that roll south to North Carolina and Tennessee, this area is, at least to the rest of the state, the unknown hinterland. Nevertheless, it's home to a broad cross-section of people who probably represent a more diverse bunch than any other group in the Old Dominion. Coal miners, truckers, tobacco farmers, and smalltown professionals mind their own businesses here, apparently just as happy to remain "undiscovered" and left alone. Interstate 81 cuts a line through the southwest quadrant, breaking its longtime isolation. Here and there a few picture-perfect towns sprout, but the genteel tone of the Shenandoah and the Piedmont is not the predominant voice. After all, places like Harlan, Kentucky, lie just over the mountains—far closer, both geographically and attitudinally, than a place like Richmond.

Coal and railroads brought a quick prosperity to much of this area more than a century ago. Times were tough before that, and they were tough again too soon. Though the boom era was short-lived, mining and railroading remain economic backbones to this day, and they've produced some compelling things—rough-and-tumble pockets of coal country with their own distinctive character and a few highly urbane spots where the money of industry oils the local culture into a high gloss of traditional Virginia refinement.

If Virginia has an "empty quarter," it's in its isolated southwest corner, surrounded by Kentucky, West Virginia, Tennessee, and North Carolina. Good roads, besides I-81, are few here, but on the snaking backroads you come upon pockets of classic hill country—images that stay with you of black-and-white cows grazing in the shadow of the Alleghenies or of smalltime tobacco farms warped into hillsides, their weathered, earth-brown barns hung with bundles of the drying, burnished leaves. Along the southwest edge of the state, you share the twists and bends of these backroads with high-sided coal trucks that shuffle along like big, dumb beasts. To them, cars are of no more consequence than an ant is to an elephant. Be forewarned: The laws are a little different in these parts. The beasts have the right-of-way, no matter what the rules of the road say. (After a couple of days of sharing two-lane roads with these slow-moving behemoths, it's actually a relief to pull into the fast-moving lanes of an interstate.)

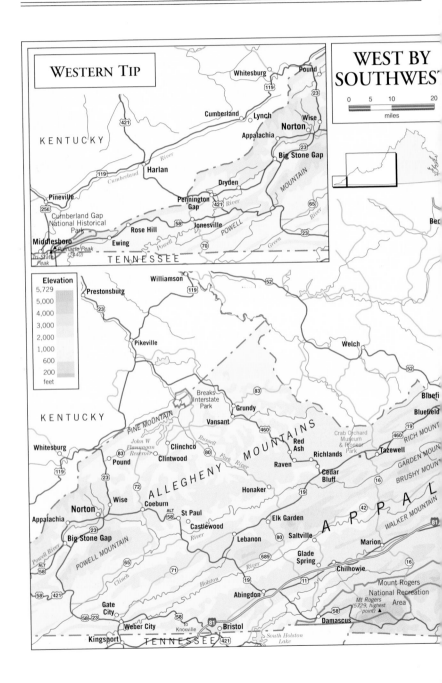

WESTERN TIP

Whitesburg · Pound
119 · 23

Cumberland · Lynch · Wise
Norton

KENTUCKY · Appalachia · 23

Big Stone Gap

River

119 · Harlan · Dryden · MOUNTAIN

Cumberland

Pineville · Pennington · 421 · River · 65
Gap

25E · Cumberland Gap · 58 · Jonesville · POWELL
National Historical
Park · Rose Hill · 23
Middlesboro · Ewing · Green · Bec
Pinnacle Peak · 70
Tri-State (2440) · Powell
Peak · TENNESSEE

WEST BY SOUTHWES

0 · 5 · 10 · 20
miles

Elevation

5,729	
5,000	
4,000	
3,000	
2,000	
1,000	
600	
200	
feet	

Williamson · 52

Prestonsburg
23

Pikeville · Welch

52

Breaks · 83 · Bluefi
Interstate
Park · Grundy · Bluefield

KENTUCKY · Vansant · 19
PINE MOUNTAIN · 460 · Crab Orchard · 460 · RICH MOUNT
John W · Russell · Museum
Flannagan · Clinchco · Red · & Pioneer
Whitesburg · 83 · Reservoir · 80 · Ash · Park · Tazewell
Pound · Clintwood · Fork · Richlands · 16 · GARDEN MOUN
119 · River · Raven · BRUSHY MOUN
23 · 72 · ALLEGHENY · MOUNTAINS · Cedar
Bluff · 16
Honaker · 19

Wise · Coeburn · 42 · APPAL
Norton · ALT · St Paul · 81
Appalachia · 58 · Castlewood · Elk Garden · WALKER MOUNTAIN
23 · River · 80 · Saltville
Big Stone Gap · Lebanon · Marion
ALT · POWELL MOUNTAIN · 65 · 71 · Glade · 16
58 · Spring · Chilhowie
Clinch · Holston · 19 · 11
58 · 421 · Abingdon · Mount Rogers
National Recreation
Gate · Mt Rogers · Area
City · (5729, highest
58 · 23 · 58 · point) ▲
Weber City · 81 · Bristol · 58
Knoxville · South Holston · Damascus
Kingsport · TENNESSEE · 421 · Lake

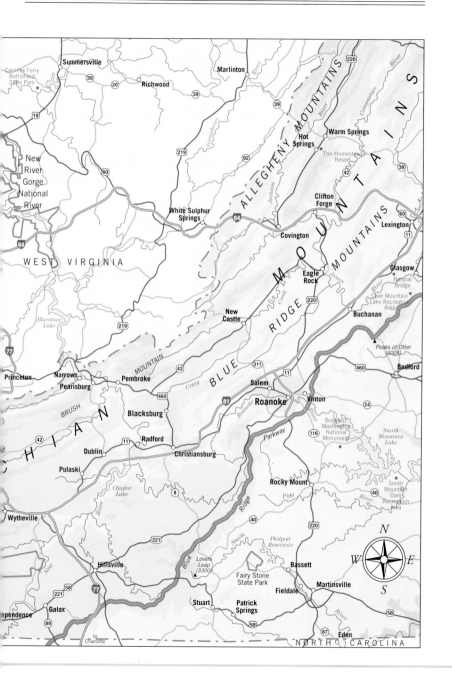

■ CUMBERLAND GAP

In some ways, it's ironic that this area has lapsed back into isolation, because it was through here that the westward-hoing settlers poured on their way to Kentucky and the far wilderness. These days, you have to be just about as determined as they were to get to that famous gateway to the West, the Cumberland Gap. Two-lane, truck-bearing Route 58 shambles for long, tedious miles toward the tip end of the state where lies the gap. For years determined voices have been raised, insisting that good old 58, the only road that travels across the entire width of the state, from coast to mountains, be improved. So far only a small part has been upgraded to four-lane status, and not the part that heads toward the Cumberland Gap.

The gap itself and the surrounding mountains have been proclaimed the **Cumberland Gap National Historical Park,** a long narrow strip lying along the Virginia/Kentucky/Tennessee border. Here, soon after it enters the park and hits the Kentucky border, Route 58 unceremoniously ends, dumping its travelers onto Route 25 E, a superhighway that funnels traffic to the park visitors center. As you round the bends of this freeway, pay attention, because you are actually traveling through the historic gap itself. It's easy to miss, as it seems no more than another twist on the highway, and that is exactly the point. The Cumberland Gap is, and always was, easily traversible, the only natural break in the formidable wall of the Appalachians as they stretch from Maine to Georgia.

Humans have used this pass farther back in time than history records. Before white settlers ever even heard of it, Native Americans were treading the gap in search of game and of each other, as the gap lay along the famous Warrior's Path running from the Potomac River to the Ohio. In 1750 Albemarle County's Dr. Thomas Walker, a neighbor of Thomas Jefferson, explored this break in the mountains. Others came after him, most notably Daniel Boone, a Pennsylvania-born boy with a taste for the wilderness. No great flood of humanity poured through the gap, however, until the 1775 Treaty of Sycamore Shoals brought about peace with hostile tribes in the region. After that, the stampede west began, thanks in large part to Boone. He was hired to build the **Wilderness Road** through the gap and into Kentucky. In three weeks, he and 30 woodsmen had cut the 208-mile (335-km) road that would accommodate pioneers, livestock, and the nation's dreams of manifest destiny.

As the western lands were settled, the Wilderness Road became a commercial thoroughfare for goods and produce moving east as well. By the 1820s and '30s, though, traffic along the gap declined as newly built canals and steamboats offered easier passage. History moved on and left the mountains in peace.

The park service, wisely, hasn't disturbed that peace—not much, anyway. Most of the 200,000 acres of high, green wilderness is accessible only by foot. If you're not a hiker, you can opt for the snaking, four-mile (6.4-km) drive up to 2,440-foot (743-m) **Pinnacle Peak.** From here, the Blue Ridge seems to roll off in waves toward the horizon. If stateline geography appeals to you, you might climb the .9-mile (1.5-km) trail up to Tri-State Peak, and stand (or lie?) simultaneously in Virginia, Kentucky, and Tennessee.

■ BIG STONE GAP

They call Big Stone Gap, near the western edge of that far southwest corner off U.S. 58, the "Gateway to the Coalfields." These days that sobriquet doesn't necessarily ring with commercial or tourist potential, but in the past century, a slogan like that meant a lot. Now a small, unremarkable town, Big Stone Gap is nonetheless the cultural mecca for the Old Dominion's far reaches. The town's arrow-straight streets boast several museums, all of which recount, in one form or another, the gap's blink-of-an-eye heyday.

That occurred in the 1880s, when Northern entrepreneurs descended on the area, ready to exploit its wealth in coal, timber, and iron ore. In a matter of just a few years, the town went from being a little crossroads called Three Forks to Mineral City to Big Stone Gap, a major city and railroad junction for the newly developed mineral fields. The come-here industrialists settled in grandly, putting up ostentatious Victorian mansions on Poplar Hill and bringing all kinds of "culture" to the town. Virtually overnight the gap was being touted as the "Pittsburgh of the South." That name proved a little overzealous. The iron ore here had its own soft, genteel Virginianess—not the kind of stuff to make into steel, or to make of the town a new Pittsburgh. Still, the coal was abundant, and the town flourished into the 1890s. Coal is still king in the outlying hills around Big Stone Gap, in little towns like Appalachia. (Pronounce it with a short second and third "a," or the locals will take you for a know-nothing city slicker.)

(following pages) The town of Monterey, nestled in an Appalachian valley.

FIGHTING ON THE VIRGINIA FRONTIER

After attacks by the French and Indians on the Virginia frontier in 1755, the Virginia militia was in dire need of volunteers. Samuel Davies, a noted Presbyterian educator, made this appeal in 1758, and stimulated such a rush of recruits that some were turned away.

Ye young and hardy men, whose very faces seem to speak that God and nature formed you for soldiers, who are free from the encumbrance of families depending upon you for subsistence, and who are perhaps but of little service to society while at home, may I not speak for you and declare as your mouth, "Here we are, all ready to abandon our ease and rush into the glorious dangers of the field, in defense of our country?" Ye that love your country, enlist, for honor will follow you in life or death in such a cause. You that love your religion, enlist; for your religion is in danger. Can Protestant Christianity expect quarters from heathen savages and French Papists? Sure in such an alliance, the powers of hell make a third party. Ye that love your friends and relations, enlist; lest ye see them enslaved or butchered before your eyes. Ye that would catch at money, here is a proper bait for you— £10 for a few months' service, besides the usual pay of soldiers.

◆ ◆ ◆

Perhaps some may object that should they enter the army their morals would be in danger of infection, and their virtue would be perpetually shocked with horrid scenes of vice . . . I wish I could remove it by giving you a universal assurance that the army is a school of religion and that soldiers, as they are more exposed to death than other men, are proportionably better prepared for it than others. But, alas! the reverse of this is too true; and the contagion of vice and irreligion is perhaps nowhere stronger than in the army; where, one would think, the Supreme Tribunal should be always in view, and it should be their chief care to prepare for eternity, on the slippery brink of which they stand every moment.

But, Gentlemen Officers, I must again appeal to you that, as for this company, you will not willingly allow any form of vice to be practised in it with impunity, but will always endeavor to recommend and enforce religion and good morals by your example and authority and to suppress the contrary.

—Rev. Samuel Davies, *The Curse of Cowardice,* 1758

"Washington on his Mission to Ohio" during the French-Indian War. These early battles gave George Washington the experience necessary to fight the British army in the Revolution years later. (Virginia State Library and Archives)

In an old stone mansion at 10 W. First Street, up on Poplar Hill, the state's **Southwest Virginia Museum** celebrates the town's glory days, explaining how industry quickly came and then just as quickly went. The fine china and clothing, the rich furniture, and the other accouterments of those heady days are exhibited here. So are the tales of the early pioneers who pressed through the area on their way west, as are the quilts and other crafts created by present-day residents. The museum also extols the architecture of the Gilded Age by offering guided walking tours past the mansions of Poplar Hill.

Down in the heart of town, the big attraction revolves around writer John Fox, Jr. A Northerner and later one of Teddy Roosevelt's Rough Riders, Fox was drawn here during the boom days, and he recorded them in his romantic classic, *The Trail of the Lonesome Pine.* All about the unlikely love affair between an educated mining engineer and a local mountain girl, the tale is retold every summer in an outdoor dramatization. Beside the theater on Climpon Avenue is the **June Tolliver House,** where the actual mountain girl lived while attending school in the "big city" (Fox's tale is based loosely on a true story). Now a museum, the Tolliver House consists of a parlor, June's bedroom, and a craft shop. **John Fox's house,** a few blocks away on Shawnee Avenue, is an appealing, low-slung shingle home still decorated with Fox family memorabilia. A block away from it at 112 E. Fifth Street North lies Fox's old library and study, now the **Harry W. Meador Coal Museum,** with mining history and exhibits.

■ Breaks Interstate Park

Buried high in the heart of Appalachia off U.S. 460 is a little jewel of a place called Breaks Interstate Park. With a liberal dash of hyperbole, it bears the designation "Grand Canyon of the South." At 1,600 feet (488 m) deep and five miles (8 km) long, the Breaks canyon does rank as the largest gorge east of the Mississippi.

It's called "interstate park" because the canyon cleaves Pine Mountain as it angles between Virginia and Kentucky. While park lands lie in both states, all the facilities—the pleasant little restaurant and lodge rooms overlooking the gorge, the visitor center, campgrounds, and a small, recreational lake—lie on the Virginia side.

Down in the gorge, the **Russell Fork River** riffles desultorily along, with a patience that over millions of years has carved the gorge out of the soft shale of Pine Mountain. Erosion also produced some fantastic formations, like the

*Coal miners working by candlelight in a Cumberland area mine in 1939.
(Virginia State Library and Archives)*

sandstone-capped Towers and the Chimney, both rising sentinel-like from the canyon floor. Before the gorge became parkland, it served the railroads, and if you stand at one of the several overlooks, you can see the track laid by the Clinchfield Railroad in 1915. It clings to a low bench just above the Russell Fork River and still serves passing coal trains treading this mining country.

The Virginia cliffs above the canyon are hardly the wild place they were when moonshiners hid out here or when the Kentucky Hatfields and McCoys carried their blood feud across the border into this area. The seasons move gracefully above the canyon. In early spring redbud and dogwood dapple the forest, giving way as the season progresses to thickets of white and pink mountain laurel and rhododendron. In fall, the forests here blaze orange and gold, and winter brings an occasional blanket of snow.

Beyond its natural beauty, the Breaks holds the appeal of being deep in the heart of nowhere. To the southeast, **Grundy**, the nearest town as the crow flies, is one of those vestiges of the past. Though not exactly picturesque, it does have a kind of coal-country mystique. Towering tipples, waiting to load coal cars, line the railroad tracks that follow Route 460 as it winds up and through Grundy. The town feels sewn into a long, narrow seam in the mountains, far from the high-tech

Livestock auction in Christianburg.

tones of the encroaching future. While life here may be a little rough, the townspeople are not. That overlay of Virginia hospitality has seeped up out of the ground and given them a softness not found in every state's coal country.

■ ABINGDON

After wandering Virginia's southwest backcountry, stumbling into Abingdon feels like discovering an oasis in the desert. On U.S. 58, off of I-81, Abingdon is compact and cultured, compassing a few broad tree-lined streets graced by big, well-kept homes. Around the old Washington County Courthouse, antique shops, craft shops, and a few galleries proclaim this to be a town with taste.

Many residents attribute Abingdon's good breeding to its most famous feature—the old **Barter Theatre.** Housed in a slightly dilapidated redbrick structure on West Main Street, the theatre has been going strong for 60 years, making it one of the oldest "art spaces" in the country. Far more than a regional playhouse, the Barter counts among its past players Gregory Peck, Hume Cronyn, Ned Beatty, Patricia Neal, Ernest Borgnine, and more.

It all began with necessity. In the midst of the Depression, an aspiring actor and

The Barter Theatre has fostered the careers of many famous actors and acresses.

Appalachian home of Fannie Corbin, photographed by Arthur Rothstein for the Farm Security Administration in the 1930s. (The Chrysler Museum)

native of southwest Virginia named Robert Porterfield found himself in New York City, out of work and hungry. He needed work to eat, as did many of his fellow actors. So why not, he reasoned, open a theater in a rural area where food was plentiful, and instead of charging moneyless local farmers cash for a ticket, let them barter produce for plays? Porterfield chose his native Virginia and a little town called Abingdon to try out his idea. It proved a roaring success. Over the years, such luminaries as Noel Coward and Tennessee Williams have exchanged their playwriting royalties for Virginia hams, and theater-goers from every continent on the globe have come to attend performances at this, the official state theater of Virginia.

Though you have to pay in cash at the Barter these days, the modest ticket price is more than worth the fine performance you'll see. Productions in the old hall range from traditional classics to contemporary dramas. Across the street, the Barter has opened an "adventure theater" in the remains of an old building.

Close by both Barter theaters rises another Abingdon landmark, the **Martha Washington Inn**, located at 150 W. Main Street. The grand old antebellum mansion, affectionately known as "The Martha," has enjoyed a number of incarnations. The prominent Preston family built it in 1832 and lived there until 1858, when the building was transformed into Martha Washington College, a fashionable school for women. That incarnation lasted 70 years, until the college fell on hard times and closed in 1932. A few years later, it reopened as a stylish hotel, and since then its clientele has included presidents and celebrities. In the mid-1980s the hotel was extensively renovated and modernized, though its old-style charm was carefully preserved. The critics of the hotel world have anointed it with multistars and diamonds, but these first-rate ratings pall compared to the classiness of the ghosts that haunt the inn. You'll have to rate these yourself, since poltergeist appeal is a very subjective thing.

At the east end of Abingdon, you can pick up the **Virginia Creeper Trail**, a footpath that winds 34 miles (55 km) from here to Damascus. On its way it passes through serene pastures and deep forests, and crosses bridges above stone-laced riverbeds. The trail follows an old Indian trace that later became a railroad bed through the mountains. Because the steam trains traveling this line had a long, slow pull through rough terrain, they were known as Virginia Creepers. In the 1980s, the Norfolk and Western railroad sold this right-of-way, and the old roadbed entered the post-industrial area of the recreationalist. Now hikers, bikers, joggers, and horse lovers steam along the old path.

Falling Springs in Allegheny County is a popular summer picnic spot.

The Crab Orchard Museum and Pioneer Park sits right beside U.S. 19/460, close to, well, nothing. Yet another cluster of log buildings dedicated to explaining the life of Virginia's early white settlers, this site does have a compelling twist. It's located on a prehistoric hunting ground frequented by Cherokee and Shawnee braves. Archaeological digs here have turned up their stone tools and other artifacts, and modern descendants of the Cherokee have reconstructed the kinds of dwellings used by their ancestors.

■ MOUNT ROGERS NATIONAL RECREATION AREA

Mount Rogers National Recreation Area (or in governmentese, the MRNRA) sprawls across the southeast side of I-81, encompassing 117,000 acres and enclosing Virginia's highest peak, 5,729-foot (1,746-m) Mount Rogers. Under the National Forest Service mandate for multiple use, this wooded land welcomes loggers, hunters, and cattlemen, as well as hikers, skiers, and campers—though there are three pristine and protected wilderness areas. The Appalachian Trail corkscrews through much of the area and across the shoulder of Rogers itself, with a spur trail leading off to its wooded summit. The Virginia Creeper Trail also creeps through the southern end of the MRNRA, so the hiking options here are enticing. Among the roads lacing the area, graveled and twisting Routes 689 and 80, in the south-central region, lead up to Elk Garden and views of Rogers. Forest Service headquarters are located on Route 16, several miles south of the Marion exit off I-81. Information is also available in the visitors center in Wytheville's Fort Chiswell Mall, off I-81.

■ ROANOKE

Roanoke, "Capital of the Blue Ridge," is a pleasure. Lively, upbeat, and innovative, this old railroad town has turned what could have been a passé downtown into an inviting mecca in the mountains. Jefferson Street, the city's main stem, tunnels between the nostalgic architecture of mid-century-style office buildings and storefronts, then opens up unexpectedly onto a vintage Farmer's Market, where produce vendors sell seasonal wares from outdoor stalls. Across from them, the city's old enclosed marketplace operates now as a "food court" and boutique bevy, with clothes that look more West Coast than western Virginia. Loose African and Asian print dresses flutter in shop windows, and there's nary a hound-hunting scene to be found.

The whole flavor of downtown Roanoke is distinctly artsy, thanks in large part to the city's pièce de résistance—its **Center in the Square.** Once an old warehouse, the four-story structure at One Market Square was converted into an arts center in the early 1980s. It now houses a playhouse and three museums in a creative, accessible setting. The **Mill Mountain Theatre** and its Theatre B offer the whole theatrical smorgasbord—new works, comedies, musicals, Shakespeare, and experimental productions. The center's **Science Museum of Western Virginia** gears itself to students and focuses on flora, fauna, ecology, and the stars, attempting to be as interactive as its budget will allow. The **Art Museum of Western Virginia** is slightly misnamed. While it does an admirable job showcasing the works of up-and-coming artists in the Southern Appalachian region, it also displays pieces from all places and times. Finally, the **Roanoke Valley History Museum** starts with the stone age cultures in this area, moves through the days when the place was no more than a salt marsh crossroads called Big Lick, and then into the railroad heyday of the last century. For Center in the Square information call (703) 342-5700.

Railroads and transportation have remained the backbone of the area ever since it became a railroad junction in 1882. Not long after that, the newly created city of Roanoke (the old name, Big Lick, seemed unbecoming a new metropolis) was on its way to becoming the urban hub of the Blue Ridge. It still is that, with a population of about 100,000 and a decidedly forward-looking focus.

A good place to trace the history of railroading here is at the **Virginia Transportation Museum.** Its exhibits include old cars, automobiles, a model circus exhibit, and "the largest collection of diesel engines in the South." Unfortunately, much of the rolling stock displayed in its rail yard can't be boarded, so you have to be content with peering into the windows of old passenger cars and cabooses.

If you drive through Roanoke's **Old Southwest Historic District,** you can get a clear picture of the prosperity that railroading brought to Roanoke. Columned, turreted, verandahed manses dignify the streets of this designated National Historic Area. On the other end of town, an entirely different heritage is celebrated at the **Harrison Museum of African American Culture** (523 Harrison Avenue N.W.). Housed on the ground floor of what served as the first black public high school in western Virginia, the museum devotes itself to the "achievements of

African Americans, especially in Western Virginia . . . and greater knowledge of African American culture." Besides art exhibitions in its two galleries, the museum periodically sponsors performing arts presentations, festivals, and celebrations.

■ BOOKER T. WASHINGTON NATIONAL MONUMENT

The Booker T. Washington National Monument is in stark contrast to the urbane atmosphere of Roanoke. Here, in the countryside 20 miles (32 km) south of the city (on Route 122), tumbling meadowlands ripple off into forests that sweeten the air. The air must have smelled even sweeter in Booker Taliafero Washington's day, but the air would have been all that was sweet for this boy slave. When you visit his birthplace, the old Burrough's tobacco farm, you are struck by the poverty and yearning that must have shaped this great man's early life. Born into slavery in 1856, he lived out his first nine years here, sharing a tiny one-room cabin with his mother and three sisters. Laws barred him from being educated at all, but the boy nonetheless had a desperate yearning to learn. "From the time that I can remember having any thoughts about anything, I recall that I had an intense longing to learn to read." Happily for Washington, he was born on the cusp of change, and when

The Farmers Market in Roanoke (above). The city's skyline (right).

CHILDHOOD IN THE SLAVE QUARTERS

*O*f my ancestry I know almost nothing. In the slave quarters, and even later, I heard whispered conversations among the coloured people of the tortures which the slaves, including, no doubt, my ancestors on my mother's side, suffered in the middle passage of the slave ship while being conveyed from Africa to America. I have been unsuccessful in securing any information that would throw any accurate light upon the history of my family beyond my mother. She, I remember, had a half-brother and a half-sister. In the days of slavery not very much attention was given to family history and family records—that is, black family records. My mother, I suppose, attracted the attention of a purchaser who was afterward my owner and hers. Her addition to the slave family attracted about as much attention as the purchase of a new horse or cow. Of my father I know even less than of my mother. I do not even known his name. I have heard reports to the effect that he was a white man who lived on one of the near-by plantations. Whoever he was, I never heard of his taking the least interest in me or providing in any way for my rearing. But I do not find especial fault with him. He was simply another unfortunate victim of the institution which the Nation unhappily had engrafted upon it at that time.

The cabin was not only our living-place, but was also used as the kitchen for the plantation. My mother was the plantation cook. The cabin was without glass windows; it had only openings in the side which let in the light, and also the cold, chilly air of winter. There was a door to the cabin—that is, something that was called a door—but the uncertain hinges by which it was hung, and the large cracks in it, to say nothing of the fact that it was too small, made the room a very uncomfortable one. In addition to these openings there was, in the lower right-hand corner of the room, the "cat-hole,"—a contrivance which almost every mansion or cabin in Virginia possessed during the ante-bellum period. The "cat-hole" was a square opening, about seven by eight inches, provided for the purpose of letting the cat pass in and out of the house at will during the night. In the case of our particular cabin I could never understand the necessity for this convenience, since there were at least a half-dozen other places in the cabin that would have accommodated the cats. There was no wooden floor in our cabin, the naked earth being used as a floor. In the centre of the earthen floor there was a large, deep opening covered with boards, which was used as a place in which to store sweet potatoes during the winter. An impression of this potato-hole is very distinctly engraved upon my memory, because I recall that during the process of putting the potatoes in and taking them out I would often come into possession of one or two, which I roasted and thoroughly enjoyed. There was no cooking-stove on our plantation, and all the cooking for the whites and slaves my mother had to do over an open fireplace, mostly in pots and "skillets." While the poorly built cabin caused us to suffer with cold in the winter, the heat from the open fireplace in summer was equally trying.

The early years of my life, which were spent in the little cabin, were not very different from those of thousands of other slaves. My mother, of course, had little time in which to give attention to the training of her children during the day. She snatched a few moments for our care in the early morning before her work began, and at night after the day's work was done. One of my earliest recollections is that of my mother cooking a chicken late at night, and awakening her children for the purpose of feeding them. How or where she got it I do not know. I presume, however, it was procured from our owner's farm. Some people may call this theft. If such a thing were to happen now, I should condemn it as theft myself. But taking place at the time it did, and for the reason that it did, no one could ever make me believe that my mother was guilty of thieving. She was simply a victim of the system of slavery. I cannot remember having slept in a bed until after our family was declared free by the Emancipation Proclamation. Three children —John, my older brother, Amanda, my sister, and myself—had a pallet on the dirt floor, or, to be more correct, we slept in and on a bundle of filthy rags laid upon the dirt floor.

—Booker T. Washington,
Up From Slavery, 1901

Booker T. Washington as a young man at Hampton University.
(Hampton University Archives)

the Emancipation Proclamation was read in 1865, Booker and his family found themselves free.

They migrated to Malden, West Virginia, and the boy took work in local salt and coal mines and managed to attend school as well. One day, he overheard miners describing a school devoted to black education in Hampton, Virginia, and the young Washington "resolved at once to go to that school." And so at 16, he took an eastbound stagecoach, heading in the general direction of Virginia. But early in his pilgrimage he ran out of money and took to walking and "begging rides" all the way to Richmond. Here, hungry and penniless, he halted and took work as a dockhand loading pig iron on an outgoing ship. To save money, he slept underneath the board sidewalk, something he recalled years later when he was feted in Richmond as a celebrity.

When he finally made it to the doors of Hampton Normal and Agricultural Institute, he looked, according to his own description, like a tramp. The head teacher apparently had serious doubts about admitting him, and so she set him to cleaning the school's recitation room. This he did—dusting and sweeping it several times before asking her to inspect it. She was impressed enough with his thoroughness to admit him, and he became what he had dreamed of becoming—a student.

In his autobiography, *Up From Slavery,* Washington recounts with humor and grace those hard early years, relating heartfelt stories of slave life and of his new life in Hampton. So different was the one from the other that he confessed he didn't even know how to sleep correctly at the institute. "The sheets were quite a puzzle to me," he recalled. "The first night I slept under both of them, and the second night I slept on top of both of them . . . ."

Once finished with his studies in Hampton, he returned to Malden to teach, then went on for more schooling at the Wayland Institute in Washington, D.C. In 1879, his mentor in Hampton, Samuel Armstrong, called him back to help in the institute's experiment to educate American Indians. After two years of teaching at the Institute, Armstrong approached Washington with another project. A new black school was being established in Tuskegee, Alabama, and the search was on to find someone to head it. Would Washington like to be considered?

Tuskegee Institute became Booker T. Washington's life work. Over the course of 30-some years, he took it from classes held in what he called a "shanty" to a distinguished institution. In the process, he established his own reputation as a leading educator and social thinker. As much as his life and accomplishments have been written about and recorded, nothing leaves quite such a lasting impression of the man as a trip to his birthplace.

The monument, like most park service projects, is faithful to the facts. Split rail fences bound the pastures where the Burroughs family once farmed and where Washington lived as an impoverished slave. This was a modest tobacco farm of only 206 acres and the owners themselves lived in a small house whose foundations have been outlined in stone. A re-creation of the chinked-log Washington cabin is situated nearby, dirt floored and grimly dark inside. Off below the houses stands a horse barn, and livestock area. The stock, by the way, is truly live (horses, chickens, etc.), and the park service also maintains a vegetable and tobacco plot. Inside the small visitors center, a slide presentation does an affecting job of chronicling the life of this exemplary Virginian.

■ THE HOMESTEAD

In the last century, the hills of Virginia cosseted a dozen different spa resorts, where the weary, the ailing, or simply the indulgent came to soothe their aching bones in warm mineral waters. Many of these old resorts closed their doors or burnt down long ago. A few were retrofitted as modern nursing homes or retreats. Happily, though, the great grande dame of them all has managed to survive into the present.

An immense and awesome brick edifice ensconced in the heart of the Alleghenies, The Homestead reigns over—or more precisely, is the raison d'être for—the little village of Hot Springs. Skirted by iridescent green golf courses, the resort is probably best described in the words of Lyndon Johnson, who commented something to the effect of, "My God, what a spread." In all, the spread covers some 15,000 acres, taking in tennis courts, swimming pools, riding trails, skeet and trap shooting fields, ski runs, mineral bath spas, and even wooded nature trails. Oh, yes, and three 18-hole golf courses, one designed by Robert Trent Locke. The resident pro, by the way, is none other than Sam Snead, a local boy who grew up in Bath County.

The Homestead Resort is the largest of Virginia's mountain getaways.

For all that, The Homestead does not rest on a reputation of overstated hauteur. There remains something downhome about it all. The verandah along the entrance feels like a front porch, complete with a line of rockers facing out on the view. The old lobby, where tea and chamber music are served up every afternoon, stretches in a long corridor of wing-backed chairs and Corinthian columns, reminiscent of the spas of yesteryear. As one journalist perspicaciously put it, there are no waterfalls in the lobby here.

Pools, of course, are what gave impetus to this living legend of a place. As far back as the sixteenth century, Native Americans apparently had discovered the healing waters of the area's hot springs. Tradition holds that a young brave, traveling between the western Appalachians and the coast, discovered a shallow pool of warm water hereabouts on a rainy night. He curled up in its warmth and slept the night, waking renewed and invigorated. Naturally, he spread the word about these healing waters and others passing through stopped to bathe in them.

Early in the 1700s, white explorers filtered into the area, but they did little to settle what is now Hot Springs. Not until the 1760s was a rustic guest lodge called The Homestead put up. It never amounted to much until the 1830s, when a Dr. Thomas Goode arrived on the scene. From a well-established Virginia family, the good doctor took the reins of development, enlarged the old hotel, built cabins

Warm Springs was a resort as early as 1800.

and bathhouses, and began to attract the "right kind of people" from as far away as Philadelphia.

With the war, the hotel became a Confederate hospital, but at war's end, it re-established its reputation as a watering hole for the well-heeled, and by the twentieth century Vanderbilts, Rockefellers, and Fords were entertaining here. In 1901, the charming old clapboard hotel, with its wraparound porches, burned to the ground, a fate that overtook so many hotels of that era. The new brick structure that began to go up within a year is still part of the current hotel today, with a great deal of additions and modifications, including its hallmark tower. One remarkable feature remaining from that era is the gracious old indoor tiled pool, built in 1903. Light pouring into it from surrounding windows creates an almost ethereal atmosphere.

For decades The Homestead had its own dairy, raised its own livestock, and grew its own vegetables to supply the dining room. Those inhouse luxuries, however, are long gone, which is too bad because the food in the dining room has reverted to uninspired, resort-style fare. From 1891 to late 1993 the place remained a homegrown affair, under the direction of the Ingalls family. They had become its owners after the good Dr. Goode and had shepharded the old resort through its twentieth-century heyday. The Ingalls family has recently turned control of The Homestead over to a Dallas-based conglomerate, Club Resorts, Inc.

Perhaps The Homestead's most original offering lies five miles (8 km) north of the main complex, in the hamlet of **Warm Springs.** Long ago eclipsed by the glamour of nearby Hot Springs, Warm Springs nonetheless came to fame first. Settled in 1727, it was a bustling little place by mid-century, and by 1800 a sought-after resort. The mineral waters attracted all sorts of Virginians, including Thomas Jefferson. Against common sense, he once spent two hours in the baths and emerged believing that his health, far from being improved, had been permanently impaired by the experience.

In those days, taking the waters was a segregated affair for men and women, with the gentlemen and ladies switching off every two hours. Today, it's still segregated, which encourages a more "natural," less encumbered bathing experience. For the modest, of course, bathing suits are an option, as is the quaint costume called the Mother Hubbard romper suit. Provided to ladies free of charge, these slip-on one-piece pantalets recall the days when Mrs. Robert E. Lee came here to take the waters for her crippling arthritis. The chair in which they lowered her is still on display inside the bathhouse.

About the bathhouse, or bathhouses: These two simple octagonal clapboards charm with an aged beauty. The men's spa dates back to 1761 and the women's to 1836. No more than structures built above large mineral pools, they are filled with streaming natural light that pierces the waist-to-chest-deep water and highlights the natural colors of the stones lining the floor of the pools. The water temperature here hovers around 96 degrees (35°C), so winter bathing feels fine, though the undressing and dressing process can be a little chilly in the unheated dressing rooms that rim the pools.

(following pages) Winter snows occasionally blanket the entire state; however, they're not so common in this Tidewater town of Reedville.

MR. FRANK'S ENCOUNTER

One winter weekend in the late 1920s Frank Schairer and his friend Charlie Williams were hiking in the mountains, chatting with the people they met along the way. Both men were active members of the Potomac Appalachian Trail Club which at that time was constructing the Appalachian Trail and side trails through the Blue Ridge. An experience they had on this hike was still a vivid memory nearly four decades later. Schairer recounted the story at the fortieth anniversary celebration of the Potomac Appalachian Trail Club in 1967:

All of a sudden around a sharp bend in the trail came two mountaineers. One was an older man with a white beard, and the other was a younger man carrying a gunny sack in which it was quite obvious there were four two-quart jars of corn liquor. So we just sat there. And there was an awkward pause. And then the conversation got going as they do in the great circle of the mountains. . . .

You start with the weather . . . And the next thing you talk about is the crops, which are important to the mountain people, for if the crops are bad they might starve. And then the talk was about illness, miseries, as they called it. And about that time everybody was sick, with inadequate food and inadequate housing, and so forth. And then another adequate topic of conversation was this proposed Shenandoah National Park, was that all nonsense or was it going through . . . And we got back to the weather; if it was a good day, it was a good day for a drink; or if it was a bad day, we needed a drink.

And the fellow says, "Do you fellows ever drink?"

And I said, "I don't mind if I do."

And he brought out a two-quart fruit jar.

Charlie is a nice guy, but he doesn't drink. It was the most embarrassing thing in the world. I rushed up to Charlie and grabbed the two-quart fruit jar. I nearly knocked him down. I swung the fruit jar up, took a swig, and swung it down again, and I said, "Charlie doesn't drink, but I drink for him." And I took another swig.

So they thought it was so cute that I got Charlie's drink. And then there was an awkward pause. And it suddenly dawned on me that I had a drink in my pack, and I said, "Won't you have a drink of my liquor?"

And I went over to get it out of my pack . . . pulled out this pint thermos bottle and handed it to the fellow. And he took a drink and he looked very startled. He took another little drink and he handed it back. I put it back in the pack and tied up the pack and we sat down and there was an awkward pause.

Then the old fellow said, "I can tell you where you-all got that liquor."

And I said, "You can?"

And he said, "Yes. That is Hazel Hollow liquor." (And Hazel Hollow was about 30 or 40 miles to the north.)

And I said, "Yes?"

And he said, "I can tell you who made that liquor."

And I said, "Can you?"

And he said, "That is Jack Dodson's liquor. And I can tell you when you got that liquor."

"How can you tell me that? When I got it, it was in a two-quart jar." (But he was right all the time.)

And he looks at me and said, "You must be Mr. Frank."

Here I give a guy a drink of liquor and he tells me my name! And I said, "Would you mind telling me how you do it?"

He said, "Each hollow has its own formula. There is only one make of liquor in Hazel Hollow, and this is Jack's. And Jack has only made three batches this year. The first batch he was terribly thirsty, so he let the batch burn. It couldn't have been that, because it was burned. And having burned the first batch he was terribly cautious, and the second batch was perfect."

(That was the batch I had. In fact, it was so good that word got around and it lasted only three days. So he knew within three days when I bought it.)

"It couldn't have been the third batch, because he stored it. And Jack never sells any of his liquor to anybody outside the mountains but this fellow Frank, and so you must be Mr. Frank."

—Carolyn and Jack Reeder, *Shenandoah Heritage,* 1920s

(following pages) A bucolic view along the Colonial Parkway between Jamestown and Yorktown.

PRACTICAL INFORMATION

■ AREA CODES

The area code for the southeastern third of Virginia is 804; the rest of the state uses 703.

■ GETTING THERE

Virginia has major domestic and international airports in Norfolk, Richmond, Loudoun, and between Alexandria and Arlington (National Airport). Amtrak has a line that runs north-south from Alexandria to Newport News, and east-west from Washington, D.C., to Chicago, making stops in northern, central, and western Virginia along the way. Greyhound-Trailways buses also serve much of the state.

■ WEATHER

Virginia's climate is relatively temperate and predictable. The greatest shock to travelers' systems here is the humidity, which makes summers feel hotter and winters colder than the actual temperatures warrant. The humidity is, naturally, higher in coastal areas, though the mountains too tend to be plenty moist. The coastal areas also have milder winters, because of the moderating effects of the ocean and bay.

Spring and fall are the optimum seasons, though heavy rains can occur in either of them. Summers are unrelentingly hot, winters unpredictable. Some years, the state gets several serious snowfalls and extremely cold temperatures; other years winters are quite moderate. Obviously, the higher elevations experience more snow and lower temperatures than the rest of the state.

In general, daytime temperatures average as follows. Winter: 30 degrees to low 40s; Spring: 60 degrees to low 80s; Summer: 80s and 90s; Fall: 50s to low 70s.

CITY	FAHRENHEIT TEMPERATURE			PRECIPITATION	
	Jan. Avg. High/Low	July Avg. High/Low	Record High/Low	Avg. Annual	Avg. Snow
Alexandria	43 28	88 70	106 -15	41.74"	17"
Charlottesville	45 27	87 67	107 -9	45.22"	24"
Norfolk	48 32	87 70	105 -3	40.45"	8"
Richmond	47 27	88 67	107 -12	40.80"	15"
Roanoke	44 27	85 64	105 -12	40.80"	8"
Big Stone Gap	41 22	81 59	97 -26	50.34"	60"

■ ACCOMMODATIONS

Virginia has the typical collection of roadside motels, and you'll never find yourself in a location too remote to find one of these. In addition, however, the state offers an impressive collection of Bed & Breakfasts and small inns, particularly in the northwest and Shenandoah Valley. Most of these are truly charming, and many are housed in historic structures. Antiques and Virginia hospitality predominate in almost all of them.

The state offers a **reservation service** through a toll-free number (800) 934-9184 or (202) 659-5523. You can also stop by for information or to make reservations at the Virginia Tourism Office located at 1629 K St. NW in Washington, D.C. Inns and B&Bs in the Charlottesville area also can be accessed through a private, and extensive, reservation service called Guesthouse Bed & Breakfast; Box 5737, Charlottesville, 22905; (804) 979-7264.

Prices
Prices based on double occupancy, per night, are indicated as follows:

B (Budget): up to $50; **M** (Medium): $50 to $100;
E (Expensive): $100 to $150; **L** (Luxury): $150 to $200;
XL (Extra-luxurious): over $200

■ ABINGDON

Martha Washington Inn. Once a private home, then a women's college, this historic four-star place maintains an antebellum grace in its small but elaborate parlors and well-appointed rooms, some with fireplaces. 150 W. Main St., (800) 533-1014. **M-XL**

Pete Sheffey, bell captain at the Martha Washington Inn in Abingdon for over 30 years.

Summerfield Inn. In this part of the state, the prices are lower but the quality isn't. This charming 1920s Virginia home, within a couple of blocks of the Barter Theatre, features fine antiques and an exceptionally competent innkeeper. Terry-cloth guest robes and breakfasts served on fine china are among the inn's memorable touches. 101 W. Valley St., (703) 628-5905. **M**

■ ALEXANDRIA

The Morrison House. In the heart of historic Old Town Alexandria, this newly built, elegant reproduction of a Federal-style house blends old charms with new amenities, like marble-tiled bathrooms. 116 S. Alfred St., (800) 367-0800. **E-XL**

■ CHARLES CITY

Edgewood Plantation. Built in 1849 and once part of Berkeley Plantation, this old Carpenter's Gothic clapboard is stuffed with Victorian antiques and a kind of *Gone With the Wind* atmosphere. Perfectly situated for visiting the nearby James River plantations. 4800 John Tyler Memorial Hwy. (Rte.5), (804) 829-2962. **M-E**

North Bend Plantation. This fine old Greek Revival home, in plantation country, is itself an early 1800s plantation and continues to function as a working farm. What the hostelry lacks in sumptuousness, it makes up for in history, authenticity, and the hospitality of its owners. 12200 Weyanoke Rd., (804) 829-5176 (call after 5 P.M.). **M-E**

■ CHARLOTTESVILLE AND ALBEMARLE

Boar's Head Inn. Considered the area's most upscale resort, this 1830s grist mill-turned-inn is now surrounded by new Colonial-style clapboards and courts a distinctly hunt-country tone. Rte. 250, (804) 296-2181. **L**

Clifton. Though this columned, clapboard home has plenty of history behind it (it was built by Jefferson's son-in-law Thomas Randolph), it nonetheless has a comfortable, lived-in feel and such twentieth-century charms as a lap pool and tennis court. Rooms in the main house are more traditional, while suites in the dependencies are done in Malibu style. Rte. 13, Box 26. (804) 971-1800. **E-L**

High Meadows Inn. Out in the pleasant, rural town of Scottsville, this B&B combines an eclectic mix of Italianate, Federal, and late-Victorian styles—and comes up with a particularly appealing result. On request, owners will fix afternoon and evening "meals in a basket" that you can enjoy in your room. Rte. 4, Box 6, Scottsville, (804) 286-2218. **M-E**

Prospect Hill. This elegant frame home claims the distinction of being the oldest continuously occupied frame manor house in the state. Victorianized since its colonial days, it offers five pleasant rooms in the main house and six stunning dependencies, with such touches as whirlpools and large Palladian windows. Dinner is served to those desiring it with formal, but inspiring, ceremony. Rte. 3, Box 430, Trevilians, (800) 277-0844. **E-L**

The Silver Thatch Inn. At the center of this semicircular compound of buildings north of Charlottesville is an old log structure built by Hessian prisoners during the Revolution. The inn's pleasant guest rooms offer antiques, comforters, and, in some cases, fireplaces. 3001 Hollymead Dr., (804) 978-4686. **E**

200 South Street. The small hotel is well situated for rambling through Charlottesville's pedestrians-only downtown, and sampling its wide array of fine restaurants. Actually two Victorian houses filled with European antiques and contemporary art, the hotel offers some rooms with whirlpools and fireplaces. 200 South St., (804) 979-0200. **M-E**

■ CHINCOTEAGUE

The Channel Bass Inn. The rambling, unpretentious inn belies an interior filled with sybaritic pleasures: seven guest rooms with original art, fine linens and thick towels, plus an exceptional restaurant. 100 Church St., (804) 336-6148. **E-XL**

Miss Molly's. With its back to the Chincoteague channel and its front to Main Street, the simple rambling house is decorated in pleasant, unfussy decor appropriate to an island hostelry. Writer Marguerite Henry forever honored the house by staying here while writing the island classic, *Misty.* 113 N. Main St., (804) 336-6686. **M-E**

■ COVINGTON

Milton Hall Bed & Breakfast Inn. In the Allegheny Mountains, this English country manor offers rural delights and fine accommodations. 207 Thorny Lane, (703) 965-0196. **M-E**

■ F A I R F A X

The Bailiwick Inn. The old Greek Revival townhouse offers distinguished hospitality and pleasant decor in its 13 guest rooms. In the middle of historic Fairfax County Courthouse, the inn itself is preserved from, though surrounded by, the sprawl of Northern Virginia suburbia. 4023 Chain Bridge Rd., (800) 366-7666. **E**

■ H A R R I S O N B U R G

Joshua Wilton House. This fine old Queen Anne cottage offers lovely Victorian guest rooms, elegant breakfasts, and a central location for exploring the Shenandoah Valley and Blue Ridge. 412 S. Main St., (703) 434-4464. **M**

■ H O T   S P R I N G S

The Homestead. Virginia's grande-dame resort has been a first-rate hostelry for better than a century. The mammoth town-in-a-town offers three golf courses, hiking and riding trails, skiing, tennis, ice-skating, spas, and a sense of Virginia hospitality. Rates are MAP or European plan. Hot Springs, (800) 336-5771. **XL**

■ I R V I N G T O N

Tides Inn. This upscale resort on the banks of Carter's Creek has long been a favorite with old-school Richmonders and other Virginians who want to be pampered in tradition style. The resort particularly caters to golfers and their kind of socializing. Rates are MAP. Route 200, (800) TIDESIN. **XL**

■ L E E S B U R G

Fleetwood Farm B&B. The historic old farmhouse, in Loudoun county horse country, dates to 1745. Though the exterior, surrounded by fields of grazing sheep, is pleasantly unpretentious, the interior gleams with polished wood and brass, and rooms have all the charms of past and present. Sumptuous breakfasts include products from the owners' own gardens. Rte. 1, Box 306A, (703) 327-4325. **M-L**

The Norris House. An elegant Federal-style inn in the heart of downtown Leesburg, the place is noted for such touches as its wild-cherry bookcases and fresh flowers. 108 Loudoun St. SW, (703) 777-1806. **M-E**

(following pages) Rounding up the wild ponies of Chincoteague.

■ L U R A Y

The Ruffner House. This historic manor, built over 200 years ago in the foothills of the Blue Ridge and Massanutten mountains, has been elegantly restored. It features period antiques, house-cooked breakfasts, a pool, and horses pastured on the grounds. Box 620, Rte. 4, Luray, (703) 743-7855. **B-E**

■ L Y N C H B U R G

Langhorne Manor. This neoclassical home in the Diamond Hill Historic District features period furnishings and a fine sense of its antebellum past. 313 Washington St., (804) 846-4667. **M**

Lynchburg Mansion Inn. The impressive Spanish Georgian Mansion, with its columned porte-cochere and soaring grand hall, recalls life in Lynchburg's glory days, early in this century. Rooms are well-appointed, with many modern conveniences; breakfasts are served on fine china and silver. 405 Madison St., (800) 352-1199. **M-E**

■ M I D D L E B U R G

The Red Fox Inn. Built in the 1720s, the old yellow fieldstone inn has witnessed a lot of historic goings-on. Its tavern today is often frequented by the area's horsey set, as well as passing tourists. The inn's quieter rooms are located in two annexes —the Stray Fox Inn and the McConnell House. Rte. 50, Box 385, (800) 223-1728. **E-XL**

Welbourne. This ancestral antebellum house, built in 1775, is located in hunt country, with six rooms available in the house itself and two cottages outside. Included are large southern breakfasts. Rte 1, Box 300, Middleburg, 22117, (703) 687-3201. **M**

■ M I D D L E T O W N

Wayside Inn. A hostelry since the eighteenth century, this lovely old inn maintains its charm with antiques, art, and Colonial-style cuisine in the dining room. 7783 Main St., (703) 869-1797. **M-L**

■ M O N T E R E Y

Highland Inn. The turn-of-the-century inn stands in the quiet little Allegheny foothill town of Monterey, "Virginia's Switzerland." The inns broad Eastlake porches are lined with rocking chairs, and rooms feature antiques and a pleasant coziness. Main St., (703) 468-2143. **M**

■ **NELLYSFORD**

Trillium House. Only a couple of miles from the Wintergreen Resort complex, this rambling frame building, built in 1983, offers simply furnished rooms and an impressive Great Room, where guests gather to chat and read. Box 280, (800) 325-9126. **M-E**

■ **NEW CHURCH**

The Garden and the Sea. This B&B in the little hamlet of New Church features Victorian decor in its two guest rooms and a place to relax, as the name promises, near the sea. Box 275, (804) 824-0672. **M-E**

■ **NORFOLK**

The Page House Inn. Set in the Ghent Historic District and close to major attractions, the Georgian Revival home is decorated in antiques and offers amenities such as whirlpool baths and a European soaking tub. Full breakfasts are served on fine china. 323 Fairfax Ave., (804) 625-5033. **M**

■ **ORANGE**

Mayhurst. On a hill above the charming town of Orange, this white Italianate villa is an architectural play of cupolas, porticoes, and gables set amid 36 rolling acres. Box 707, (703) 672-5597. **E**

The Shadows. Near Montpelier, President Madison's home, this American Craftsman-style bungalow of wood and fieldstone is a refreshing change from the typical Colonial or Victorian decor. Huge breakfasts are part of the big-hearted hospitality here. 14291 Constitution Hwy., (703) 672-5057. **M**

■ **PARIS**

The Ashby Inn. A true country inn, this one is nestled in the picturesque hamlet of Paris and offers antique beds, quilts, and a pleasantly simple tone. Hefty breakfasts are included in the room price, and the inn is famous for its fabulous dinner cuisine. Rte. 1, Box 2A, (703) 592-3900. **M-L**

■ REEDVILLE

Cedar Grove. Looking out across the Chesapeake Bay, this Colonial Revival home offers formal Victorian furnishings, tennis, croquet, and a taste of bayside living. Full breakfasts are served on fine china and silver. Rte. 1, Box 2535, (804) 453-3915. **M-E**

■ RICHMOND

The Emmanuel Hutzler House. A classic Monument Avenue mansion, this Italian Renaissance jewel features such architectural details as a mahogany-paneled living room. 2036 Monument Ave., (804) 353-6900. **E**

Linden Row Inn. At the west edge of downtown, within walking distance of the capitol, this series of connected, Greek Revival townhouses were built in 1847 and retain their nineteenth-century charm. Though the inn has 71 rooms, it feels intimate, especially in its small parlor/lobby. 100 E. Franklin St., (800) 348-7424. **M-E**

Jefferson Grand Heritage Hotel. This famous turn-of-the-century hotel at the edge of downtown has been restored to its past splendor, with sweeping staircases, polished marble, and gleaming chandeliers. This is a memorable, wonderful place to stay. The tasteful guest rooms feature reproduction antiques, and guests are embraced by Southern hospitality. Franklin and Adams Sts., (800) 424-8014. **E**

■ SPERRYVILLE

The Conyers House. More or less in the middle of nowhere, this fine old clapboard was built as a country store in the early 1800s and now serves as a hostelry for hikers climbing Old Rag and weekenders looking for an indulgent getaway. The seven inviting guest rooms all have fireplaces, and if you arrange in advance, the owners will prepare a multicourse gourmet dinner for you. Rte 1, Box 157, Slate Mills Rd., (703) 987-8025. **E-L**

■ STANLEY

Jordan Hollow Farm. Set amid 45 acres of rolling fields, the 200-year-old farmhouse, built partially of chinked logs, still serves as the hub of a working horse farm. The main attraction here are the trail rides offered daily to guests. Rte. 626, (703) 778-2209 or 2285. **M-E**

■ STAUNTON

Bell Grae Inn. Set in a renovated Victorian manse just a few blocks from Staunton's downtown, this inn offers a mix of antiques and latter-day comforts, such as thick carpeting and luxurious bathrooms. 515 W. Frederick St., (703) 886-5151. **M-E**

The Sampson Eagon Inn. This classic antebellum inn features antiques, including canopied beds, and a location convenient to Staunton's historic sites and fine old neighborhoods. 238 E. Beverly St., (800) 597-9722. **E**

■ WARM SPRINGS

The Inn at Gristmill Square. As its name implies, this hostelry occupies part of a restored mill and blacksmith shop in the little burg of Warm Springs, just down the road from the renowned Homestead resort. Rooms are cozy and close by the famous old antebellum bath houses at Warm Springs, where you can take the waters for whatever ails you. Rte. 645, (703) 839-2231. **M**

■ WASHINGTON

The Inn at Little Washington. Best known for its elegant cuisine, this lovely old inn also offers guest rooms with decor by Joyce Evans, whose theatrical design

The Inn at Gristmill Square in Warm Springs.

background shows up in wonderfully fantastical touches. In the countryside below the Blue Ridge, the inn is a fine place to enjoy natural scenery and more sybaritic pleasures. Middle and Main Sts., (703) 675-3800. **XL**

■ WATERFORD

The Pink House. Pink it is and decidedly homey, and, most appealing of all, it occupies the heart of Waterford, one of Virginia's most charming villages. The house holds two guest suites, both with fireplaces and one with its own baby grand piano. Waterford, (703) 882-3453. **M**

■ WHITE POST

L'Auberge Provencale. Best known as for its outstanding French restaurant, the Victorianized, mid-eighteenth-century stone house also houses nine guest rooms, all decorated with classic French flair. Box 119, (703) 837-1375. **E-L**

■ WILLIAMSBURG

Liberty Rose Situated on a wooded knoll a mile from the historic area, this clapboard B&B is filled with romantic touches, such as a floor taken from an old plantation and an eclectic mix of antiques. 1022 Jamestown Rd., (804) 253-1260. **M-L**

Williamsburg Inn. This elegant establishment, a block from Duke of Gloucester Street, offers hospitality in the high style. Rooms are decorated in English Regency decor and the tone in general is decidedly formal. The inn and its owner, Colonial Williamsburg, also offer rooms in historic houses and taverns throughout the historic area. 136 E. Francis St., (800) 447-8679. **L-XL**

■ WINTERGREEN

Wintergreen Resort. This 10,000-acre resort at the edge of the Blue Ridge features upscale condominiums and the Mountain Inn, two championship golf courses, 25 tennis courts, six pools, miles of hiking and horseback riding trails, an equestrian center, and one of the South's best downhill ski complexes. Rte. 151, (800) 325-2200. **E-L**

■ WOODSTOCK

The Inn at Narrow Passage. Hugging the North Fork of the Shenandoah River, this log inn, with its huge fireplace, is the place to come to rusticate. After a hearty breakfast, guests can tube, fish, or swim along the river. The three guest rooms in the original building are far more charming than the nine rooms in the new wing. Rte. 11S, (703) 459-8000. **M**

■ RESTAURANTS

Seafood is Virginia's special forté, and almost any restaurant will offer some kind of fish or shellfish. What the state is not noted for is its diversity of authentic ethnic cuisines. Of course, every town has its American version of Italian and Chinese eateries, but only in Northern Virginia, and somewhat in Charlottesville, will you find a healthy selection of true Asian, Mediterranean, and Latin American restaurants.

Prices
Prices for complete meal (entrée, drink, dessert or appetizer):

B (Budget): under $10; **M** (Medium): $10 to $20;
E (Expensive): $20 and up

■ A B I N G D O N

Martha Washington Inn. Upscale dining in the area's classiest inn. Menu includes such treats as roast quail and mountain trout stuffed with crabmeat. 150 W. Main St., (703) 628-3161. **E**

The Tavern. In a cozy, old historic building, it offers well-prepared fresh seafood, cornish hen and rack of lamb. 222 E. Main St., (703) 628-1118. **M**

■ A L E X A N D R I A / A R L I N G T O N

Cafe Dalat. Probably the most well-respected restaurant in this area of Asian eateries, the cafe specializes in well-prepared Vietnamese noodle and seafood dishes. 3143 Wilson Blvd., (703) 276-0935. **B**

Duangrat's Thai Restaurant. Critically acclaimed for its Thai food, this restaurant occupies an unlikely building ensconsed in the strip centers of deepest suburbia. 5878 Leesburg Pike, (703) 820-5775. **M**

Le Gaulois. Offers French country cuisine, in a classy but simple bistro setting. Specialties include cassoulets and rich stews. 1106 King St., (703) 739-9494. **M**

Peking Gourmet. This cavernous, old-fashioned Chinese restaurant, located in the 1950s-style Culmore shopping plaza, offers the best Peking duck this side of, well, Peking. Beware, however, that other offerings are somewhat bland by current standards. 6029-33 Leesburg Pike, (703) 671-8088. **M**

Santa Fe East. A fun, funky two-story eatery offering all kinds of Tex-Mex fare. 110 Pitt St. S, (703) 548-6900. **B-M**

RT's. Also in an unlikely location in a rundown shopping area, this popular, up-scale place offers innovative entrées amid friendly, but professional service and pleasant decor. 3804 Mount Vernon Ave., (703) 684-6010. **M**

■ CHINCOTEAGUE

Channel Bass Inn. One of the state's most respected seafood restaurants, the fresh fish and shellfish are prepared with true gourmet finesse. All this skill comes at a price, however, so be prepared to pay handsomely. 6228 Church St., (804) 336-6148. **E**

■ CHARLOTTESVILLE AND ALBEMARLE

C&C Restaurant. Housed near the old train depot downtown, this starkly classy restaurant is renowned for its elegant French cuisine. Downstairs an informal bistro offers lighter fare, still finely prepared. 515 E. Water St., (804) 971-7044. **E**

Crozet Pizza. Now a county landmark, this family-run restaurant in the little town of Crozet easily has the best pizza in the state, with innovative fresh-vegetable toppings, as well as stand-bys like pepperoni, anchovies, etc. On weekends, make a reservation at least a day in advance—even for carry out! Rte. 240, (804) 823-2132. **M**

Eastern Standard. Imaginative nouvelle entrées characterize this upscale restaurant. Their downstairs bistro menu includes pasta and less sumptuous offerings. Downtown Mall, (804) 295-8668. **E**

■ HAMPTON

Fisherman's Wharf. Overlooking Hampton Creek, this cavernous old building now sports nautical decor, and an extensive seafood buffet. 14 Ivy Home Rd., (804) 723-3313. **M**

■ LEXINGTON

Maple Hall. A former plantation house offering elegant dining, and classic veal, beef, and chicken entrées. Outdoor patio open in good weather. Rte. 11, (703) 463-4666. **E**

Menhadden fishermen hauling in the catch from a smaller "purse" boat on Chesapeake Bay.

The Palms. In a converted Victorian ice cream parlor with pressed metal ceilings, the Palms offers well-prepared soups, charbroiled meats, and chicken. 101 W. Nelson St., (703) 463-7911. **B**

■ **L U R A Y**

Parkhurst Inn. Pleasant inn atmosphere with gourmet menu that includes veal Oscar and roast duck. Good selection of Virginia wines. Rte. 211 W, (703) 743-6009. **M-E**

■ **N E W P O R T N E W S**

Herman's Harbor House. Tucked into a residential area, this place is famous for its crab cakes, though it also offers other fine seafood and meat dishes. 663 Deep Creek Rd., (804) 930-1000. **M**

■ **N O R F O L K**

Freemason Abbey Restaurant and Tavern. Lobster and prime rib are specialties at this restaurant in the city's Waterside area. Housed in an old church, the place offers views of the river. 333 Waterside Dr., (804) 627-4400. **M**

La Galleria. Surrounded by Italian urns and columns, diners at this impressive restaurant are treated to perfectly prepared pastas and other well-prepared entrées. 120 College Pl., (804) 623-3939. **E**

The Ship's Cabin. Seafood, of course, is the focus in this well-known Norfolk establishment. To complement the menu and decor, some tables overlook Chesapeake Bay. 4110 E. Ocean View Ave., (804) 362-4659. **E**

■ **R I C H M O N D**

Amici Ristorante. The classic, northern Italian cuisine here includes calamari, pastas, quail, duck, and veal. 3343 W. Cary St., (804) 353-4700. **M**

The Frog and the Red Neck. Part of the new Richmond, this restaurant focuses on nouvelle presentations of seafood, pastas, and meats amid an informal, engagingly trendy atmosphere and very competent staff. The crème brulée is a knock-out here. 1423 E. Cary St., (804) 648-3764. **M**

Joe's Inn. At this Fan district eatery, the focus is on spaghetti, served Greek-style with melted feta and provolone cheese. 205 N. Shields Ave., (804) 355-2282. **B**

Mr. Patrick Henry's Inn. A nineteenth-century atmosphere permeates the dining rooms in these two joined houses, which function now as both a well-respected inn and restaurant. Try their crisp roast duck and crab cakes in puff pastry. 2300 E. Broad St., (804) 644-1322. **E**

■ **R O A N O K E**

The Homeplace. Down-home fried chicken, mashed potatoes, beans, and hot biscuits are featured here. Rte. 311 N, near Salem, (703) 384-7252. **M**

La Maison du Gourmet. In a 1920s Georgian Colonial home, the restaurant offers superb veal, chicken and lamb. 5732 Airport Rd., (703) 366-2444. **M-L**

■ **T A N G I E R   I S L A N D**

Hilda Crockett's Chesapeake House. Literally in a house, this landmark restaurant serves up true down-home Bay cuisine at long, family-style tables. Platters of crab cakes, clam fritters, vegetables, and home-baked breads keep on coming. (804) 891-2331. **M**

■ **W A R M   S P R I N G S**

Waterwheel Restaurant. Part of a charmingly restored gristmill complex, it features a walk-in wine cellar, with an extensive wine collection. Changing menu features nouvelle offerings with local ingredients. Gristmill Square, (703) 839-2231. **E**

■ **W A S H I N G T O N**

The Inn at Little Washington. Though it's a good ways from the Washington suburbs, this inn's reputation for stellar cuisine draws crowds from the metropolitan area into the countryside. The decor, like the food, is whimsically elegant. Middle and Main Sts., (703) 675-3800. **E**

■ **W I L L I A M S B U R G**

Regency Room. Elegance marks both the decor and cuisine in the dinning room of the Williamsburg Inn. Rack of lamb, lobster bisque and similar classics are impeccably served under the glow of crystal chandeliers. S. Francis St., (804) 229-1000. **E**

The Trellis. Because it's at the edge of the historic buildings, this fine restaurant can break with the omnipresent Colonial and offer a California decor and more innovative nouvelle cuisine, as well as an eclectic wine selection. Merchants Square, (804) 229-8610. **E**

(following pages) The "Grand Illumination" at the magazine in Williamsburg.

■ **Y O R K T O W N**

Nick's Seafood Pavilion. Long a peninsula tradition, this rambunctious Greek-owned restaurant on the Yorktown waterfront offers fabulous seafood, salads, baked Alaska and baklava desserts, as well as a virtual army of classical statuary. Water St., (804) 887-5269. **M-E**

■ WINERIES

There are over 40 wineries in Virginia's wine country, each with its own distinctive products. Following is a selective list of those open to the public. Because days and times of tours frequently change, **we recommend you call wineries prior to visiting.** For more information, see the brochure *Virginia Wineries—Festival and Tour Guide.* Also see the essay "Virginia Wines" in the "PIEDMONT" chapter of this book.

■ **C E N T R A L   V I R G I N I A   W I N E R I E S**

Afton Mountain Vineyards. Nine and a half acres in Nelson County, this beautiful winery features fine wines in mountain grandeur. Open daily except Tues, 10-6 (5 in winter). Closed major holidays. *Directions:* From Charlottesville, take I-64 West to Exit 107, west on U.S. 250 for 6 miles to Rte. 151. South on 151 for 3 miles to Rte. 6. West on Rte. 6 for 1.8 miles to Rte. 631. South on 631 for 1 mile to entrance. (703) 456-8667.

Autumn Hill Vineyards/Blue Ridge Winery. Eight and a half acres in Greene County, this is an award-winning winery overlooking the Blue Ridge Mountains. Dates and times vary, call ahead. *Directions:* 6 miles north of Charlottesville on Rte. 29. Left on Airport Rd. (Rte. 649), left at Rte. 606, right on Rte. 743 to Earlysville. Left on Rte. 663 for 1.5 miles, right on Rte. 663 for .5 miles, left on 663 for 3.7 miles. Right at Rte. 603 for 2 miles, winery on right. (804) 985-6100.

Barboursville Vineyards. Seventy-five acres in Orange County, with the historic ruins of Governors Barbour's mansion designed by Thomas Jefferson. Tours: Sat 10-4:30. Tastings and sales: Mon-Sat, 10-4; call for Sun hours. *Directions:* At Rtes. 20 and 33, take 20 South for 200 yards, left on Rte. 678 for .5 miles. Right on Rte. 777 (Vineyard Rd.) for 500 yards, right at first driveway and sign. Follow Barboursville Ruins and grape cluster signs. (703) 832-3824.

Burnley Vineyards. Twenty acres in Albemarle County. Tasting and banquet rooms overlooking Virginia countryside. Tours and tastings: Jan-Feb weekends only; Mar-Dec, Wed-Sun, 11-5. *Directions:* From Charlottesville, go north 15 miles on Rte. 20, left on Rte. 641 for .3 miles to winery. (703) 832-2828.

Chermont Winery, Inc. Twelve acres in Albemarle County. Established in 1978 amid the rolling hills of South Albemarle County. Tours: Tues-Sat, 12-5; and Sun by appointment. Closed major holidays and heavy snow days. Tours: Jan-Mar by appointment only. *Directions:* From Charlottesville, Rte. 20 South for 15 miles, right on Rte. 626 for 7 miles to entrance on right. (804) 286-2211.

Dominion Wine Cellars. Spectacular view under 25-foot post and beam roof. Sells wine from 17 privately owned vineyards throughout Virginia. Wine shop open noon-5, Tues-Sun. Closed major holidays and heavy snow days. *Directions:* From Rte. 29 bypass, Culpeper, exit at Rte. 3 West, right on McDevitt Dr. to Winery Ave. (703) 825-8772.

Lake Anna Winery. Thirteen acres in Spotsylvania County. Two miles from scenic Lake Anna on Route 208 (Courthouse Rd.). Tour times vary with season, call ahead. *Directions:* From Rte. 95 take the Thornburg exit. West on Rte. 606 for 2.5 miles. Cross intersection at Snell to Rte. 208. Continue on 208 for 11.5 miles to winery entrance on left. (703) 895-5085.

Misty Mountain Vineyards, Inc. Twelve acres in Madison County. Award winning, traditionally made wines of classic elegance and structure. Tours: Mon-Sat, 11-4, Sun by appointment; Nov-Jan by appointment only. *Directions:* From Rte. 29, go north on Rte. 231 at Madison, left on Rte. 651, right on Rte. 652 and follow signs. (703) 923-4738.

Montdomaine Cellars. Fifty acres in Monticello. Charlottesville's largest winery, built into a hillside overlooking 10 acres of vineyards. Tour times vary, call ahead. *Directions:* From I-64, take Monticello Exit 121, to Rte. 20 South past the Thomas Jefferson Visitors Center for 10 miles, right on Rte. 720 for 1 mile to entrance. (804) 971-8947.

Mountain Cove Vineyards. Twelve acres in Nelson County. Located in a scenic cove, it is Central Virginia's oldest winery. Tours: Apr-Dec, 1-5 daily. Jan-Mar, Wed-Sun, 1-5. *Directions:* From Lovingston, U.S. Rte. 29 North. Turn left on Rte. 718, right on Rte. 651. Winery on right. (804) 263-5392.

Oakencroft Vineyard and Winery. Seventeen acres in Albemarle county. Idyllic farm setting with Blue Ridge Mountain views. Free tours: Apr-Dec, 11-5 daily; Jan-Mar by appointment only. Bus tours by appointment; groups of 10 or more $1 per person. *Directions:* From Rte. 29, west on Barracks Rd., for 3.5 miles. Entrance on left. (804) 296-4188.

Prince Michel Vineyards. One hundred and ten acres in Madison County. This French Provincial winery houses a restaurant, museum, and gift shop. Open 10-5 daily, except major holidays. *Directions:* From Culpeper, 10 miles south on Rte. 29 West. (703) 547-3707.

Rebec Vineyards. Five acres in Amherst County. Estate listed on Historic American Building Survey. Tours: Mar 15-Dec 15, 10-5 daily; Dec 15-Mar 15 by appointment. *Directions:* On Rte. 29 West, 5 miles north of Amherst and 11 miles south of Lovingston. (804) 946-5168.

Rockbridge Vineyard. Five acres in Rockbridge county. Virginia's newest winery. Call for tours. *Directions:* From I-81, take exit 205 to Rte. 606. Vineyard 1 mile on 606 on right. (703) 377-6204.

Rose Bower Vineyard and Winery. Ten acres in Prince Edward County. An estate-bottled winery featuring a rental chalet overlooking a 10-acre fishing lake and a newly constructed champagne cellar. Tours by appointment. *Directions:* From Farmville, take Rte. 15 to Worsham. Right on Rte. 665 for 2 miles. Bear left at second fork in road onto Rte. 604. 3 miles on 604 and right onto Rte. 686. 1.5 miles to sign on right. (804) 223-8209.

Rose River Vineyards and Trout Farm. One hundred and seventy-seven acres in Madison County. Distinctive wines with elegantly silk-screened labels and fresh or smoked trout available for all occasions. Tours: Mar-Dec, 11-5, Sat and Sun; Oct, 10-5 daily; or by appointment. *Directions:* From Syria, go west on Rte. 670 passing Graves Mountain Lodge, left on Rte. 648 to vineyard. (703) 923-4050.

Simeon Vineyards, Ltd. Sixteen acres in Albemarle County. Tastings of the largest selection of *vinifra* variety wines in the state. Tours: Mar-Nov, 11-5 daily, except major holidays; Dec-Feb by appointment only. *Directions:* Located on Rte. 795 off Highway 53 between Monticello and Ashlawn. (804) 977-3042 or (804) 977-0800.

Stonewall Vineyard. Seven acres Appomattox County. Family-run winery located within easy distance from Appomattox and Lynchburg. Tours: Mar-Dec, Wed-Sun, 1-6, or by appointment. *Directions:* From Lynchburg, 15 miles east on Rte. 460 at Concord. Go north 6 miles on Rte. 608, left on Rte. 721. First farm on the left. (804) 993-2185.

Totier Creek Vineyard, Ltd. Twenty-two acres in Albemarle County. Nestled in the Green Mountain Range, this winery offers free tastings, tours, and a gift shop. Hours: Tue-Sat, 11-5; Sun, 1-5. *Directions:* From I-64, exit 121A. Follow

Rte. 20 South past Thomas Jefferson Visitor's Center approx. 10.5 miles, then right at Rte. 720 for approx. 1 mile to entrance. (804) 979-7105.

Wintergreen Vineyards and Winery. Eight acres in Nelson County. Historic plantation on South Fork of the Rockfish River, adjoining Wintergreen Ski Resort. Open daily 10-6 (5 in winter), except major holidays. *Directions:* From Charlottesville, take I-64 west to Exit 107, west on U.S. 250 for 5 miles to Rte. 151. South on 151 for 14 miles to Rte. 664, and west on 664. .5 miles to entrance. (804) 361-2519.

■ EASTERN VIRGINIA WINERIES

Ingleside Plantation Vineyards. Fifty-acre vineyard on a 3,000-acre estate. Features a European-style courtyard, museum with Native American artifacts, gift shop, picnic and banquet facilities. Free tours and tastings. Open daily except major holidays: Mon-Sat, 10-5; Sun, 12-5. *Directions:* Located 35 miles east of Fredericksburg on Rte. 3, south of Oak Grove 2.5 miles on Rte. 638. (804) 224-8687.

Williamsburg Winery, Ltd. Unique 17th- and 18th-century era buildings with Old World barrel cellar among over 50 acres of vineyards. Tours: Tues-Sun until 5; no tours Jan 15-Feb 15. Small fee charged. *Directions:* From I-64, Exit 242A to Rte. 199 West. Left onto Brookwood Lane, left onto Lake Powell Rd. for .75 miles. Winery entrance on left. (804) 229-0999.

■ NORTHERN VIRGINIA WINERIES

Farfelu Vineyard. Six and a half acres in Rappahannock County. This is a small winery being revitalized. Tours and tastings: 11-5 daily. Please call ahead. *Directions:* Leave Rte. 66 at Exit 27, take Rte. 647 West for 12.5 miles. (703) 364-2930.

Harwood Winery. Twelve acres in Stafford County. Outstanding wines, and special wine tasting receptions, celebrations, and private labels available. Free tours and tastings: Sat-Sun, 11-5, except major holidays; extended summer hours. *Directions:* From Rte. 17 and I-95 intersection, 5 miles north on Rte. 17. Right for 1.5 miles on Rte. 612 (Hartwood Rd.). Winery on left. (703) 752-4893.

Linden Vineyards. Eleven acres in Fauquier County near Skyline Drive and Shenandoah National Park. Dramatic mountain views and beautiful picnic areas. Tours: Jan-Feb, Sat and Sun, 11-5; Mar-Dec, Wed-Sun, 11-5. Closed major holidays. *Directions:* One hour from D.C. Beltway; From I-66 Exit 13 at Linden, go 1 mile east on Rte. 55, right on Rte. 638 for 2 miles. Winery on right. (703) 364-1997.

Loudoun Valley Vineyards. Twenty-two acres in Loudoun County. Panoramic mountain views, cozy fires, and European-style fine wines. Tours: Sat-Sun, 11-5; and by appointment. *Directions:* From Leesburg, take Rte. 7 West 2 miles to Rte. 9 West. Proceed 5 miles to the winery on right. (703) 882-3375.

Meredyth Vineyards. Fifty-six acres in Fauquier County. Vines located in Bull Run Mountains just south of Middleburg, a scene of transcendant natural beauty. Tours: 10-4 daily, except major holidays. *Directions:* From D.C., I-66 Exit 31, north on Rte. 245 to Rte. 55. Right on 55 for 1 block, left on Rte. 626 for 3.75 miles. Right on Rte. 679 for 1 mile to Rte. 628 on left. Winery entrance on left. (703) 687-6277.

Naked Mountain Vineyard. Five acres in Fauquier County. Discover sensational views from a chalet-like winery on the east slope of the Blue Ridge. Tours: times vary, call ahead. Closed major holidays. *Directions:* From D.C., take I-66 to Markham. Exit 18 on Rte. 688 North, 1.5 miles to winery. (703) 364-1609.

Oasis Vineyard. Seventy-five acres in Fauquier County near Skyline Drive in a spectacular setting facing the Blue Ridge Mountains. Tours: Daily 10-4 (sales until 5). *Directions:* From D.C., take I-66 West. Exit 27 at Marshall on Rte. 647 for 4 miles, right on Rte. 635 for 10 miles. Winery on left. (703) 635-7627.

Piedmont Vineyard. Thirty-seven acres in Fauquier County. Virginia's first commercial *vinifera* vineyard. Located on the pre-revolutionary farm of Waverly. Tours and tastings: 10-5 daily, closed major holidays. *Directions:* From Middleburg, approx. 3 miles south on Rte. 626. (703) 687-5528.

Swedenburg Estate Vineyard. Fifteen acres in Loudoun County on historic Valley View Farm (c. 1762). Open daily, 10-4. *Directions:* From Middleburg, 1 mile east, on U.S. 50 South. (703) 687-5219.

Tarara Vineyard and Winery. Fifty acres in Loudoun County. Premium wines aged in a 6,000 sq ft cave overlooking the Potomac River. Tours: Thu-Mon, 11-5, or by appointment; weekends only in Jan and Feb. *Directions:* From Leesburg, Rte. 15 North, 8 miles to Lucketts. Right onto Rte. 662, 3 miles to sign. Driveway on left. (703) 771-7100 or (703) 478-8161.

Willowcroft Farm Vineyards. Five acres in Loudoun County, on top of Mt. Gilead in a rustic barn overlooking the Blue Ridge. Tours: Sat and Sun, 12-5, or by appointment. *Directions:* From Leesburg, south on Rte. 15, right on Rte. 704, immediate left on Rte. 707 (dirt road). 3 miles to winery. (703) 777-8161.

■ SHENANDOAH VALLEY WINERIES

Deer Meadow Vineyard. Seven acres of vineyards on a 120-acre farm in Frederick County. This small estate winery produces quality wines in a remote wilderness setting. Tours: Mar-Dec, Wed-Sun, 11-5, or by appointment. *Directions:* Located between U.S. Rtes. 50 and 55, off 608. From Rte. 50, turn south on 608 for 6.5 miles, left on Rte. 629, 1 mile. Driveway on right. (800) 653-6632 or (703) 877-1919.

North Mountain Vineyard and Winery. Ten acres in Shenandoah County. Tours: Sat, Sun and holidays, 11-5; groups by appointment. *Directions:* From D.C., go west on I-66 to I-81. 10 miles to Exit 291 (Tom's Brook). West 1 mile on Rte. 651 to Mt. Olive. South 2 miles on Rte. 623, left on Rte. 655. Follow signs .5 miles to vineyard. (703) 436-9463.

Shenandoah Vineyards. Forty acres in Shenandoah County. Premium award-winning wines in a country setting. Tours: 10-6, daily. *Directions:* From I-81, exit 279 at Edinburg. West on Rte. 675, right on Rte. 686. 1.5 miles to winery on left. (703) 984-8699.

■ SOUTHWEST VIRGINIA WINERIES

Chateau Morrisette Winery, Inc. Forty acres in Floyd and Patrick Counties. A "French Country" winery with spectacular views and a restaurant on premises. Tours, tastings, and sales Mon-Sun, 12-5, except major holidays. *Directions:* From Blue Ridge Parkway at Mile post 171.5, turn right on Rte. 726 and immediate left on Winery Rd. Winery .25 miles on right. (703) 593-2865.

Tomahawk Mill Winery. Pittsylvania County. Enjoy fine Chardonnay in a historic water-powered gristmill and vineyard overlooking the mill pond. Tours and tastings Sat, 9-5, Mar-Dec 24, or by appointment. *Directions:* From Rocky Mount, Rte. 40 East, right on Rte. 626 South for 8 miles. Left on Rte. 649 to winery on right. (804) 432-1063.

■ HISTORIC HOMES

Nearly one hundred of Virginia's homes are open to the public. Below is a selective list of major historic homes; it does not include those in Colonial Williamsburg, owing to the concentration of historic buildings there.

■ HOMES OF PRESIDENTS

Ash Lawn-Highland, James Monroe Pkwy, Charlottesville, (804) 293-9539. Home of James Monroe. Open year round.

Berkeley Plantation, Rte. 5, Charles City, (804) 829-6018. Home of William Henry Harrison. Open year round.

George Washington Birthplace National Monument, Rte. 204, (804) 224-1732. Washington's Birthplace. Open year round.

Jefferson's Poplar Forest, Rte. 661, Lynchburg, (804) 525-1806. Home of Thomas Jefferson. Open April-November, Wednesday-Sunday, and major holidays.

Monticello, Rte. 53, Charlottesville, (804) 295-8181. Home of Thomas Jefferson. Open year round.

Montpelier, Rte. 20, Orange, (703) 672-2728. Home of James Madison. Open mid-March-December.

Mount Vernon, Rte. 235, Mount Vernon, (703) 780-0200. Home of George Washington. Open year round.

President Woodrow Wilson's Birthplace, 18-24 N. Coalter St., Staunton, (703) 885-0897. Open year round.

Sherwood Forest, Rte. 5, Charles City, (804) 829-5377. Home of John Tyler. Open year round.

Tuckahoe, 12601 River Rd., Richmond, (804) 784-5736. Boyhood home of Thomas Jefferson. Open during Historic Garden Week and by appointment.

■ OTHER HISTORIC HOMES

Abram's Delight, 1340 Pleasant Valley Rd., Winchester, (703) 662-6519. Open April-October.

Adam Thoroughgood House, 1636 Parish Rd., Virginia Beach, (804) 627-2737. Open year round.

Agecroft Hall, 4305 Sulgrave Rd., Richmond, (804) 353-4241. Open year round.

Appomattox Manor, Petersburg, (804) 458-9504. Open year round.

Arlington House: Robert E. Lee Memorial, Turkey Run Pkwy., Arlington, (703) 557-0613. Open year round.

Bacon's Castle, off Rte. 617, Surry, (804) 357-5976. Open daily April-October and on weekends in March and November.

Belle Grove, Rte. 11, Middletown, (703) 869-2028. Open year round.

Belmont, 224 Washington St., Fredricksburg, (703) 899-4860. Open year round.

Booker T. Washington National Monument, Rte. 3, Hardy, (703) 721-2094. Open year round.

Boyhood Home of Robert E. Lee, 607 Oronoco St., Alexandria, (703) 548-8454. Open Febraury to mid-December.

Brandon Plantation, Rte. 611, Spring Grove, (804) 866-8416/8486. Grounds open daily; house during Historic Garden Week.

Campbell House, 101 E. Washington St., Lexington, (703) 463-3777. Open weekday mornings May-October.

Carlyle House, 121 N. Fairfax St., Alexandria, (703) 549-2997. Open year round.

Carter's Grove, Carter's Grove Country Rd., Williamsburg, (804) 220-7452. Open year round.

Centre Hill Mansion, Petersburg, (804) 733-2401. Open year round.

Chatham Manor, 120 Chatham Lane, Fredricksburg, (703) 373-4461. Open year round.

Chippokes Plantation, Rte. 1, Surry, (804) 294-3625. Grounds open year round. Mansion open Memorial Day-Labor Day, Wednesday-Sunday from 1-4.

Daniel Harrison House at Fort Harrison, Rte. 42, Dayton, (703) 433-0373. Open May-October, Saturday-Sunday, 1-5.

Edgewood, Rte. 5, Charles City, (804) 829-2962. Open year round.

Evelynton, 6701 John Tyler Memorial Highway, Charles City, (804) 829-5075 or (800) 473-5075. Open year round.

Flowerdew Hundred, 1617 Flowerdew Hundred Rd., (800) 541-8897. Open April-November.

Francis Land House, 3131 Virginia Beach Blvd., Virginia Beach, (804) 340-1732. Open Tuesday-Sunday year round.

Gunston Hall Plantation, 10709 Gunston Road (VA Route 242), Lorton, (703) 550-9220. Open year round.

Hill House, 221 North St., Portsmouth, (804) 393-0241. Open April-December on Wednesday, Saturday, and Sunday, except major holidays, 1-5.

Hunter House Victorian Museum, 240 W. Freemason St., Norfolk, (804) 623-9814. Open April-December.

John Marshall House, 818 E. Marshall St., Richmond, (804) 648-7998. Open year round.

Kenmore, 1201 Washington Ave., Fredricksburg, (703) 373-3381. Open year round.

Lee-Fendall House, 614 Oronoco St., Alexandria, (703) 548-1789. Open Tuesday-Sunday.

Lloyd House, 220 N. Washington St., Alexandria, (703) 838 4577. Open year round.

Long Branch, P.O. Box 241, Millwood, (703) 837-1856. Open weekends April 15-October 31, noon-4.

Lynnhaven House, 4405 Wishart Rd., Virginia Beach, (804) 460-1688. Open April-October, Tuesday-Sunday, noon-4 P.M.

Maggie L. Walker House, 3215 E. Broad St., Richmond, (804) 226-1981. Open year round.

Mary Washington House, 1200 Charles St., Fredericksburg, (703) 373-1569. Open year round.

Maymont House, 1700 Hampton St., Richmond, (804) 358-7166. Open year round.

McCormick's Birthplace: Walnut Grove Farm, Rte. 56, Steele's Tavern, (703) 377-2255. Open year round.

Meadow Farm, 3400 Mountain Rd., Glen Allen, (804) 672-5024. Open March-December.

Morven Park, off Rte. 698, Leesburg, (703) 777-2414. Open April-October, except Mondays.

Moses Myers House, 323 E. Freemason St., Norfolk, (804) 627-2737. Open year round.

Nelson House, Main St., Yorktown, (804) 898-3400. Open daily in summer.

Newsome House, 2803 Oak Ave., Newport News, (804) 247-2360/2380. Open weekday afternoons.

Oatlands Plantation, Rte. 15, Leesburg, (703) 777-3174. Open year round.

Old Stone House, 1914 E. Main St., Richmond, (804) 648-5523. Open year round.

Point of Honor, off Cabell St., Lynchburg, (804) 847-1459. Open year round.

Prestwould Plantation, off Rte. 15, Clarksville, (804) 374-8672. Open daily May-September and weekends in October.

Red Hill Plantation, Rte. 2, Box 127, Brookneal, 24528, (804) 376-2044. Closed New Year's, Thanksgiving, and Christmas.

Shirley Plantation, 501 Shirley Plantation Rd., Charles City, (804) 829-5121. Open year round.

Smithfield Plantation, off Bypass 460, Blacksburg, (703) 951-2060. Open April-October, Thursday-Sunday, 1-5.

Smith's Fort Plantation, Rte. 31, Surry, (804) 294-3872. Open Tuesday-Sunday, April-October.

Stonewall Jackson House, 8 E. Washington St., Lexington, (703) 463-2552. Open year round.

Stratford Hall Plantation, Rte. 214, Stratford, 22558, (804) 493-8038. Open year round.

Sully Plantation, Sully Rd. (Rte. 28), Chantilly, 22003, (703) 437-1794. Open daily March-December, weekends January-February.

Sutherlin House, 975 Main St., Danville, (804) 793-5644. Open year round.

Weems-Botts Museum, 300 Duke St., Dumfries, (703) 221-3346. Open year round.

Westover, 7000 Westover Road, Charles City, 23030, (804) 829-2882. Open year round.

White House of the Confederacy, 1201 E. Clay St., Richmond, (804) 649-1861. Open year round.

Wickham-Valentine House, 1015 Clay St., Richmond, (804) 649-0711. Open year round.

Willoughby-Baylor House, 601 E. Freemason St., Norfolk, 23510, (804) 627-2737.

■ NATIONAL MONUMENTS AND HISTORIC SITES

Appomatox Court House National Historical Park, (804) 352-8987.

Arlington House, The Robert E. Lee Memorial, (703) 557-0613.

Booker T. Washington National Monument, (703) 721-2094.

Colonial National Historical Park, (804) 898-3400.

Fredericksburg and Spotsylvania County Battlefields Memorial National Military Park, (703) 373-4461.

George Washington Birthplace National Monument, (804) 224-1732.

Green Springs Historic District, (703) 373-4461.

Lyndon Baines Johnson Memorial Grove on the Potomac, (703) 285-2598.

Maggie L. Walker National Historic Site, (804) 780-1380.

Manassas National Battlefield Park, (703) 754-7107.

Petersburg National Battlefield, (804) 732-3531.

Red Hill, The Patrick Henry National Memorial, (804) 376-2044.

Richmond National Battlefield Park, (804) 226-1981.

Theodore Roosevelt Island, (703) 285-2598.

Wolf Trap Farm Park for the Performing Arts, (703) 255-1800 (TDD).

■ MUSEUMS

A selective list of Virginia museums follows. Also see "Homes of Presidents" and "Other Historic Homes" in this section, as many are virtually museums in themselves.

■ BIG STONE GAP

Southwest Virginia Museum. 10 W. First St.; (703) 523-1322. Celebrates the town's glory days and tales of the early pioneers who pressed through the area on their way west. The museum also extols the architecture of the Gilded Age by offering guided walking tours past the mansions of Poplar Hill.

■ FREDERICKSBURG

James Monroe Museum. 908 Charles St.; (703) 373-8426. Monroe memorabilia, including the Louis XVI desk on which he wrote his inaugural address, which was to form the basis of his famous Monroe Doctrine.

■ HAMPTON

Casemate Museum at Fort Monroe. Fort Monroe in Hampton; (804) 727-3391. Exhibits on the history of the fort and Civil War.

Hampton University Museum. I-64, Exit 267; (804) 727-5308. Collection includes African Art, Harlem Renaissance paintings, Native American art and craft work, and art from Oceania.

Virginia Air and Space Center. Off I-64 (Exit 267) on 600 Settlers Landing Rd.; (804) 727-0800. Architectural tour de force, housing two museums: the Air and Space Center and the Hampton Roads History Center. Air and space exhibits include ten historic aircraft and the Apollo 12 command capsule. An IMAX theater, with its five-story screen, is the only one of its kind in Virginia.

■ J A M E S T O W N

Jamestown Festival Park. On the Colonial Parkway, Box JF; (804) 229-1607. A fine museum explains the conditions in seventeenth-century England and Europe that forced the Elizabethans to look for new horizons beyond their cramped Motherland. Exhibits here also do justice to the Powhatan culture and to the endurance of the early colonists. Outside, the park re-creates a Powhatan village, and leather-clad "natives" cook native foods, tend fires, and explain how the Powhatan hunter-gatherers and farmers lived off the abundance of Virginia's woodlands and rich river shores.

■ L E X I N G T O N

George C. Marshall Museum. Located on grounds of Virginia Military Institute, adjacent to Washington and Lee University; (703) 464-7232. Memorabilia of the former cadet and Nobel Peace Prize winner who created the post–World War II Marshall Plan.

■ N E W P O R T   N E W S

Mariners' Museum. Located off I- 64, Exit 258A at 100 Museum Dr.; (804) 595-0368. Nautical museum "devoted to the culture of the sea." Entrance gallery is enhanced by gleam of the old Cape Charles Lighthouse lens. Other exhibits cover 3,000 years of maritime history. Exquisite ship models produced by woodcarver August Crabtree.

Virginia Living Museum. 524 J. Clyde Morris Blvd., about a mile (1.6 km) west of Mariners' Museum; (804) 595-1900. Houses native animal life. State-of-the-art indoor exhibits feature aquariums filled with bay and river critters, as well as woodpeckers, owls, and flying squirrels. Planetarium; outside, a boardwalk trail, cantilevered above a serene lake.

U.S. Army Transportation Museum. On the grounds of Fort Eustis, headquarters for Army transportation, at the northern edge of Newport News, off I-64, Exit 250A, at Besson Hall, building 300; (804) 878-1109. Dioramas and artifacts that trace the history of army movement from horse-drawn Revolutionary wagons to "the world's only captive flying saucer."

War Memorial Museum of Virginia. 9285 Warwick Blvd. (Rte. 60); on the north side of the James River Bridge; (804) 247-8523. Over 50,000 artifacts reveal the human impact of war—from its hardships and tragedies to its hyped-up propaganda. Array of weaponry—pre-World War I howitzers, tanks, anti-tanks, and more.

■ NORFOLK

The Chrysler Museum. Located amid mansions of the city's Hague neighborhood at 245 W. Olney Rd.; (804) 622-1211. One of this country's finest art collections, including exhibits of antique and art glass; Greco-Roman, Egyptian, and pre-Columbian antiquities; art nouveau and art deco works. Paintings by Americans Charles Willson Peale, Asher Durand, Winslow Homer, Edward Hopper, Jackson Pollock, and Richard Diebenkorn. Works by European masters from the fourteenth to the twentieth century, including pieces by Filipino Lippi, Gauguin, Renoir, and Matisse.

■ PORTSMOUTH

Hill House. 221 North St. functions as a museum and headquarters of the Portsmouth Historical Association; (804) 393-0241. A dignified old brick Federal built in the early 1800s, the home holds furnishings collected by the long-time owners, the Thompson/Hill family, who lived here until 1961.

Lightship Museum. Docked along the waterfront near Water St. is a fine piece of the maritime past. The ship's spit-and-polish interior gives a good sense of what life was like for crews living aboard. This one saw service from 1915 to 1964.

Naval Shipyard Museum. Corner of High and Water Sts.; (804) 393-8591. Model ships ride the immobile seas of display cases and wartime and maritime memorabilia is exhibited.

■ RICHMOND

Edgar Allan Poe Museum. 1914 E. Main St. on the southeast edge of downtown;

(804) 648-5523. Poe memorabilia are here, as well as his writings, even architectural parts of Richmond buildings that he lived or worked in. The complex also holds a separate piece of history—the **Old Stone House,** built in the late 1730s and the oldest structure still standing in the city.

John Marshall House. 9th and Marshall Sts.; (804) 393-8591. "The Great Chief Justice," became the country's third chief justice in 1801.

Valentine Museum. 1015 E. Clay St.; (804) 649-0711. Has taken as its mission a "reinterpretation of the city's history" that locates "Richmond in the mainstream of American history." Dramatic recordings in several rooms of the house effectively capture conversations between house slaves and the members of the family who lived here.

Virginia Museum of Fine Arts. At Boulevard and Grove Ave.; (804) 367-0844. A rambling, elegant museum that can hold its own with virtually any museum in the country. Founded in 1936, it boasts a collection that spans 5,000 years, from Egyptian, Roman, and Greek works, to twentieth-century decorative arts, impressionist and post-impressionist paintings, and an outstanding collection of Fabergé Easter eggs.

White House of the Confederacy. 1201 E. Clay St.; (804) 649-1861. Important Civil War memorabilia.

■ R O A N O K E

Center in the Square. One Market Square; information for museums listed below call (703) 342-5700. **Science Museum of Western Virginia** focuses on flora, fauna, ecology, and the stars. **Art Museum of Western Virginia** showcases the works of up-and-coming artists in the Southern Appalachian region.

Roanoke Valley Historical Society. Starts with the stone age cultures in this area, moves through the days when the place was no more than a salt marsh crossroads called Big Lick, and then into the railroad heyday of the last century.

Virginia Transportation Museum. Its exhibits include old cars, automobiles, a model circus exhibit, and "the largest collection of diesel engines in the South." Unfortunately, much of the rolling stock displayed in its rail yard can't be boarded, so you have to be content with peering into the windows of old passenger cars and cabooses.

Harrison Museum of African American Culture. 523 Harrison Ave. NW. Devoted to the achievements of African Americans, especially in Western Virginia and greater knowledge of African American culture. Besides art exhibitions in its two galleries, the museum periodically sponsors performing arts presentations, festivals, and celebrations.

Roanoke Museum of Fine Art. Center on Church; (703) 342-5760. Strong in regional work, especially folk art.

■ **S T A U N T O N**

Statler Brother's Mini-Museum. 501 Thornrose Ave.; (703) 885-7297. For years, the Statlers have treated their neighbors to a free Fourth of July country music extravaganza, "to repay the townsfolk for helping us out in the beginning."

■ **V I R G I N I A   B E A C H**

Virginia Marine Science Museum. 717 General Booth Blvd. just south of the Rudee Inlet Bridge; (804) 425-3474. 50,000-gallon aquarium, examples of local wildlife, explanations of weather movements, and a chance to tong oysters. An outdoor boardwalk crosses a pristine salt marsh, with explanations of what life is like in a Virginia wetland.

■ **W I L L I A M S B U R G**

Abby Aldrich Rockefeller Folk Art Center. One of the nation's premier folk art museums. Collection of weathervanes, folk portraits, and wood carvings.

DeWitt Wallace Decorative Arts Gallery. One of the finest collections in the world of seventeenth- through early nineteenth-century British and American decorative arts. Among its masterworks are Charles Willson Peale's military portrait of George Washington; mid-seventeenth and eighteenth-century furniture, ceramics, silver, and pewter; and an extraordinary collection of historic prints.

■ **W I N C H E S T E R**

George Washington's Office. Small stone cabin at 32 W. Cork St. (703) 662-4412. Served Washington when, as a young man, he was surveying and guarding Virginia's western frontier.

■ **Y O R K T O W N**

Watermen's Museum. 309 Water St. Evokes the centuries-old culture of the Bay's oystermen, crabbers, and fishermen.

■ EVENTS

Fairs, festivals, exhibits, and tournaments take place throughout the state almost every weekend in the spring, summer, and fall. For a list of upcoming events, contact the Virginia Division of Tourism. The list below represents major annual festivals, as well as a few smaller, but uniquely appealing, local happenings.

■ JANUARY

Lexington: Stonewall Jackson's Birthday celebration honors this Lexington native son and famous Confederate general with free tours of his home and birthday festivities.

■ FEBRUARY

Alexandria: George Washington Birthday Parade. Some 200 floats, marching bands, fife-and-drum corps, and more twist through the streets of historic Old Town.

Fairfax: Great Tastes of Virginia. Thirty-some Virginia vintners offer tastes of their wares, as do 3- and 4-star restaurants from the state and nearby Washington, D.C. Live music adds to the festivities.

■ MARCH

Monterey: Highland County Maple Festival. One of the southernmost maple sugar harvests in the country. Tours of maple-producing farms, arts and crafts, maple products for sale.

Mount Vernon: Woodlawn Needlework Exhibition. With more than a thousand entries from both amateurs and professionals, this competition is the oldest and largest such exhibition in the country.

■ APRIL

Chincoteague: Easter Decoy and Art Festival. Features the works of more than 150 local and national artists. Seafood and down-home cooking also.

Gloucester: Daffodil Festival. Tours of the famous Daffodil Mart, where several varieties of daffodils are in bloom. Carnival, arts and crafts, parade, and bus tours to local historic sites.

Norfolk: International Azalea Festival. Four-day celebration of Norfolk's role in

NATO. The festival's parade, ball, and airshow are presided over by an azalea queen and 15 princesses, chosen from the NATO countries. Coronation at Norfolk Botanical Gardens.

Richmond: Strawberry Hill Races. Major steeplechase race. Festivities also include a carriage drive, tailgate competition, and carriage promenade through city streets.

Statewide: Historic Garden Week. Perhaps Virginia's most famous event, in which some 200 private homes and gardens—both historic and contemporary—are open for tours.

Winchester: Shenandoah Apple Blossom Festival. Parade, entertainment, and other festivities presided over by a young apple blossom queen and her court.

■ MAY

Crozet: Crozet Arts and Crafts Festival. Juried crafts festival with exceptionally fine crafts. Features the works of woodworkers, potters, weavers, photographers, artists, and other craftsmen from throughout the state. Live entertainment and food. Also held in October.

Harrisonburg: Virginia Poultry Festival. Honors the Shenandoah Valley's poultry industry with golf and tennis tournaments, galas, parades, and more.

The Plains: Virginia Gold Cup. One of the country's premier steeplechase events. Seven races held at the Great Meadows Race Course, in the heart of hunt country.

Roanoke: Festival in the Park includes art and craft shows, parades, numerous sports competitions, performing arts, and food.

Upperville: Virginia Hunt Country Stable Tour. Some of the state's most respected Thoroughbred breeding and training farms and private estates are open for tours.

Wintergreen: Wildflower Weekend. Botanists and other experts give lectures and lead nature walks in search of native wildflowers.

■ JUNE

Fairfax: Virginia Wineries Festival. Billed as the largest wine festival on the East Coast, this one gives guests a chance to sample wines from forty different vineyards. Arts and crafts and Virginia foods as well.

Lynchburg: James River Batteau Festival. This eight-day event begins in Lynchburg, as reproductions of batteaux, eighteenth-century shallow-draft merchant boats, start off down the James, heading for their destination in Richmond. The boats stop daily at various towns along the river.

Norfolk: Harborfest. An extravagant waterfront festival held on Town Point Park and featuring all kinds of seafood, soul food, tall ships, water and air shows, military demonstrations, and parades of sail.

The Plains: Vintage Virginia. The Virginia Wineries Festival features about three dozen of the state's wineries who offer samples of their wares. Also jazz, blues, and reggae bands and arts and crafts purveyors.

■ J U L Y

Chincoteague: Annual Pony Swim and Auction. This two-day event draws crowds from throughout the Northeast to the island of Chincoteague. The wild ponies of Assateague Island are rounded up and swum across the channel to Chincoteague, where the foals are sold in a public auction. Carnival, seafood, and entertainment.

Hampton: Hampton Jazz Festival. Now in its third decade, this annual two-day festival attracts musicians from throughout the country. Held at the Hampton Coliseum.

■ A U G U S T

Abingdon: Virginia Highlands Festival. Devoted to showcasing Appalachian artists, craftsmen, writers, and musicians. Antique market, wine tastings, hot-air balloons, and a variety of live performances.

Galax: Old Fiddlers' Convention. Claims to be the oldest and largest such "convention" in the country. Old-time, bluegrass, and folk music competitions, as well as clogging and flat-foot dancing.

■ S E P T E M B E R

Hampton: Hampton Bay Days. Celebrates the Chesapeake Bay with water and sporting events, arts and crafts shows, entertainment, and bay-related exhibits.

Virginia Beach: Neptune Festival. Held along the oceanfront, festivities include a parade, sandcastle building, surfing, sailing, arts and crafts, a parade and airshow.

Mathews: Mathews Days. Held in the county's picturesque court house, this smalltown festival features fine, homemade seafood dishes, waterman demonstrations, arts and crafts.

■ OCTOBER

Charlottesville: Virginia Festival of American Film. A gathering of filmmakers and scholars join with the public to explore traditions in American cinema.

Danville: Harvest Jubilee. Celebrates tobacco harvest, the crops' farmers and auctioneers. Nationally known entertainers, arts and crafts, sports events, and farm exhibits.

Waterford: Waterford Homes Tour and Crafts Exhibit. This quaint eighteenth-century village hosts more than 130 juried craftsmen, as well as street performers. Ten of the town's historic homes open for tour.

■ NOVEMBER

Urbanna: The state's official oyster festival includes tall ships, oyster and work boat exhibits, parades, arts and crafts, and oysters served in every conceivable fashion.

■ DECEMBER

Alexandria: Scottish Christmas Walk. Bagpipers, fife-and-drum corps, and other marching bands parade through streets decorated for Christmas. Historic home tours, arts and crafts, Christmas greenery, and foods sold throughout town.

Colonial Williamsburg: Grand Illumination. Candles are lit throughout the historic area, accompanied by caroling, fife-and-drum corps music, musketry and artillery salutes, and fireworks. Homes throughout town are decorated in eighteenth-century style.

■ STATE PARKS

The Virginia Department of Conservation and Recreation operates the following state parks. Some are small parcels, others are large tracts with accommodations and other guest facilities. For camping and cabin reservations, call (804) 490-3939. For general information, contact the Dept. of Conservation and Recreation, 203 Governor St., Suite 302, Richmond 23219; (804) 786-1712, TDD (804) 786-2121. Also see the booklet, *Virginia State Parks,* available at most state visitor and welcome centers.

■ MOUNTAINS

Breaks Interstate Park, (703) 865-4413
Claytor Lake State Park, (703) 674-5492
Douthat State Park, (703) 862-7200
Grayson Highlands State Park, (703) 579-7092
Hungry Mother State Park, (703) 783-3422
Natural Tunnel State Park, (703) 940-2674
Shot Tower and New River Trail State Park, (703) 699-6778
Sky Meadows State Park, (703) 592-3556

■ PIEDMONT

Bear Creek Lake State Park, (804) 492-4410
Fairy Stone State Park, (703) 930-2424
Twin Lakes State Park, (804) 392-3435
Holliday Lake State Park, (804) 248-6308
Lake Anna State Park, (804) 854-5503
Occoneechee State Park, (804) 374-2210
Pocahontas State Park, (804) 796-4255
Sailor's Creek Battlefield Historical Park, no phone
Smith Mountain Lake State Park, (703) 297-6066
Staunton River State Park, (804) 572-4623
Staunton River Bridge Battlefield Historical State Park, no phone

■ COASTAL

Chippokes Plantation State Park, (804) 294-3625
False Cape State Park, (804) 426-7128
George Washington's Grist Mill Historical State Park, (703) 780-3383
Kiptopeke State Park, (804) 331-2267
Leesylvania State Park, (703) 670-0372
Mason Neck State Park, (703) 550-0960
Seashore State Park and Natural Area, (804) 481-2131

Westmoreland State Park, (804) 493-8821

York River State Park, (804) 566-3036

■ NATIONAL PARKS, FORESTS, AND RECREATION AREAS

Blue Ridge Parkway. Stretches south for 469 miles, from the south end of Shenandoah National Park into North Carolina. (703) 259-0779

George Washington National Forest. Over a million acres spread across northwest Virginia and into West Virginia. (703) 433-2491

Jefferson National Forest. Woodlands covering 690,000 acres of mountains and valleys in western Virginia. (703) 982-6270

Mount Rogers National Recreation Area. A 115,000-acre tract within the Jefferson National Forest. (703) 783-5196

Shenandoah National Park. About 200,000 acres of hardwood forests along the slopes of the Blue Ridge. Includes Skyline Drive. (703) 999-2243

■ CAVERNS

Virginia's western corridor offers an impressive array of limestone and dolomite caverns, with winding passages and spectacular stalactites, stalagmites, flowstone, and draperies. Of the 3,000-some caves and caverns, most are on private property, and strictly closed to the public. The following, however, are major commercial caverns, where guided tours are given. Also, Inner Quest, Inc., in Purcellville, offers one-day caving programs. (703) 478-1078.

Augusta County: Grand Caverns, (703) 249-5705

Luray: Luray Caverns, (703) 743-6551

Roanoke County: Dixie Caverns, (703) 380-2085

Rockbridge County: Caverns of Natural Bridge Village, (703) 291-2121

Rockingham County: Endless Caverns, (800) 544-CAVE

Shenandoah County: Shenandoah Caverns, (703) 477-3115

Warren County: Skyline Caverns, (703) 635-4545

■ SKIING

Bryce Resort. On the northwest side of the Shenandoah Valley, Bryce is a small-scale ski resort with two major runs and, consequently, a somewhat less frenetic atmosphere than other, larger ski resorts. P.O. Box 3, Basye, (703) 856-2121.

The Homestead. The posh old resort has developed a scenic but unremarkable ski area as part of its larger resort facilities. It also maintains an Olympic-size skating rink. Hot Springs, (800) 336-5771 or (703) 839-5500.

Massanutten. One of the state's larger ski resorts, Massanutten is located about midway down the Shenandoah Valley, on its eastern flank. The resort operates six lifts and claims Virginia's longest vertical drop (110 feet). P.O. Box 1227, Harrisonburg, (800) 207-MASS.

Wintergreen. Another of the state's major ski resorts, Wintergreen has more than a dozen slopes, as well as compelling mountain views. It's located on the slopes of the Blue Ridge, between Charlottesville and Staunton. Wintergreen, (800) 325-2200.

■ GOLF

Below is a listing of 18-hole courses open to the public throughout the state. It does not include nine-hole courses or the many private and semi-private clubs in Virginia. For a complete listing of golf courses, see the brochure, *Virginia Golf,* available through visitor centers and the Virginia Tourism Development Group; 1021 East Cary St., Richmond 23219; (804) 786-4484.

Afton: Swannanoa Country Club, (703) 942-9877

Alexandria: Greendale, (703) 971-6170

Bastian: Wolf Creek, (703) 688-4610

Basye: Bryce Resort, (703) 856-2121

Centreville: Twin Lake, (703) 631-9099

Charlottesville: Meadowcreek, (804) 977-0615

Danville: Ringold, (804) 799-8728

Fairfax: Burke Lake, (703) 323-6600

Fancy Gap: Skyland Lakes, (703) 728-4923

Hadensville: Royal Virginia, (800) 642-0505 or (804) 784-4589

Hampton: Hampton Golf and Tennis Center, (804) 727-1195; also Hamptons, (804) 766-9148

Harrisonburg: Lakeview, (703) 434-8937; also Massanutten Village, (703) 289-9441

Herndon: Herndon Centennial, (703) 471-5769

Hopewell: Jordan Point, (804) 458-0141

Hot Springs: Cascades, (703) 839-5660; also Lower Cascades, (703) 839-5600; also The Homestead, (703) 839-5500

Irvington: Golden Eagle, (804) 438-5501; also The Tides Tartan, (804) 438-6000

Jonesville: Cedar Hill, (703) 346-1535

Laurel Fork: Olde Mill, (703) 393-2638

Leesburg: Algonkian Park, (703) 450-4655; also Goose Creek, (703) 729-2500

Lorton: Pohick Bay Regional Park, (703) 339-8585

Lynchburg: Poplar Forest, (804) 525-0473

Manakin: Sycamore Creek, (804) 784-3544

Manassas: Prince William, (703) 754-7111

Martinsville: Beaver Hill, (703) 632-1526

Natural Bridge: The Links, (703) 291-GOLF

New Market: Shenvalee, (703) 740-3181

Newport News: Deer Run, (804) 886-2848; also Kiln Creek, (804) 988-3220; also Kingsmill, (804) 253-3906

Norfolk: Lake Wright Resort, (800) 228-5157; also Ocean View, (804) 480-2094

Pembroke: Castle Rock, (703) 626-7276

Petersburg: Prince George, (804) 991-2251

Portsmouth: Bide-A-Wee, (804) 399-9562; also Sleepy Hole, (804) 393-5050

Reston: Reston, (703) 620-9333

Richmond: Belmont, (804) 266-4929; Birkdale, (804) 739-8800; Brookwood, (804) 737-0519; Confederate Hills, (804) 737-4716; The Crossings, (804) 226-2254; Glenwood, (804) 226-1793; The Lakes, (804) 737-4716; Oak Hill

Country Club, (804) 784-5718; Pine Lakes Country Club, (804) 226-9859; River's Bend Country Club, (804) 530-1000; Spring Lake, (804) 226-9859

Salem: Hanging Rock, (703) 389-8193

Smithfield: Smithfield Downs, (804) 357-3101

Staunton: Gypsy Hill, (703) 387-9802; also Ingleside Red Carpet Inn, (703) 248-1201

Stuart: Gordon Trent, (703) 694-3805

Suffolk: Suffolk, (804) 539-6298

Virginia Beach: Bow Creek, (804) 431-3763; also Hell's Point, (804) 721-3400; also Honey Bee, (804) 471-2768; also Kempsville Greens, (804) 474-8441; also Owl's Creek, (804) 428-2800; also Red Wing Lake, (804) 437-4845; also Stumpy Lake, (804) 467-6119

Warrenton: South Wales, (703) 347-1401

White Stone: Windjammer, (804) 435-1166

Williamsburg: Ford's Colony, (804) 258-4130; also Golden Horseshoe, (804) 229-1000; also The Summit, (703) 888-4188

Winchester: Carper's Valley, (703) 662- 4319

Wintergreen: Devils Knob, (804) 325-2200; also Stoney Creek, (804) 325-2200

■ VIRGINIA IN BLOOM

Virginia provides a spectacular show of color, both in its wild and domestic flowers and in its fall color, which begins at lower elevations in early October and makes its way into the mountains by mid- to late October. Herewith is a blooming schedule of the state's showiest flora; bear in mind that the coastal areas can be a couple of weeks ahead of the north and the mountains:

March: Crocuses, daffodils, and redbud trees

April: Azaleas and Virginia bluebells; dogwood and fruit trees

May: Mountain laurels and rhododendrons

June: Roadside vetch

July and August: Crepe myrtle trees, roadside vetch, brown-eyed Susans, Queen Anne's lace, and butterfly weed

■ LYME DISEASE

In the last decade, Lyme Disease has become an increasing problem in Virginia. The disease is carried by the minuscule deer tick and has been reported in many locations in the state. Experts suggest that the best precaution against the disease is simply to try and avoid tick bites. They recommend using insecticides, wearing long pants and socks when hiking, and avoiding high grasses where the ticks tend to congregate. Also, you should check yourself carefully for ticks after being outdoors, although the deer ticks are so small they often look like no more than a dot on the skin. The first symptoms of the disease are a large red ring on the skin around the area where an infected tick has lodged, and flu-like symptoms. If you have these indications, you should see a doctor at once. Lyme Disease is treatable, especially if detected in the early stages.

■ VISITOR INFORMATION

VIRGINIA DIVISION OF TOURISM, (800) 932-5827
Abingdon, (703) 676-2282
Alexandria, (703) 838-4200
Arlington, (703) 358-5720 or (800) 677-6267
Bath County, (703) 839-5409
Charlottesville/Albemarle, (804) 293-6789
Eastern Shore, (804) 787-2460
Fairfax County, (703) 550-2450 or (800) 7-FAIRFA
Fredericksburg, (703) 373-1776 or (800) 678-4748
Front Royal/Warren County, (703) 635-3185 or (800) 338-2576
Hampton, (804) 727-1102 or (800) 800-2202
Harrisonburg-Rockingham County, (703) 635-3185
Lexington, (703) 463-3777
Loudoun, (703) 777-0518 or (800) 752-6118
Lynchburg, (804) 847-1811
Norfolk, (804) 393-8481 or (800) 368-3097

Petersburg, (804) 733-2400 or (800) 368-3595
Portsmouth, (804) 393-8481 or (800) 338-8822
Richmond Metro Area, (804) 782-2777 or (800) 365-7272
Roanoke, (703) 740-3132
Staunton, (703) 885-8504
Virginia Beach, (804) 437-4888 or (800) 822-3224
Williamsburg, (804) 253-0912 or (800) 368-6511
Colonial Williamsburg, (800) 447-8679

RECOMMENDED READING

■ HISTORY

Allen, Thomas B. *The Blue and The Gray.* Washington, D.C.: National Geographic Society, 1992.

Antonelli, Lisa M. *Virginia: A Commonwealth Comes of Age.* Northridge, California: Windsor Publications, Inc., 1988.

Barden, Thomas E., ed. *Virginia Folk Legends.* Charlottesville, Virginia: University of Virginia Press, 1991.

Bowers, John. *Stonewall Jackson: Portrait of a Soldier.* New York: William Morrow, 1989.

Brodie, Fawn. *Thomas Jefferson, An Intimate History.* New York: Norton, 1974.

Dabney, Virginius. *Virginia, The New Dominion.* Charlottesville, Virginia: University of Virginia Press, 1971.

Freeman, Douglas. *R. E. Lee, A Biography.* 4 Vols. New York: Charles Scribner's Sons, 1936.

Janney, Werner L. and Asa Moore. *John Jay Janney's Virginia: An American Farm Lad's Life in the Early 19th Century.* McLean, Virginia: EPM Publishing, Inc., 1978.

Jones, Katharine M., ed. *Heroines of Dixie: Spring of High Hopes.* New York: Ballantine Books, 1955.

Lawliss, Chuck. *The Civil War Sourcebook.* New York: Harmony Books, 1991.

National Park Service. *Appomattox Court House.* Washington, D.C.: United States Department of the Interior.

Reeder, Carolyn and Jack. *Shenandoah Vestiges: What the Mountain People Left Behind.* Washington, D.C.: The Potomac Appalachian Trail Club, 1980.

Rouse, Parke, Jr. *The James: Where a Nation Began.* Richmond, Virginia: Dietz, 1991.

Smith, William Francis and T. Michael Miller. *A Seaport Saga: Portrait of Old Alexandria, Virginia.* Norfolk, Virginia: The Donning Company, 1989.

Taylor, L. B., Jr. *The Ghosts of Virginia.* USA: Progress Printing Co., Inc., 1993.

Thomas, David Hurst, et al. *The Native Americans: An Illustrated History.* Atlanta: Turner Publishing, Inc., 1993.

Washington, Booker T. *Up From Slavery.* New York: Penguin Books, 1986.

Whitehead, John Hurt, III. *The Watermen of the Chesapeake Bay.* Centerville, Maryland: Tidewater Publishing, 1979.

Wilson, Charles Reagan and William Ferris, eds. *Encyclopedia of Southern Culture.* 4 Vols. New York: Anchor Books, Doubleday, 1989.

■ FICTION

Baker, Russell. *Growing Up.* New York: New American Library, 1982.

Dillard, Annie. *Pilgrim at Tinker Creek.* New York: Bantam Books, 1974.

Glasgow, Ellen. *Vein of Iron.* New York: Harcourt, Brace, Jovanovich, 1935.

—. *The Sheltered Life.* New York: Hill and Wang, 1979.

Styron, William. *The Confessions of Nat Turner.* New York: Random House, 1966.

—. *Lie Down in Darkness.* New York: Random House, 1951.

—. *Tidewater Morning.* New York: Random House, 1993.

Thom, James Alexander. *Follow the River.* New York: Ballantine Books, 1981.

■ GUIDEBOOKS

de Hart, Allen. *Hiking the Old Dominion.* San Francisco, California: Sierra Club Books, 1984.

Gooch, Bob. *Virginia Hunting Guide.* Charlottesville, Virginia: University of Virginia Press, 1985.

Miller, Skip. *Tidewater Fishing.* Newport News, Virginia: Daily Press, Inc., 1993.

Mulligan, Tim. *Virginia: A History and Guide,* New York: Random House, 1986.

Olmert, Michael. *Official Guide to Colonial Williamsburg.* Williamsburg, Virginia: Colonial Williamsburg Foundation, 1985.

Paulus, Conrad Little. *Fodor's Bed & Breakfasts and Country Inns: The South.* New York: Fodor's Travel Publications, Inc., 1992

Robertson, James I., Jr. *Civil War Sites in Virginia: A Tour Guide.* Charlottesville, Virginia: University of Virginia Press, 1982.

Virginia Atlas & Gazetteer. Freeport, Maine: DeLorme Mapping Company, 1989.

Virginia Inns Handbook: Classic Inns and Bed & Breakfasts. Leesburg: Virginia Handbooks, Inc., 1993.

Wiencek, Henry. *The Smithsonian Guide to Historic America: Virginia and the Capital Region.* New York: Stewart, Tabori & Chang, 1989.

Willis, Bob and John Bowen. *Fodor's Virginia & Maryland.* New York: Fodor's Travel Publications, Inc., 1993.

LIBERTY OR DEATH

Perhaps the greatest of Patrick Henry's speeches, the following is an excerpt from his address to the convention that gathered at Richmond after Lord Dunmore suspended the Virginia Assembly.

Gentlemen may cry, peace, peace; but there is no peace. The war is actually begun! The next gale that sweeps from the north will bring to our ears the clash of resounding arms! Our brethren are already in the field! Why stand we here idle? What is it that gentlemen wish? What would they have? Is life so dear or peace so sweet as to be purchased at the price of chains and slavery? Forbid it, Almighty God—I know not what course others may take; but as for me, give me liberty, or give me death!

—Patrick Henry, March 23, 1775

I N D E X

COMPASS AMERICAN GUIDES

Comprehensive, literate, and beautifully illustrated guides to the individual cities and states of the United States and Canada, Compass American Guides are unparalleled in their cultural, historical, and informational scope. They are to the 1990s what the WPA guidebook series was to the 1930s — insightful, resourceful, and entertaining.

"Each [Compass American Guide] pairs an accomplished photographer with a writer native to the state. The resulting pictures and words have such an impact I constantly had to remind myself I was reading a travel guide." — National Geographic Traveler

"Entertaining and well-illustrated with maps and photographs, in color and vintage black and white...good to read ahead of time, then take along so you don't miss anything." —San Diego Magazine

"You can read [a Compass American Guide] for information and come away entertained. Or you can read it for entertainment and come away informed . . . an informational jackpot." —Houston Chronicle

"Wickedly stylish writing!" —Chicago Sun-Times

Compass American Guides are available in general and travel bookstores, or may be ordered directly by calling 1-800-733-3000; or by sending a check or money order, including the cost of shipping and handling, payable to: Random House, Inc. 400 Hahn Road, Westminster, Maryland 21157. Books are shipped by USPS Book Rate (allow 30 days for delivery): $2.00 for the 1st book, $0.50 for each additional book. Applicable sales tax will be charged. All prices are subject to change. Or ask your bookseller to order for you.

"Books can make thoughtful (and sometimes even thought-provoking) gifts for incentive travel winners or convention attendees. A new series of guidebooks published by Compass American Guides is right on the mark." —Successful Meetings magazine

Consider Compass American Guides as gifts or incentives for VIP's, employees, clients, customers, convention and meeting attendees, friends and others. Compass American Guides are available at special discounts for bulk purchases (100 copies or more) for sales promotions or premiums. Special editions, including personalized covers, excerpts of existing guides, and corporate imprints, can be created in large quantities for special needs. For more information, write to Special Marketing, Fodor's Travel Publications, 201 E. 50th St., New York, NY 10022; or call 800/800-3246. Inquiries from the United Kingdom should be sent to Fodor's Travel Publications, 20 Vauxhall Bridge Rd., London, England SW1V 2SA.

CHICAGO
1st Edition
Author
Jack Schnedler
Photographer
Zbigniew Bzdak
1-878-86728-8

$16.95 Paper 288 pp.
($22.50 Canada)

Also available in a hardcover edition:
1-878-86729-6
$24.95 ($31.50 Canada)

"Great to send to anyone coming to Chicago for the first time, or anyone who left town before Wrigley Field got lights." *—Chicago Sun-Times*

LAS VEGAS
3rd Edition
Author
Deke Castleman
Photographer
Michael Yamashita
1-878-86736-9

$16.95 Paper 304 pp.
($22.50 Canada)

"Visiting this neon oasis has been made much more interesting thanks to Deke Castleman's *Las Vegas*."

—Travel & Leisure

LOS ANGELES
1st Edition
Author
Gil Reavill
Photographer
Mark S. Wexler
1-878-86717-2

$14.95 Paper 324 pp.
($19.95 Canada)

Also available in a hardcover edition:
1-878-86725-3
$22.95 ($29.00 Canada)

"No cinephile should head out L.A. way without a copy of *Los Angeles*." *—New York Daily News*

NEW ORLEANS
1st Edition
Author
Bethany Ewald Bultman
Photographer
Richard Sexton
1-878-86739-3

$16.95 Paper 304 pp.
($21.95 Canada)

Also available in a hardcover edition:
1-878-86740-7
$24.95 ($31.50 Canada)

Vibrant photography and jaunty commentary guide travelers through the heart and soul of sizzling New Orleans.

SAN FRANCISCO & THE BAY AREA
2nd Edition
Author
Barry Parr
Photographer
Michael Yamashita
1-878-86716-4

$14.95 Paper 396 pp.
($19.95 Canada)

"*San Francisco* tackles the 'why' of travel to that city as well as the nitty gritty details." *— Travel Weekly*

CANADA
1st Edition
Author
Garry Marchant
Photographer
Ken Straiton
1-878-86712-1

$14.95 Paper 320 pp.
($19.95 Canada)

"*Canada* goes a long way in presenting this country in all its complex, beautiful glory." *—Toronto Sun*

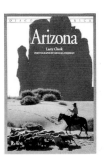

ARIZONA
2nd Edition
Author
Lawrence Cheek
Photographer
Michael Freeman
1-878-86732-6

$16.95 Paper 288 pp.
($22.50 Canada)

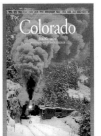

COLORADO
2nd Edition
Author
Jon Klusmire
Photographer
Paul Chesley
1-878-86735-0

$16.95 Paper 320 pp.
($22.50 Canada)

"This is my kind of guidebook."
—David Laird, *Books of the Southwest*

"A literary, historical and near-sensory excursion across the state." —*Denver Post*

MONTANA
1st Edition
Author
Norma Tirrell
Photographer
John Reddy
1-878-86710-5

$14.95 Paper 304 pp.
($19.95 Canada)

Also available in a hardcover edition:
1-878-86713-X
$22.95 ($29.00 Canada)

NEW MEXICO
1st Edition
Author
Nancy Harbert
Photographer
Michael Freeman
1-878-86706-7

$15.95 Paper 288 pp.
($19.95 Canada)

Also available in a hardcover edition:
1-878-86722-9 $22.95
($29.00 Canada)

"The most comprehensive guide to the state...will have you ready and rarin' to go." — *Travel & Leisure*

"Bold yet artful in its photography."

— *Albuquerque Journal*

UTAH
2nd Edition
Authors
Tom & Gayen Wharton
Photographer
Tom Till
1-878-86731-8

$16.95 Paper 352 pp.
($22.50 Canada)

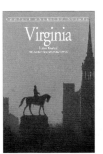

VIRGINIA
1st Edition
Author
K.M. Kostyal
Photographer
Medford Taylor
1-878-86741-5

$16.95 Paper 320 pp.
($21.50 Canada)

Also available in a hardcover edition:
1-878-86742-3 $24.95
($31.50 Canada)

"The jaunty text and eye-popping photos make this a keeper." —*Deseret News*

Winner of the Rocky Mountain Book Publishers' Award for Best Guidebook

"History haunts Virginia like a lost lover," writes author Kostyal in this fascinating guide to the history and culture of Virginia.

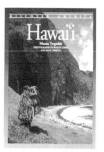

H A W A I ' I
1st Edition
Author
Moana Tregaskis
Photographer
Wayne Levin & Paul Chesley
1-878-86723-7

$15.95 Paper 364 pp.
($19.95 Canada)

Also available in a hardcover
edition:
1-878-86724-5
$22.95 ($29.00 Canada)

"A fine guide and a welcome addition to travel
collections." —*Library Journal*

1993 Award of Merit—Hawai'i Visitors Bureau

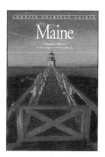

M A I N E
1st Edition
Author
Charles Calhoun
Photographer
Thomas Szelog
1-878-86751-2

$16.95 Paper 304 pp.
($21.50 Canada)

Also available in a hardcover
edition:
1-878-86752-0 $24.95
($31.50 Canada)

The leaves of this book display photographs as colorful
as Fall in Maine, and the narrative is entertaining and
informative to travelers and natives alike.

O R E G O N
1st Edition
Author
Judy Jewell
Photographer
Greg Vaughn
1-878-86733-4

$16.95 Paper 320 pp.
($21.50 Canada)

Also available in a hardcover
edition:
1-878-86734-2
$24.95 ($31.50 Canada)

Special emphasis on outdoor recreation and natural
resources highlights this first edition celebrating
Oregon's magnificent landscape.

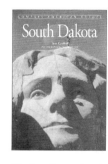

S O U T H   D A K O T A
1st Edition
Author
Tom Griffith
Photographer
Paul Horsted
1-878-86726-1

$16.95 Paper 304 pp.
($21.50 Canada)

Also available in a hardcover
edition:
1-878-86727-X
$24.95 ($31.50 Canada)

The first illustrated guide to explore the hidden
wonders, colorful characters, and legends of the Land
of Infinite Variety—South Dakota.

W I S C O N S I N
1st Edition
Author
Tracy Will
Photographer
Zane Williams
1-878-86744-X

$16.95 Paper 304 pp.
($21.50 Canada)

Also available in a hardcover
edition:
1-878-86745-8
$24.95 ($31.50 Canada)

Wisconsinite Tracy Will recounts the history and the
peopling of the state from its first inhabitants, the
Chippewa and Dakota Sioux, to the Scandinavian
pioneers of the 19th century.

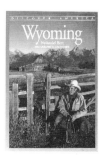

W Y O M I N G
1st Edition
Author
Nathaniel Burt
Photographer
Don Pitcher
1-878-86704-1

$14.95 Paper 396 pp.
($19.95 Canada)

Also available in a hardcover
edition:
1-878-86703-2
$22.95 ($29.00 Canada)

"Their mixture of anecdotes, history, and beautiful
photographs provide a genuine taste of the 'Wild
West.'" — *Library Journal*

■ ABOUT THE AUTHOR

Born and raised in coastal Virginia, K.M. Kostyal earned a graduate degree in social anthropology from the University of Virginia. In 1976, she joined the staff of the National Geographic Society. Initially involved in their book publications, she later became a writer and editor for the Society's *National Geographic Traveler* magazine. Since 1989, she has been a contributing editor to *Traveler* as well as a freelance contributor to *Michelin* historic travel publications and *Islands* magazine. She has won the Society of American Travel Writers Lowell Thomas Award for best magazine article on a foreign destination and a first runner-up award for best magazine article on U.S./Canada travel.

■ ABOUT THE PHOTOGRAPHER

Virginia has been home base to Medford Taylor for most of his life as he has traveled throughout the world as a photojournalist. His career started in newspapers, as staff photographer for the *Virginian Pilot* and the *Houston Chronicle.* He has also freelanced for *Time* and *Newsweek* in Washington, D.C., but his interest in people and cultures worldwide led him to *National Geographic* magazine where freelance assignments have taken him to Australia's Outback, the mountains of Russia, the icy shores of Lake Superior, and remote mountain villages on Madeira. His photographs appear in publications worldwide, and this year Taylor was a first place winner in the prestigious White House News Association Photo Competition. His plans for the future include personal book projects of his favorite places.